EMBELLISHING THE LANDSCAPE

THE IMAGES OF AMY HEAP AND FRED FLOOD 1920-1940

EMBELLISHING THE LANDSCAPE

THE IMAGES OF AMY HEAP AND FRED FLOOD 1920-1940

C.T. STANNAGE

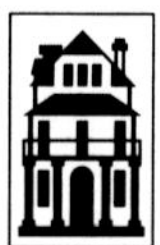

FREMANTLE ARTS CENTRE PRESS

First published 1990 by
FREMANTLE ARTS CENTRE PRESS
1 Finnerty Street (PO Box 891), Fremantle
Western Australia, 6160.

Consultant Editor B.R. Coffey.
Designed by John Douglass.
Production Manager Helen Idle.

Typeset in 10½/11½pt Goudy by City Typesetters, Perth, Western Australia. Printed on 115gsm Artpaper by Tien Wah Press (Pte.) Ltd., Singapore.

National Library of Australia
Cataloguing-in-publication data

Stannage, C.T. (Charles Thomas), 1944-
  Embellishing the Landscape: the images of Amy Heap and Fred Flood, 1920-1940.

  ISBN 0 949206 64 4.

  1. Heap, Amy, 1874-1956. 2. Flood, Fred, 1881-1965. 3. Decoration and ornament — Western Australia. 4. Photography — Western Australia — Landscapes. 5. Western Australia — Description and travel — 1901-1950 — Views. I. Title.

745.44922941.

ACKNOWLEDGEMENTS

For assistance in the preparation of *Embellishing the Landscape*, I wish to thank the following people and institutions: Mr and Mrs Wally Flood; Mr Clem Ambler; Mr John Brackenreg; Mr and Mrs Fred Harfey and Brian Harfey; Mr and Mrs Warren Tucker; Ms Katie Stannage and Mr Chris Stannage; Ms Janda Gooding; Mr and Mrs John Oldham; Dr David Bromfield, Ms Kerry Paddon and Ms Melissa Harpley; Mr Maurie Jones; Bell Publishing Group Pty Ltd; The Art Gallery of Western Australia; the National Trust; the Albany Town Council; Ms Verity James and Mr Jeff Dorrington; Mrs Vickie Mackie; Ms Ffion Murphy and Dr Richard Nile; Dr Jenny Gregory; Dr Clyde Binfield; Mr Victor France, who photographed much of the visual material for reproduction in the book; and the staff of the photographic section, J.S. Battye Library of West Australian History. I am especially grateful to the staff of Fremantle Arts Centre Press.

C.T. Stannage

Fremantle Arts Centre Press receives financial assistance from the Western Australian Department for the Arts.

ILLUSTRATION SOURCES

The following individuals and organisations provided visual material for this book and gave permission for reproduction:

Cover — Bell Publishing (*Western Mail*, 1929); Page 10 — Bell Publishing (*WM*, 1940); P12 (left) — J.S. Battye Library of West Australian History; P12 (right) — F.K. Crowley; P13 — University of Western Australia Press (*A Fine Country to Starve In*, 1972, G.C. Bolton); P14 — Art Gallery of Western Australia (c.1900); P15 — Director, Department of Fine Arts, University of Western Australia (John Barker, [Watercolour of Bush], 1935); P16 (left) — Art Gallery of Western Australia (J.R. Linton, 'A Bit of Old Guildford', reproduced in *The Westralia Gift Book*, 1916, ed. W. Murdoch, et al.); P16 (right) — Director, Department of Fine Arts, University of Western Australia (Harald Vike, 'Wharf Labourer', 1939, from *Aspects of Perth Modernism 1929-1942*, 1986, ed. D Bromfield); P17 — Director, Department of Fine Arts, University of Western Australia (Elise Blumann, 'On the Swan, Nedlands', c.1942, from the Collection of The University of Western Australia); P18 — John Oldham (John Oldham, 'Bury the Dead', poster for the Workers Art Guild, 1937); P19 (left) — Mr Wally Flood; P19 (right) — Bell Publishing (*WM*, 1927); P21 — Art Gallery of Western Australia; P23 — Bell Publishing (*WM*, 1928); P24 (top) — Bell Publishing (*WM*, 1928); P24 (bottom) — Bell Publishing (*WM*, 1935); P25 (left) — Oxford University Press (*The Romance of Reading*, 1936, eds. R.K. and M.I.R. Polkinghorne); P25 (right) — Jonathan Cape (illustration by Norman Hepple from *Gone to Earth*, 1917, Mary Webb), the Baldwin quotation is from *On England*, 1926; P26 — Oxford University Press (illustration by Roland Hilder from *The Romance of Reading*); P27 — Bell Publishing (*WM*, 1929); P28, 29 — Bell Publishing (*WM*, 1931); P30 — Bell Publishing (*WM*, 1929); P31 — Bell Publishing (*WM*, 1931); P32 — Bell Publishing (*WM*, 1932)/Mr Brian Harfey; P34 — Art Gallery of Western Australia; P35 (left) — Art Gallery of Western Australia; P35 (right) — Albany Town Council; P36 — Bell Publishing (*WM*, 1936); P38 — Bell Publishing (*WM*, 1918); P39 — Art Gallery of Western Australia; P41 — *The Westralia Gift Book*, 1916, ed. W. Murdoch, et al.; P45 — Bell Publishing (*WM*, 1929); P46 — Art Gallery of Western Australia; P48 — Bell Publishing (*WM*, 1929); P49 — Bell Publishing (*WM*, 1936); P50, 51, 52, 53 — Mr Wally Flood; P55 — Bell Publishing (*WM*, 1923); P56, 57 — Bell Publishing (*WM*, 1931); P59, 60 — Mr Wally Flood; P61 — Bell Publishing (*WM*, 1931); P63 — Bell Publishing (*WM*, 1939); P64 — Bell Publishing (*WM*, 1935); P65 — Bell Publishing (*WM*, 1941); P66 — Bell Publishing (*WM*, 1926); P68, 69 — Bell Publishing (*WM*, 1930); P70 — Bell Publishing (*WM*, 1929); P71 — Bell Publishing (*WM*, 1925); P72 — *Jarrah Leaves*, 1933, ed. J. Glascock; P73 — Bell Publishing (*WM*, 1928); P74, 75 — Bell Publishing (*WM*, 1930); P76 — Bell Publishing (*WM*, 1925); P77, 78 — Bell Publishing (*WM*, 1930); P79 — Bell Publishing (*WM*, 1928); P80 — Bell Publishing (*WM*, 1931); P81 — Bell Publishing (*WM*, 1929); P82 — Bell Publishing (*WM*, 1928); P83 — Bell Publishing (*WM*, 1923); P84 — Bell Publishing (*WM*, 1926); P85 — Bell Publishing (*WM*, 1923); P86 — Bell Publishing (*WM*, 1930); P87 — Bell Publishing (*WM*, 1924); P88 — Bell Publishing (*WM*, 1933)/Mr Fred Harfey; P89 — Bell Publishing (*WM*, 1929); P90, 91 — Bell Publishing (*WM*, 1928); P92 — Bell Publishing (*WM*, 1926); P93 — Bell Publishing (*WM*, 1930); P94, 95 — Bell Publishing (*WM*, 1926); P96 — Bell Publishing (*WM*, 1932); P98 — Mr Wally Flood; P99 — Bell Publishing (*WM*, 1926); P100 — Bell Publishing (*WM*, 1925); P101 — Bell Publishing (*WM*, 1938); P102 — Bell Publishing (*WM*, 1934); P103 — Bell Publishing (*WM*, 1931); P104 — Bell Publishing (*WM*, 1938); P105 — Bell Publishing (*WM*, 1924); P106 — Bell Publishing (*WM*, 1930); P107 — Bell Publishing (*WM*, 1941); P108 — Bell Publishing (*WM*, 1924); P109 — Bell Publishing (*WM*, 1923); P110 (top) — Bell Publishing (*WM*, 1936); P110 (bottom) — Bell Publishing (*WM*, 1930); P111 — Bell Publishing (*WM*, 1926); P112 — Bell Publishing (*WM*, 1934); P113 — Bell Publishing (*WM*, 1931); P114 — Bell Publishing (*WM*, 1930); P115 — Bell Publishing (*WM*, 1941); P116 — Bell Publishing (*WM*, 1934); P118 — Bell Publishing (*WM*, 1929); P119, 120, 121, 122, 123 — Bell Publishing (*WM*, 1930); P124 — Bell Publishing (*WM*, 1928); P125 — Bell Publishing (*WM*, 1930); P126, 127 — Bell Publishing (*WM*, 1928); P128 — Bell Publishing (*WM*, 1929); P129, 130 — Bell Publishing (*WM*, 1928); P131 — Bell Publishing (*WM*, 1929), the poem quoted in the caption is Robert Browning's 'Pippa Passes', Pt. 1; P132 — Bell Publishing (*WM*, 1934).

CONTENTS

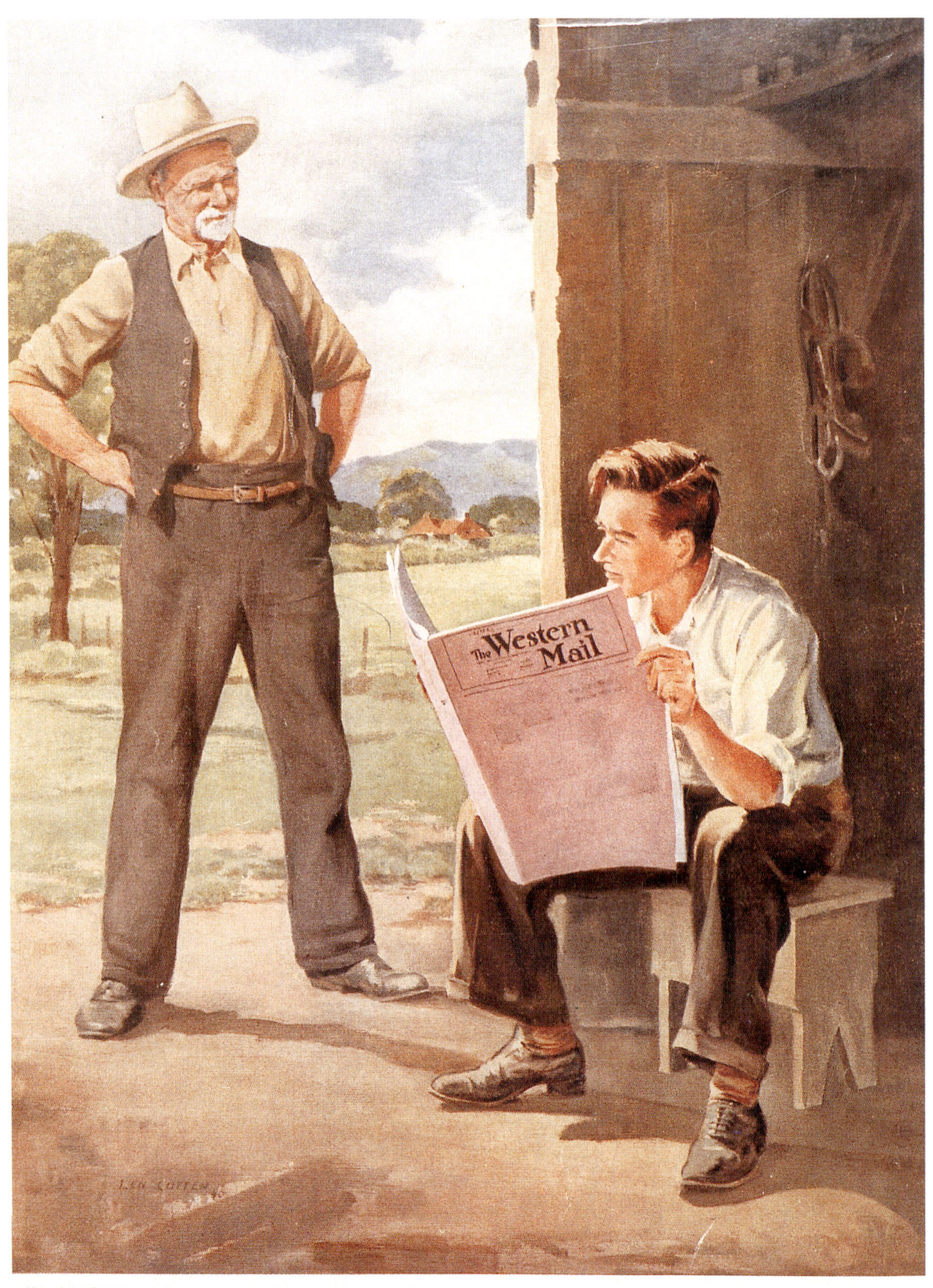

"I MIGHT HAVE KNOWN IT WAS 'MAIL' DAY!"

INTRODUCTION

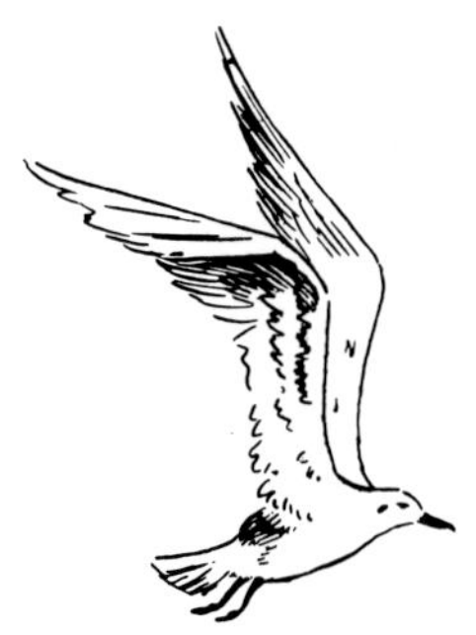

THE INTERWAR YEARS

Amy Heap and Fred Flood painted, drew and photographed Western Australia from the Great War of 1914-18 to the aftermath of the Second World War. For their images they sought out and selected what was beautiful and bountiful in nature and joyous in human nature. Their images were well known to a generation of Western Australians in the taxing interwar years through the pages of the *Western Mail*, the weekly journal of the *West Australian*, intended primarily for country readers but enjoying a wide readership in the metropolitan area as well. Especially popular was the annual or Christmas issue of the *Western Mail*, which was glossily printed and enhanced with colour illustrations. Amy Heap and Fred Flood were employed on the *Western Mail*, and their images dominated the journal's Christmas edition throughout the 1920s and 1930s.

In selecting images which were beautiful, tranquil, joyous and sentimental, Heap and Flood and the *Western Mail* provided visual and literary sustenance for those in society who saw consensus, abundance and harmony, and an absence of conflict, suffering and disorderliness as central to Western Australian history and to progress. In their stunning imagery Heap and Flood and the *Western Mail* adorned and embellished Western Australia's past, present and future. In his political rhetoric the energetic Premier of the day, Sir James Mitchell, did likewise.

In time the gap between the image and rhetoric and the reality of people's lives would become so great that the image would be taken for the reality. Amy Heap and Fred Flood, particularly within the *Western Mail*, were the very important interpreters of a

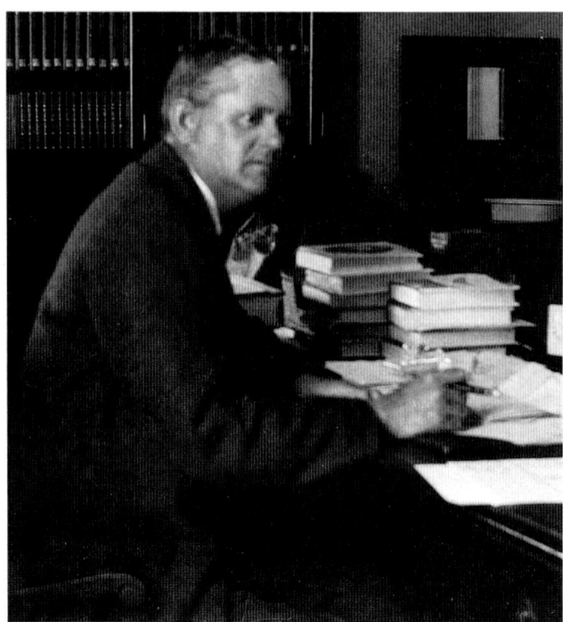
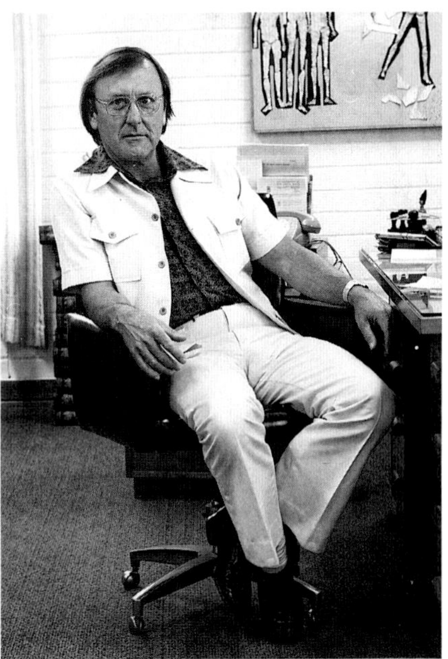

J.S. Battye and F.K. Crowley: arch-interpreters of Western Australian history.

profound conservatism in Western Australian life. Their importance has been lost from view for many years. But the values they espoused between 1920 and 1940 have remained central to historical understanding and writing about Western Australia in that interwar period.

For many years Western Australians tended to write much about the pioneering days of Swan River Settlement and little about the twentieth century. There were solid reasons for this, most acceptably that many of the older writers — like Dr Battye (1871-1954) — lived on comfortably into the twentieth century and tended to see it as current affairs rather than history. This view changed when authors born in the interwar years began to write history.

The two notable historians of this 'new' generation were F.K. Crowley and G.C. Bolton. In his 1960 book *Australia's Western Third*, Crowley quoted from Lord Acton — 'The prize of all history is the understanding of modern times'. Over half his book was devoted to post-1900 Western Australian history. Twelve years later Bolton published *A Fine Country to Starve In* (1972), an evocative rendering of the 1920s and 1930s. A challenge for both historians had been to see if the pioneer approach to Western Australian history would stand up when the focus of attention shifted from the nineteenth century to the twentieth century. Both historians answered this question in the affirmative. For Crowley the ongoing theme of Western Australian history was that of man working alongside man to tame an intractable, if at times profit-returning, environment. Mistakes were made, but the sense of community purpose prevailed even

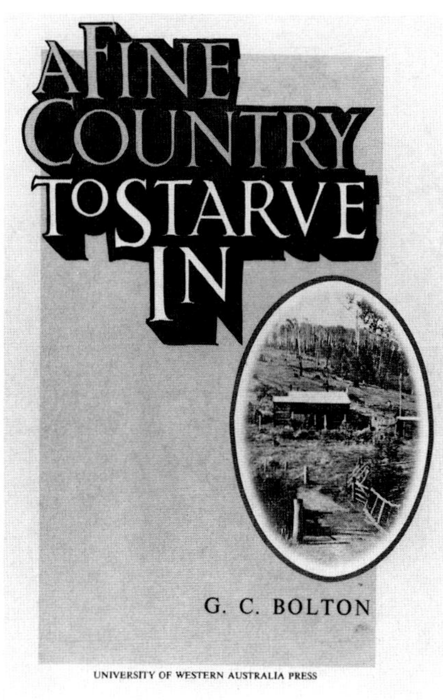

in the Great Depression of the 1930s. For Bolton, too, this remained true. His interwar society was a well-ordered one which moved forward with measured steps and a shared purpose. There was conflict, but it was marginal, not central. There was suffering, but it too was uncharacteristic, and temporary in any case. And there was no sign of class consciousness or class-based action.

This too had been the theme of one of the older writers. Sir Paul Hasluck did not write a history of Western Australia in the twentieth century, but he wrote an autobiography covering a goodly part of it. His *Mucking About*, published in 1977 when the author was a vigorous seventy-two years old, confirmed the thrust of the books by Bolton and Crowley. His interwar Western Australia was consensual, not conflict-oriented. It was harmonious and relatively tranquil. It was rural rather than urban. And it showed no evidence of class differences and class action. It stressed happiness and not suffering (other than for the Aborigines, an important exception) in the Western Australian community.

In time a post World War Two generation of Western Australian historians would challenge the views of Crowley, Bolton and Hasluck, but none would write with their flair and power — at least none has done so yet. But at thesis and article level the new work certainly knocked some holes in the older interpretations. For many Western Australians life was not simply uncomfortable in the old trials-and-tribulations-of-the-pioneers sense; but uncomfortable, even unbearable, in a society that was far less open than had been hitherto described. And perhaps more unhappy, too, as recent women's

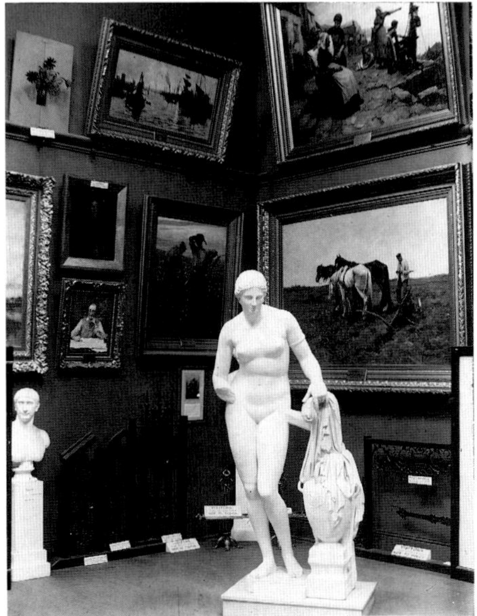

The collecting policy of the Museum and Art Gallery of Western Australia was rural, aristocratic and sentimental.

history poignantly suggests. Perhaps, however, the statue is still in the marble, and we do not know if beauty or the beast will emerge.

And where does art history come into this story of generalisation and counter-generalisation in interpreting the Westralian past? The oldest and most influential of our historians, Dr Battye, knew that art was important in shaping and reflecting social values. He was personally responsible for the collection of the Museum and Art Gallery of Western Australia being free of the contaminating influence of French and modernist paintings. Indeed the collection under his thrall was aristocratic, rural, sentimental and romantic, and altogether pioneering in a backward sense. The disturbing art, even of Whistler and definitely of the local Harald Vike, with its overtones of conflict, misery and anomie, would have no place in Battye's Public Gallery. (The Museum and Art Gallery of Western Australia were separated in 1959 into two organizations, with the Art Gallery being known as the Western Australian Art Gallery from 1959 to 1978 and The Art Gallery of Western Australia since 1978.)

In his history books Battye further marginalised art; indeed he crushed it comprehensively beneath constitutional history. His interwar-born successors Crowley and Bolton similarly bypassed art history. It was left to the less well known Barbara Chapman to harness Western Australian art history to general history, when in 1979 she published *The Colonial Eye: A topographical and artistic record of the life and landscape of Western Australia 1798-1914.* Thus to the books of deeds and words was added a book of art. Chapman was uneasily aware that her artists came from a society with a

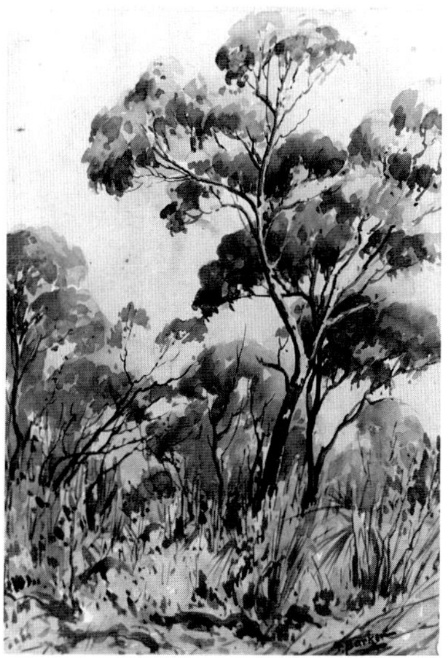

An on-going local tradition of painting compatible with England's post Great War sanctuary art and the collecting policy of the Museum and Art Gallery of Western Australia:
John Barker of Albany.

'somewhat narrow and genteel character', and that *The Colonial Eye* could be read as being within the gentry embrace of the books of deeds by Battye, Hasluck, Crowley and Bolton. But a start had to be made — and was, magnificently — even if the contours of interpretation were left relatively undisturbed. Then, too, there was the looming problem of twentieth century Western Australian art.

Scholarship in the 1980s has generated more questions than answers about the nature of the Westralian experience. Put another way, the art historians, like the general or social historians, have made Western Australians more aware of the complexity of their past. In 1983 the Robert Holmes à Court Collection, on exhibition at The Art Gallery of Western Australia, suggested strongly that Hasluck and Bolton could have used art to good effect to sustain their generalisations of peace and plenty, harmony and consensus, in the interwar years. George Benson, Walter Meston, Edith Trethowan and company all confirmed rather than dented the prevailing view. So too did the exhibition prepared by David Bromfield, of the Centre for Fine Arts, on the art of John Barker of Albany (1984). Barker, in double-breasted suit, looked all the world like Battye, and even his arts and crafts interests could be accommodated to Battye's world, if a trifle awkwardly. And trees in country lanes were certainly grist to Battye's mill! Barker was British born and trained, and the Westralia he migrated to after the Great War could easily wear, so its ideologues proclaimed, the label of Cranford by the Swan. The first painting he sold in Perth was 'An Old Swan Farmyard'. And portraits of worthies with old Western Australian names like Wittenoom suggested an artist in need of cash and

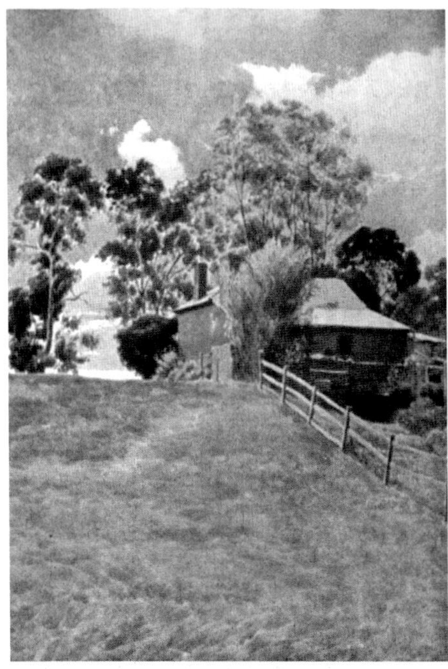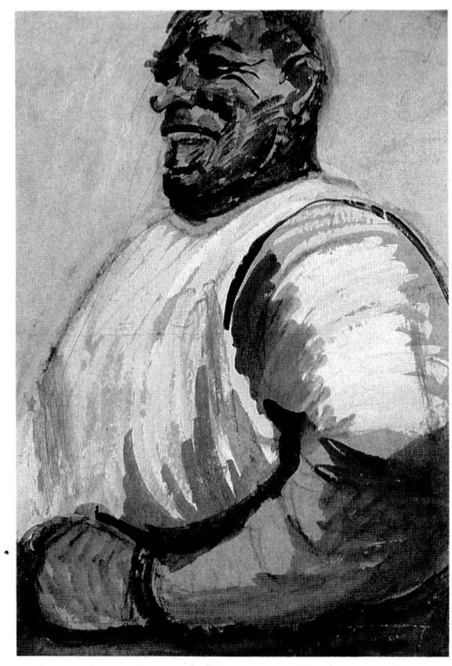

uncritical of the social values of his new society. And his relationship with the Returned Servicemen's League was a happy one. If Barker was a West Australian artist, it is clear that he was Westralian in ways acceptable to those who set the values and tone of society.

More unsettling was Bromfield's other exhibition in 1984 — on the German émigré painter Elise Blumann. Blumann arrived in 1938 as a fully fledged modernist painter of a type Battye had kept out of the Museum and Art Gallery of Western Australia from the turn of the century. Blumann too was kept out of the Gallery's collection until 1976. Her imagery, while attractive to some young artists during and after the Second World War, could not crack the visual totalitarianism of the gum-tree school.

The year which brought forward the possibility of massive shifts in understanding the art history of Western Australia in the twentieth century was 1986. In that year Anne Gray published a scholarly monograph on James Linton, *Line, Light and Shadow*. Linton, like Barker, but more spectacularly so as teacher and practitioner, was an English arts and crafts man. His most celebrated paintings, appreciated without any drawing of breath, from the 1900s onwards, are rural scenes of Guildford of great beauty, harmony and tranquillity. There could be no more compelling linking of history and art than scenes of old Guildford.

If Linton was entirely unaware of the existence of the Midland Railway Workshops just an evening's stroll from Guildford, and if he did not see the vigour of wharf life at Fremantle, there were others in the 1930s who knew both at first hand. In September

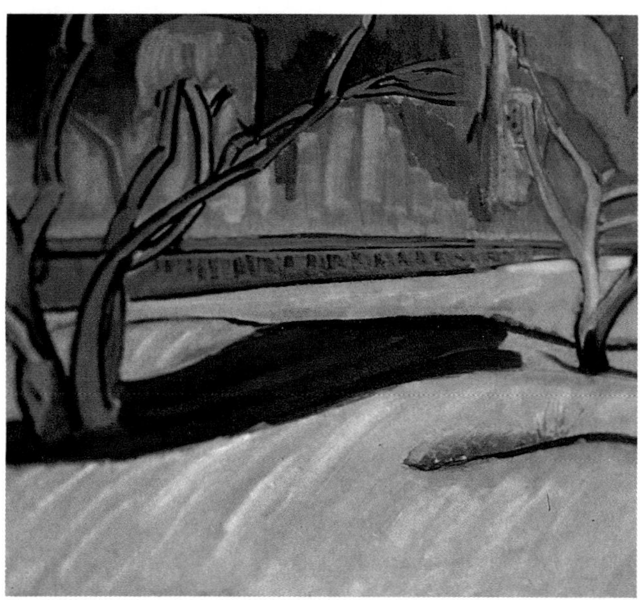

One dominant conservative image and two radical departures: James Linton in combat with Harald Vike and Elise Blumann.

1986 the indefatigable Bromfield, with Julian Goddard, published *Aspects of Perth Modernism 1929-1942*. The 'dreaming' was still there, but it was 'A Dream of New York' with images of modernity and a linking of art and radical politics, yes, even in Perth. The forgotten men and women of the 1930s — Harald Vike, John Oldham, Iris Francis, Herbert McLintock and Axel Poignant — came vividly alive for 1980s viewers in the accompanying exhibition. These artists seemed to inhabit a different Western Australia from Linton and Barker. Some were communists and shared platforms with the writer Katherine Susannah Prichard, as well as designing sets and posters for plays like the Workers Art Guild's production of *Waiting for Lefty* (1938). Here was a world apart from Battye's — disorderly, inequitable and even irrational; well apart also from the portraits of Western Australia by Hasluck, Crowley and Bolton.

And yet, and yet . . . in September 1986, too, Janda Gooding was completing her research for an exhibition and book on *Western Australian Art and Artists 1900-1950* (Summer 1986-87), produced as The Art Gallery of Western Australia's Festival of Perth show. It was in this book that the complexity of the Westralian past was fully acknowledged. Gooding argued that while the work of Vike and other 'radicals' was important and demonstrated a side of Western Australian life which had been long neglected, nevertheless it remained captive to, or overwhelmed by, a stronger tradition. However, instead of simply placing that 'stronger tradition' within the mainstream historical interpretation of Battye, Hasluck, Crowley and Bolton — namely consensus, harmony, open social mobility and so on — she contended that the stronger tradition

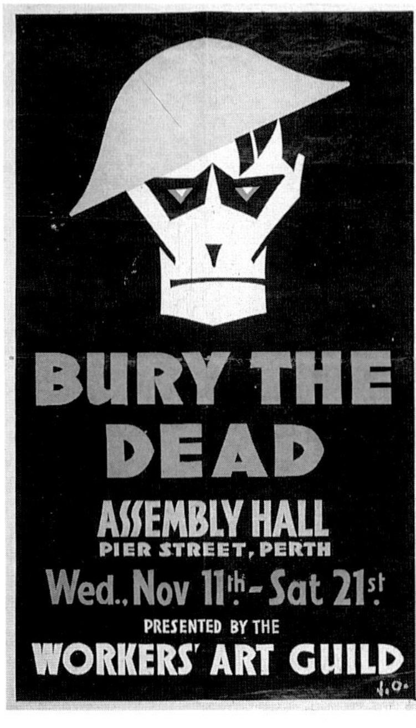

was not ideologically neutral; rather it showed a perpetuation of conservative ideology. She showed that there was a relationship between conservative art, radical art and wider divisions in society. She pointed the way towards a maturer understanding of Western Australia in the twentieth century. This study of the images of Amy Heap and Fred Flood seeks to enhance that understanding, if not embellish it.

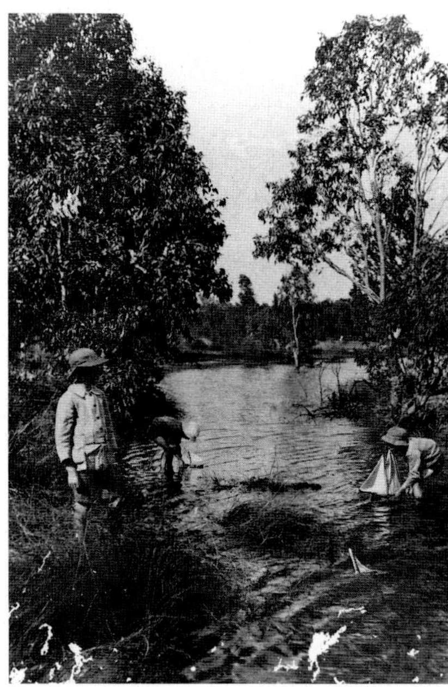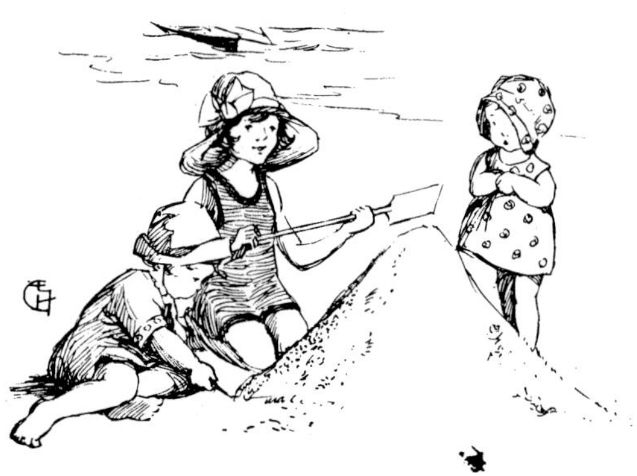

Two images of innocence in a warring world: Flood's 'real' children play in water at Jolimont near Perth; Heap's 'universal' children play on sand for people of all places and all times.

BEAUTY AND POWER

The beauty and power of the conservative imagery of the interwar years transcended chronology and remained fresh and attractive during and after the Second World War. With a few exceptions, such as J.M. Harcourt's *Upsurge* (1934) and Prichard's *Intimate Strangers* (1938), it was supported by literature. And when from the late 1940s Western Australian families began to purchase motor cars in considerable numbers (32,900 in 1947; 155,500 in 1962), and to use them for work and for leisure, including travel throughout the State, they were already heirs to a stock of images about the Westralian past, both economic and social, and about the Western Australian scenery. The stock of images stressed the bounty and beauty of nature, and the harmony, tranquillity, and enjoyment of life in Western Australia. Where struggle was portrayed, and it was usually rural in character, it always resulted in productive good and familial contentment.

The images of harmony and contentment and consensus dominated school curricula in the 1950s, especially social studies, history and literature, as well as 'nature studies'. The ideology of development undergirded these images, often in a very direct way, as in the annual booklet given free to all schoolchildren. This took them page by page through the story of agricultural, industrial and banking progress, and it displayed the beauty of the Westralian countryside.

The ideology was always present in more oblique ways, as in school texts, schoolroom prints, sponsored 'explorer' pamphlets and the like. J. Stokes *The Western State: Some of its People and Ports* (1948) and A.E. Williams and A.B. Jones *Social Studies*

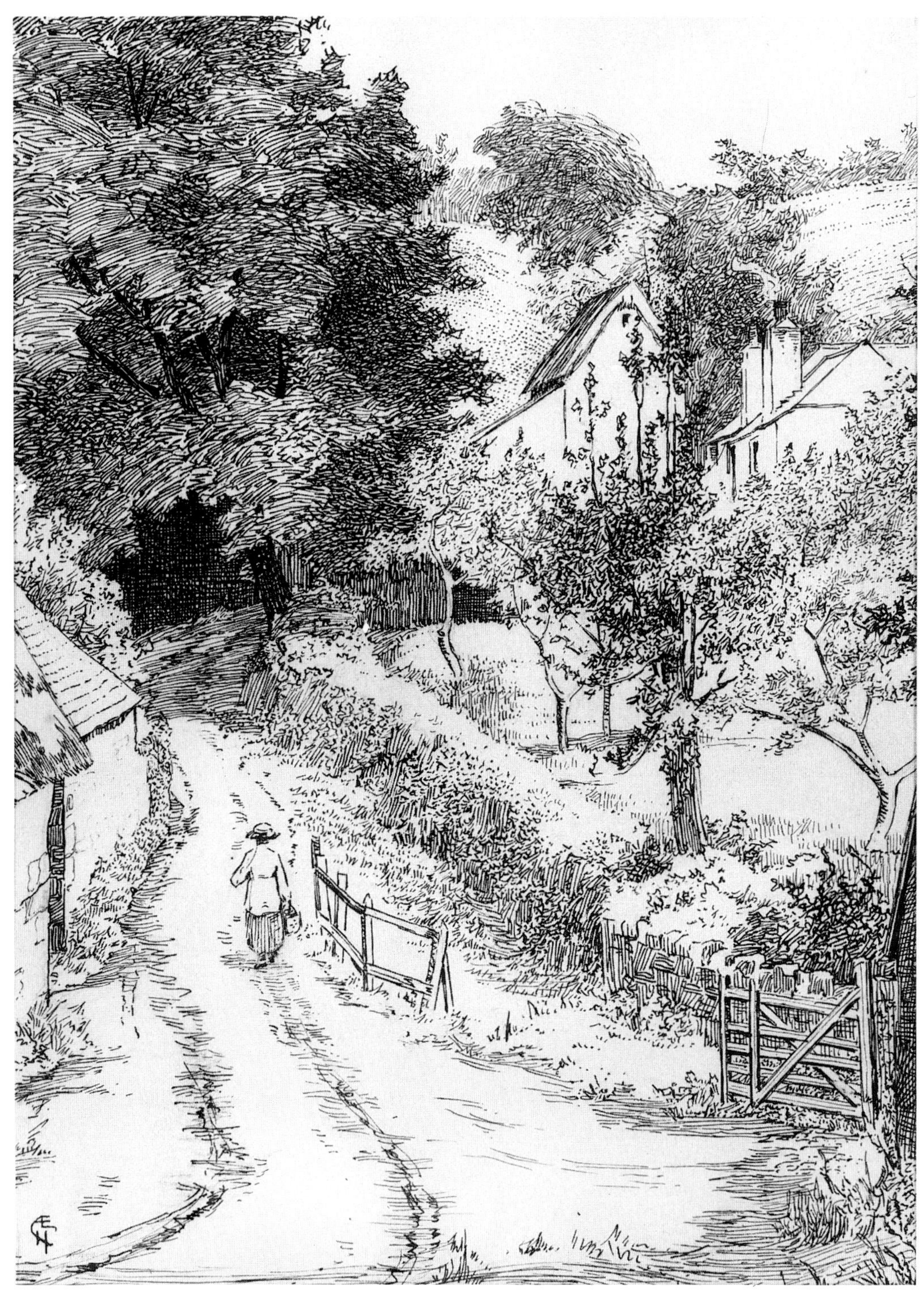

Amy Heap's love of the southern English countryside may stem from growing up in northern Bolton, described in the 1930s as a muddy pool from which all the water had been drained off. This early drawing may be of a Cornish village and lane, possibly one of three exhibited at the opening of the Linton Studio, Murray Street, Perth, in 1923.

Through Activities (1949) were examples of this. Conflict, when it appeared at all, tended to be outside Western Australia, in both location and time, except for participation in the First and Second World Wars. But the periods and experiences of conflict in Australian society were unrelated to Western Australia, events which Western Australians should be grateful for not experiencing. The Eureka Stockade, the Ned Kelly story, and the great strikes of the 1890s were events which showed by way of contrast how 'safe' and 'quiet' and 'progressive' Western Australia had been. Europe was always portrayed as societies and peoples tearing one another apart, as the much used textbook of D. Richards *An Illustrated History of Modern Europe* (1938) shows.

Even drought, fire and flood, well known to generations of Western Australians, tended to be underplayed, especially in British and Australian literature. Or, if portrayed at all, such experiences were more characteristic of the eastern states and colonies, as written about by A.B. Paterson and Henry Lawson, well used in Western Australian schools from the 1920s, probably starting with Walter Murdoch's *Oxford Book of Australian Verse* (1918).

In *The Poet's Commonwealth: A Junior Anthology for Australasian Schools* (1926), Murdoch wrote: 'Every poem is a hymn of praise of what some poet passionately loves and admires' (xi). He added that 'poetry . . . is a statement of values' (xii) and that man's deepest feeling is 'for what is beautiful in nature or in human nature, for what is great and noble in human character and destiny'.

The contents of *The Poet's Commonwealth* lock the Australian experience into the

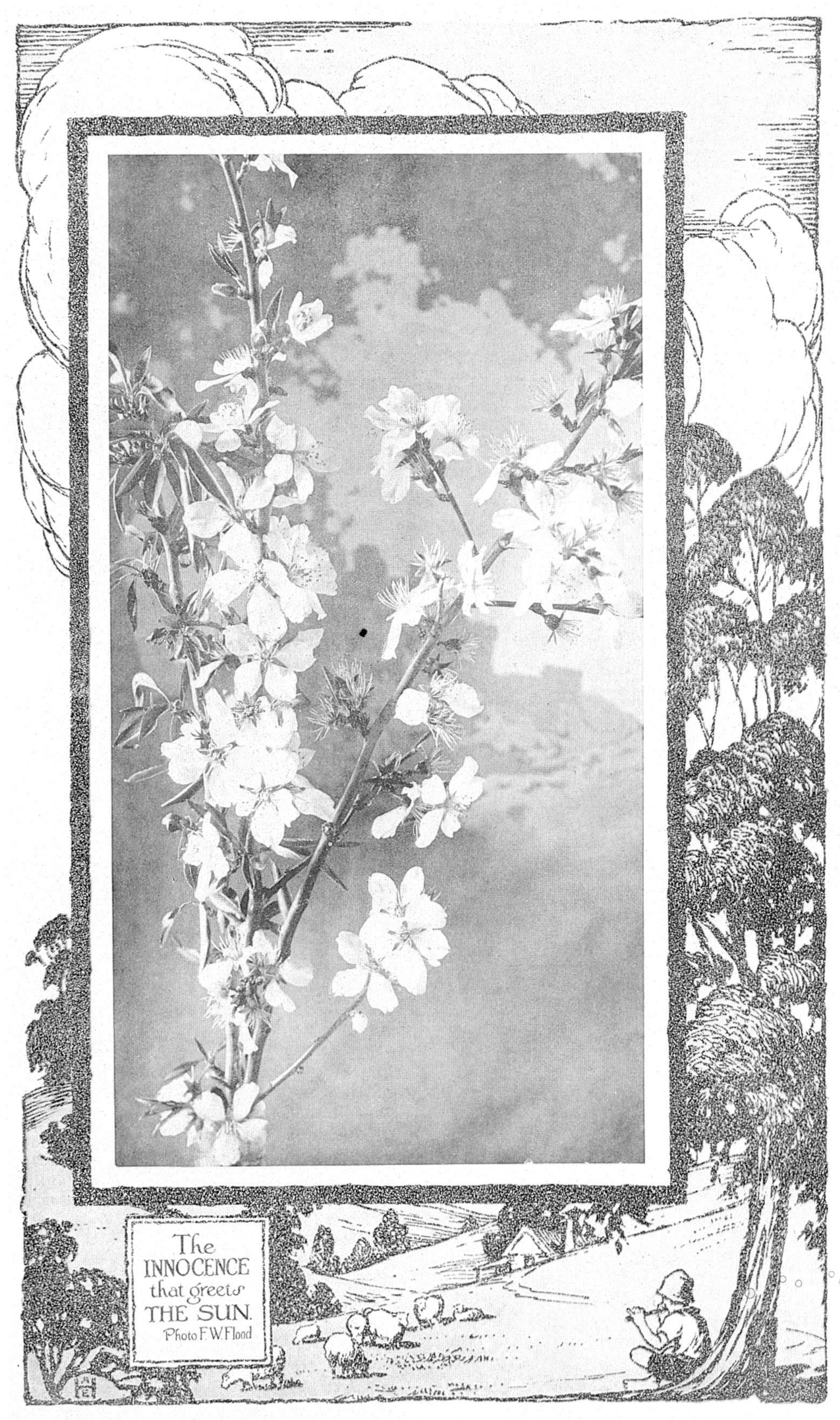

'The innocence that greets the Sun'. Amy Heap's youthful Virgilian flautist plays in a rural arcadia as decoration to nature's beauty in blossom (1928).

greater British experience. Part I, 'The Open Air', moves effortlessly from Sir Walter Scott's 'Waken, lords and ladies gay' and Thomas Hardy's 'Weathers' through 'I wandered lonely as a cloud' and 'The Brook' to Charles Harpur's 'Midsummer Noon' and James Lister Cuthbertson's 'The Australian Sunrise'. In Frank S. Williamson's now forgotten 'Magpie's Song', the bird not only carols, but is the 'Voice of happy shepherd chanting by a stream in Arcady' (p. 31).

In 'Songs of Action' (Part II), 'Agincourt' and 'Sherwood' are shared in nobility of human character and destiny by 'The Fire at Ross's Farm' and 'Clancy of the Overflow'. Murdoch found Australian poets to be unreflective (Part III) and non-elegiac (Part IV); but Adam Lindsay Gordon, William Gay and Bernard O'Dowd were linked to William Wordsworth, John Masefield and William Ernest Henley in 'Love of Country' (Part V). Gay's 'Australian Federation' struck a powerful chord:

> 'From all division let our land be free
> For God has made her one.' (p. 159)

And in the deservedly famous Australian-produced *The Pacific Readers: Southern Cross Series*, from the 1920s, William Watson's lines in 'England and her Colonies' undergird the overall mood and choice of subject matter:

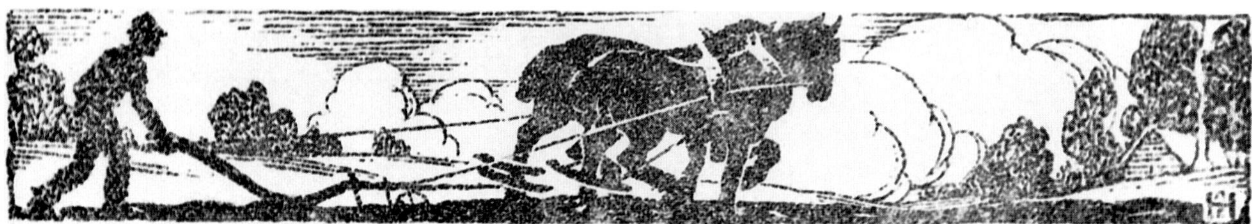

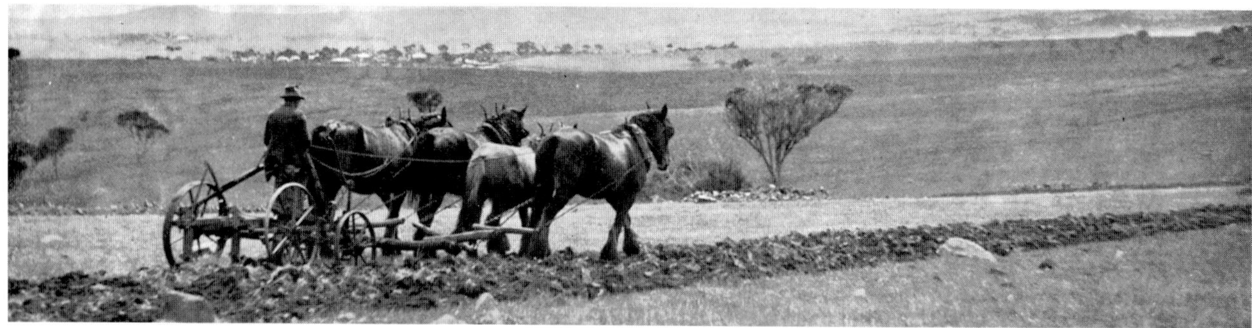

Amy Heap strikes a cultural chord with readers of the *Western Mail*: her 1928 image of a ploughman on the rim of the earth is matched by a 1935 photograph of 'The First Furrows' near Northam.

> 'Forget not whence the breath was blown
> That wafted you afar' (*Fifth Pacific Reader*, pp. 17-18)

Amy Heap and Fred Flood never forgot whence the breath was blown; nor did they question Australia's indivisibility. Both heard happy shepherds chanting by streams in a Westralian Arcady; and both sought out what was beautiful in nature and in human nature. In the images they created of Western Australia there was no room for conflict, sorrow, pain and deprivation. And they reconciled the land and people to England. They turned bush farmers into English ploughmen, the image of which came directly to Westralian schoolchildren from the 1930s as the cover picture of *The Romance of Reading* (First Series, Book IV, Oxford 1936) and in Gordon Bottomley's poem called simply 'The Ploughman'. Heap and Flood also captioned photos and paintings with lines from English romantic poets like Wordsworth early and Algernon Charles Swinburne late; while the photos and paintings themselves came less from an innocent eye than from the visual history and the observed 'reality' of the old world. The power and beauty of literature and art combined mystically in the most compelling image of all: 'I will lift up mine eyes unto the hills'.

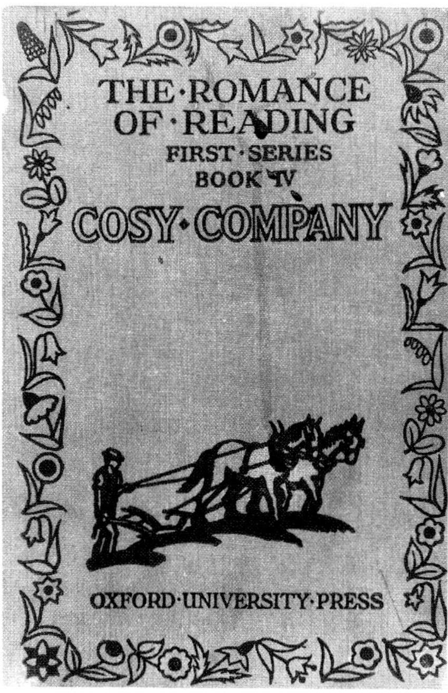

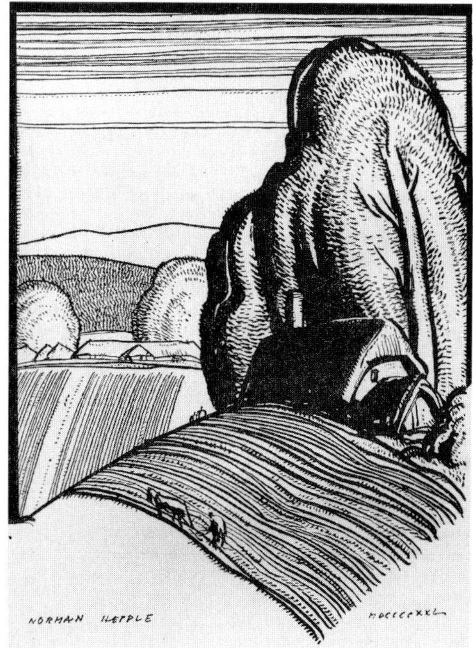

The ploughman is a characteristic image of conservative ideology in the period: as that most English of Prime Ministers, Stanley Baldwin, said, 'To me England is the country . . . the corncrake on a dewy morning . . . the sight of a plough team coming over the brow of a hill'

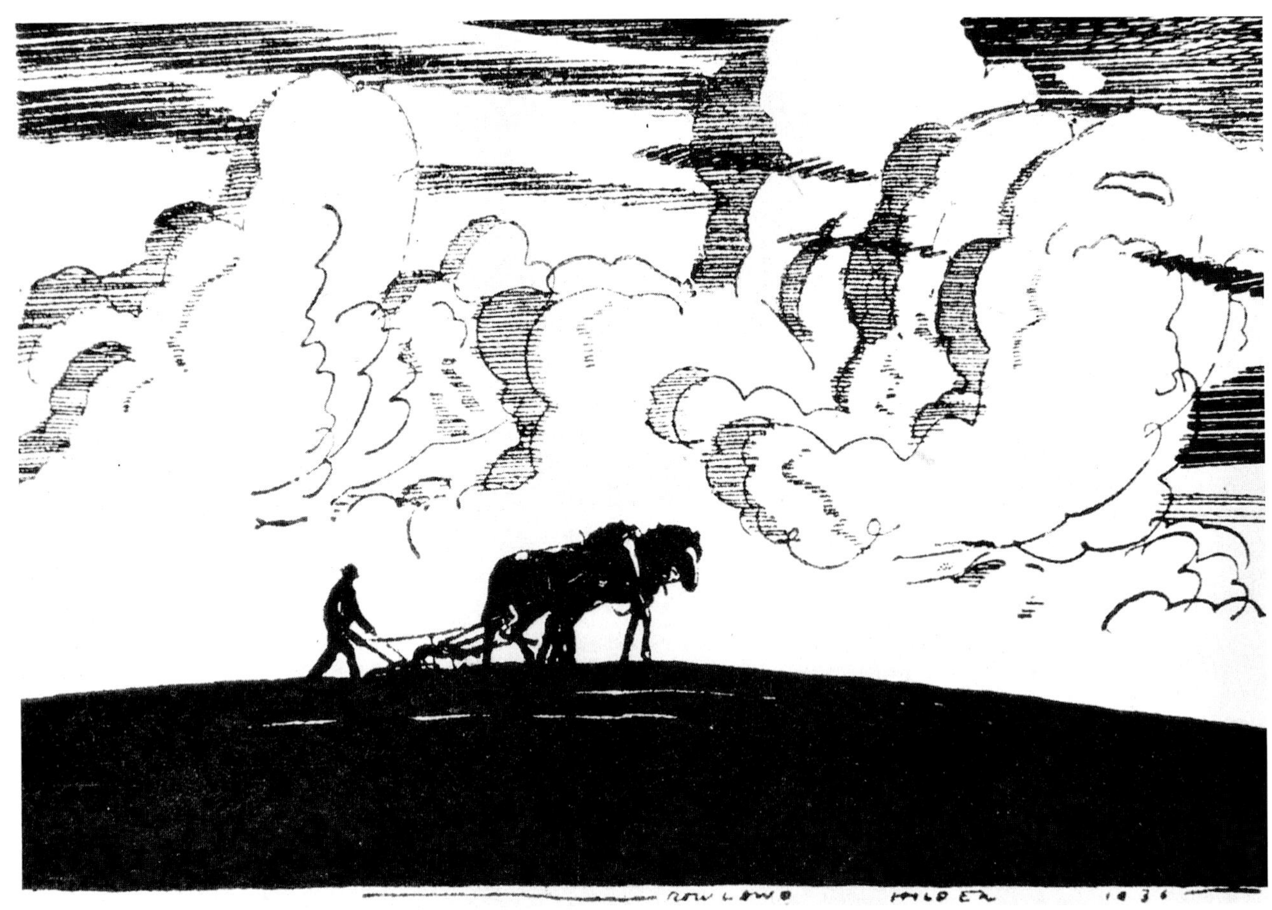

THE PLOUGHMAN

Under the long fell's stony eaves
  The ploughman, going up and down,
Ridge after ridge man's tide-mark leaves,
  And turns the hard grey soil to brown.

Striding, he measures out the earth
  In lines of life, to rain and sun;
And every year that comes to birth
  Sees him go striding on and on.

The seasons change, and then return;
  Yet still, in blind, unsparing ways,
However I may shrink or yearn,
  The ploughman measures out my days.

His acre brought forth roots last year;
  This year it bears the gloomy grain;
Next Spring shall seedling grass appear;
  Then roots and corn and grass again.

Five times the young corn's pallid green
  I have seen spread and change and thrill;
Five times the reapers I have seen
  Go creeping up the far-off hill:

And, as the unknowing ploughman climbs
  Slowly and inverately,
I wonder long how many times
  The corn will spring again for me.

Gordon Bottomley

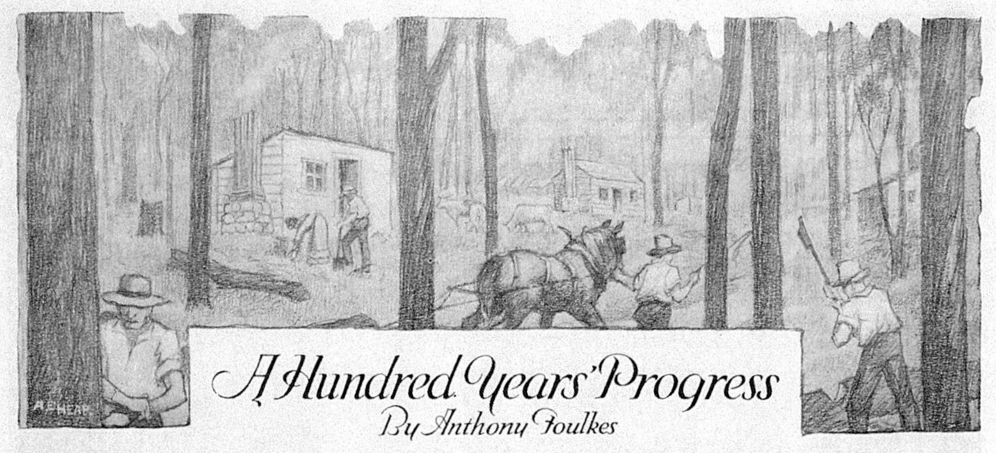

A Hundred Years' Progress
By Anthony Foulkes

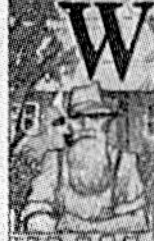

"WHAT was he? What did he accomplish?" are two questions which naturally spring to the lips of a person hearing that another has attained a great age. Age is not necessarily venerable—sometimes it is merely disreputable—and the only thing that really counts is the use to which the years have been put by an individual or a community.

The year which is passing has been celebrated as the Centenary year of Western Australia, and while 100 years is a brief span in the life of a nation, it is long enough to evoke from the interested the kind of question with which this article opens. We are, as a community, a century old: what have we accomplished?

Happily, the record is a bright one. The progress of Western Australia, while by no means steady or even of pace, has been sufficient to engender pride in her children and courage in those who are growing to maturity at the end of the first 100 years. Naturally and appropriately enough, the pace of material progress has accelerated with the passage of the years, until we are now developing faster and more surely than ever before.

A Slow Beginning

In the very early days of the colony, lack of funds, men, and knowledge of the territory and its potentialities naturally made for slow and leisurely advancement. For just over 50 years, in fact, growth was so slow as to appear insignificant from this distance, although doubtless the people of that time deemed it phenomenal. The population slowly crept up from 1,003 souls in 1829 to 29,019 in 1880, fifty-one years later; an average increase of only 549 each year. Between that date and last year, when the population was estimated at 405,908, the average increase was 7,852 each year. The increase was not, of course, as steady and even as this—during the years of the successive gold rushes, the increase in given years often exceeded 20,000—but it does serve to show that the pace of development increased vastly more quickly in the last 49 years of the State's history than in the first 51.

A portion of that last sentence betrays the secret of the sudden impetus given development just after the close of the first half century of the colony's existence. Toward the end of the 80's, the gold rushes began, and in the early 90's the human tide poured torrentially in. Production figures, as well as those of population, tell an eloquent story here. In 1870 the revenue from mining had been a meagre £26; in 1896 it was £212,407. It would be pleasant to be able to record a continuance of this amazing speed of progress in mining down to the present day, but unhappily it is not possible. In 1928 (the last figures available) revenue from mining had fallen to £18,812. The opening and exploitation of the new goldfield at Wiluna may very probably swell the figures again before very long, but for the present, mining is languishing in Western Australia. Even more startling is the contrast put in a different way. In 1870 no gold was produced in this State; in 1903 the value of gold produced was £8,770,719; last year it was £1,671,093.

Grain Follows Gold.

Happily for the State, as gold production declined the production of wealth from a different source—agriculture—swelled enormously. In 1860, by some forgotten freak of circumstance, Western Australia exported wheat to the value of £10 sterling. There followed a long period, broken only by the year 1880 (when for some equally forgotten reason £3,850 worth of wheat was exported), during which a community chiefly occupied with mining was obliged to import wheat. Last year the value of the wheat exported reached £6,994,528—proof that the virile energies of the community had been diverted to wealth production of a kind more enduring and actually more valuable to humanity than the production of gold. Wheat's companion, wool, was one of our earliest exports (£15,482 worth was exported as early as 1850), and this great source of wealth has been steadily cultivated until the export figures for 1928 were £4,962,916.

Timber was an early source of revenue, 200 loads, to the value of £2,500 being exported in 1836, seven years after the foundation of the colony. In 1927 the figures had grown to 262,225 loads and £1,658,018. Last year the value of timber exported had fallen nearly £400,000 below that of 1927, but this was due rather to industrial factors than to any real impediment in the production of wealth from this source. Parenthetically, it may here be noted with pleasure that the State's very active Forestry Department is now taking steps to ensure that the progressive denudation of our forests shall be compensated for by reafforestation. The result promises to be a transference, in the distant future, from hardwood culture to softwood culture (pines flourish in our climate, and our characteristic hardwoods defy the craft of the forester anxious to repair the ravages of the axeman); but we are now unlikely to suffer the reproach of having wasted our substance utterly.

Exports of fresh fruit grew in value from £1 (quaint sum!) in 1893 to £334,272 in 1927; seasonal conditions accounted for a drop last year, but this year's crop—of apples particularly—promised, though figures are not yet available, to excel the record of two years ago. Flour exports have grown until exports last year exceeded £1,000,000 in value. From all these figures it is evident that the good earth of the State has abundantly recompensed us for the exhaustion of mineral wealth in the parts exploited.

The Witness of Ships.

For sheer impressiveness, however, the figures relating to shipping are perhaps most telling. They are an excellent barometer of trade, and indicate growth and expansion more eloquently than any isolated figures concerning one or another commodity. In 1829, eighteen ships visited our shores bearing 5,209 tons of imports, valued at £50,284. Our total exports for that and several following years were apparently nil. In 1850, 64 ships arrived bearing 15,988 tons of imports, worth £52,351; 67 ships left, carrying 14,784 tons of exports valued at £22,135. In 1928, 792 ships arrived with 3,795,310 tons of imports valued at £18,287,633; and 812 ships left bearing 3,806,078 tons of exports, worth £18,240,775.

In a country of wide spaces, the sources of whose revenues are chiefly primary production in the hinterland, means of transport are a sine qua non. It follows that railways must grow more or less pari passu with the growth of population and production. In 1880 (the railways are only half as old as the State) Western Australia had 34 miles of Government railways open to traffic, and in that year they produced £2,626 in gross revenue. In the same year there were 38 miles of private line open. Last year there were 3,977 miles of Government railways open to traffic, and they produced a gross revenue of £3,858,051. There were also 838 miles of private line open. Western Australia has a greater railway mileage in proportion to population than any other country in the world.

The Coming State.

As a record of material progress all this is very satisfactory; sufficiently so, indeed, to justify the commonly held belief that Western Australia is "the coming State." Man does not live by bread alone, and no review of prosperity would be adequate or complete that stopped at the purely material and failed to take cognisance of those all-important factors which make for spiritual and cultural advancement. There is not in the Commonwealth a better system of free primary education than that prevailing in the 841 State schools of Western Australia. Last year 47,321 attended these schools, the total cost per head being £11/7/10. Private schools to the number of 123 were attended by 10,865 children. The University, which has the distinction of being the only completely free University in the world, has been able during the Centenary year to begin to build worthily on a new site at Crawley, thanks to the munificent bequest of the late Sir Winthrop Hackett. The year has been admirably marked, too, by the institution of a series of tutorial classes for adults. This extra-mural work, voluntarily undertaken, will do much to ensure that the cultural progress of the people keeps pace with the material progress which, alone, is apt to lead to flaccidity of mind and anaemia of the spirit.

Those of us to whom the State is dear must feel, at the close of this Centenary year, that all the auguries are happy and that given good counsel and the ability to bear success (an intoxicating beverage), ours will not be the least enviable community beneath the Southern Cross. Some of us may even hazard the opinion that the centre of gravity of the Commonwealth will eventually shift westward, drawn by the magnet of abundance and sustained success.

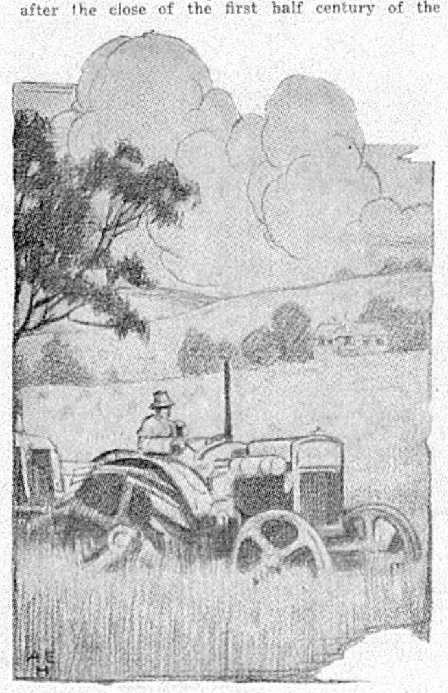

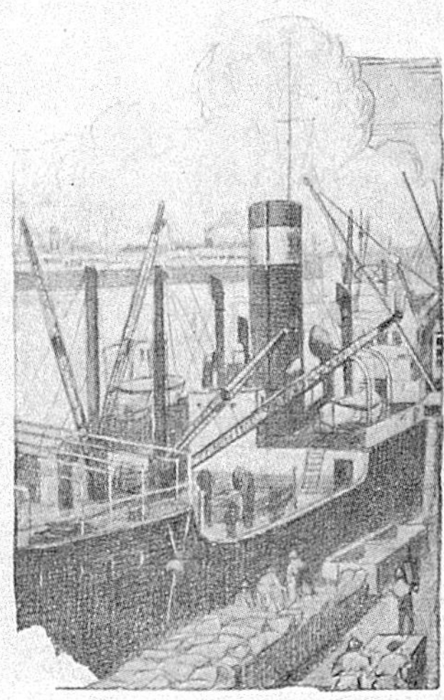

Only the ploughman is absent as Amy Heap links the Westralian and universal past with progress in the modern world.

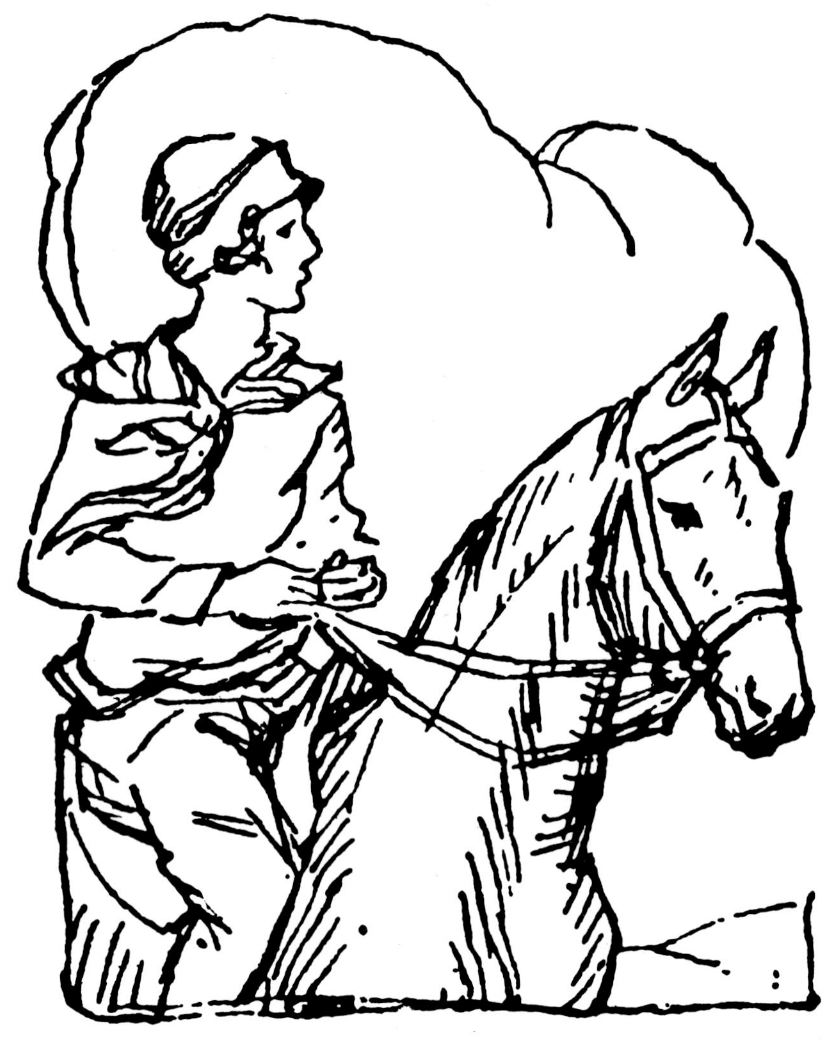

The Beau Idyll: the daughter as rural horse-woman, home on holiday from private schooling in
Perth or at Kobeelya. The image is present in British Girls' Annuals and dominates
Mary Grant Bruce's Billabong books.

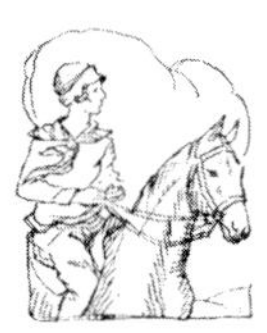
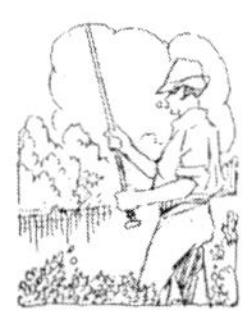

WESTERN AUSTRALIA
For Glorious Holidays

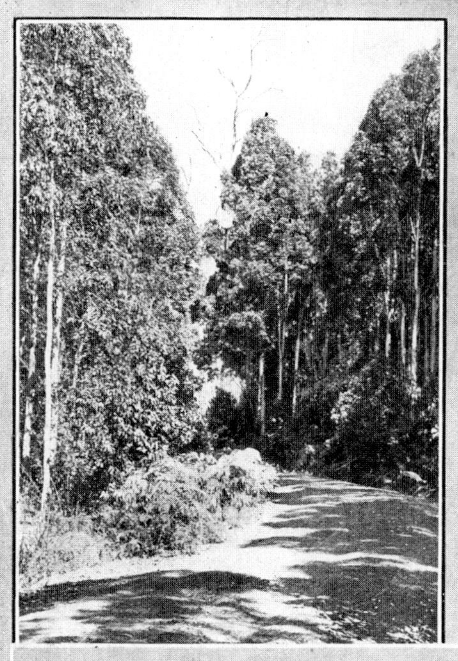

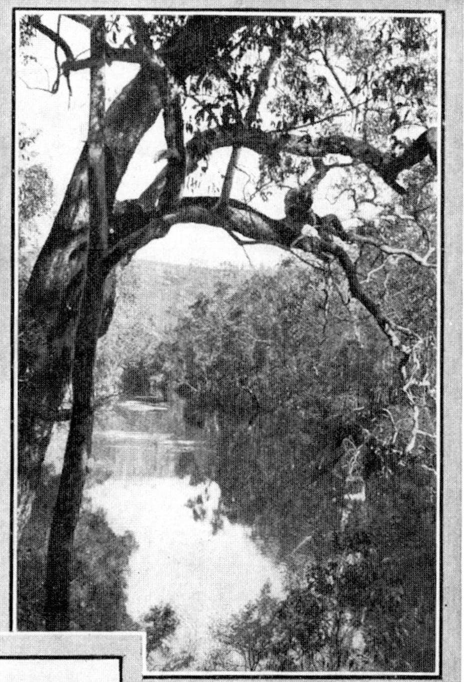

AUSTRALIA'S
Natural
Playground

CLIMATIC CONDITIONS
UNEXCELLED.

HEALTH RESORTS UNLIMITED.

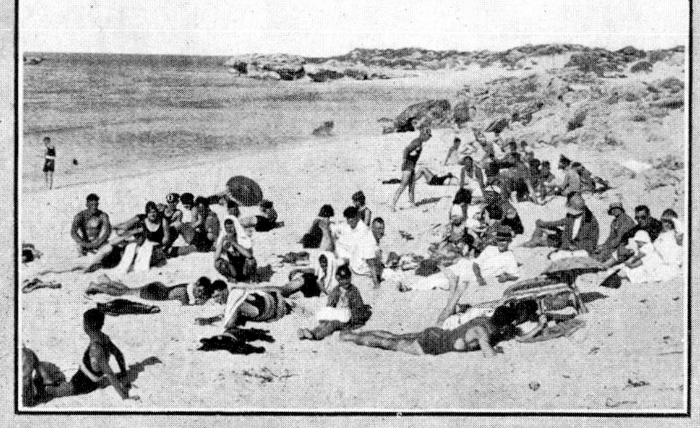

Magnificent Ocean Beaches and Inspiring Forest Scenery.

COUPON TOURS ARRANGED, ITINERARIES PREPARED, SEASIDE AND COUNTRY COMBINED.

Call or write for free literature and information.

Government Tourist and Publicity Bureau
62 BARRACK-STREET (Next Town Hall), PERTH, WESTERN AUSTRALIA.

Telephones B4376 and B9121. Cable and Telegraphic Address : "TOURIST," PERTH.

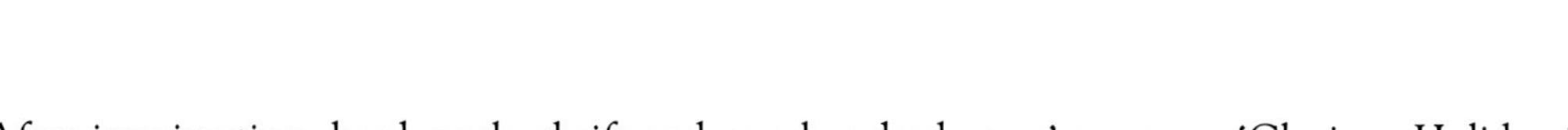

After immigration, hard work, thrift and one hundred years' progress, 'Glorious Holidays' could be enjoyed in Western Australia's 'Natural Playground', even during the depression, 1931.

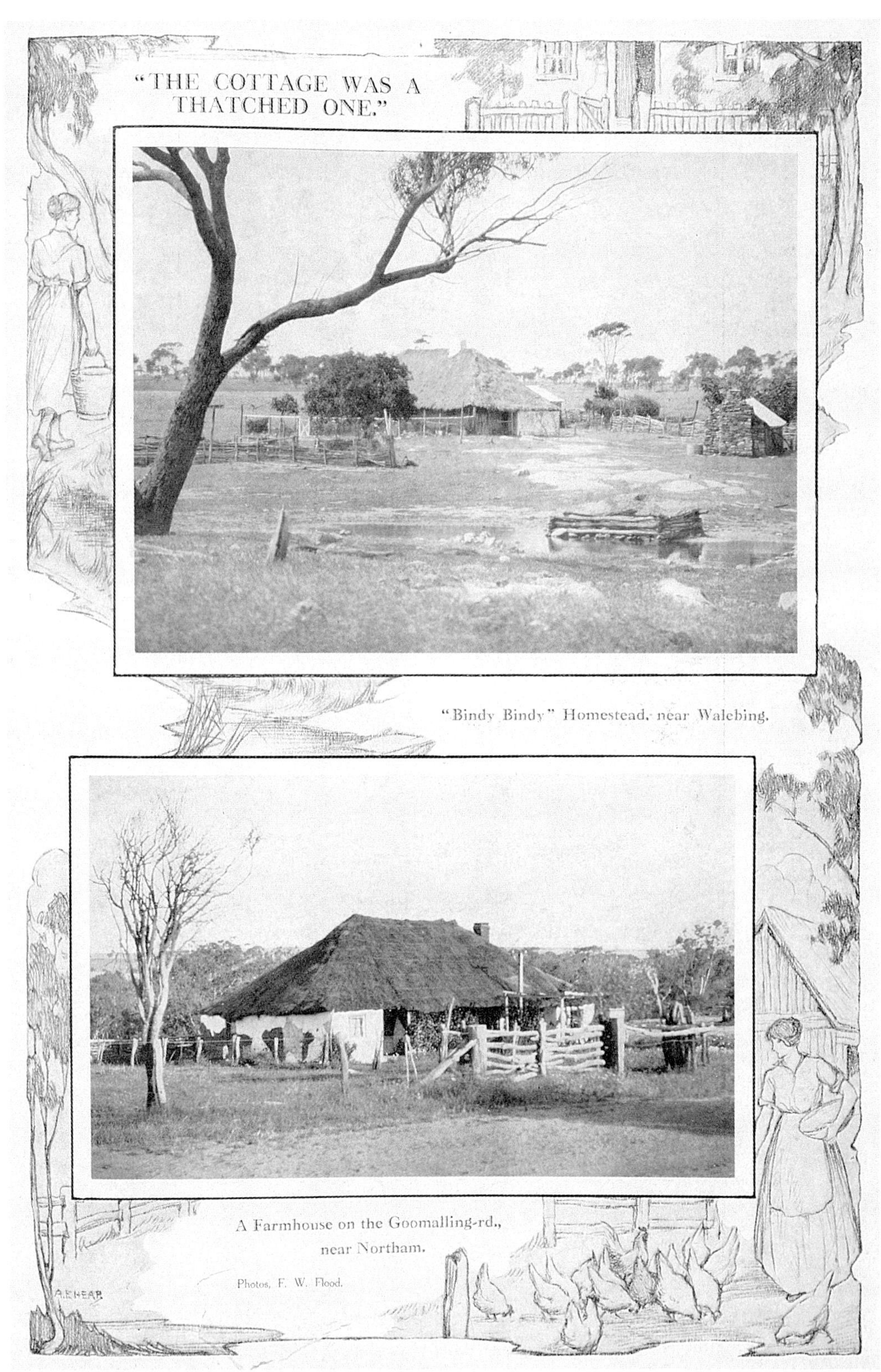

"Bindy Bindy" Homestead, near Walebing.

A Farmhouse on the Goomalling-rd.,
near Northam.

Photos, F. W. Flood.

The thatched cottage was redolent of William Shakespeare's Stratford on Avon and its image is always present in books like H.V. Morton's *In Search of England* (1928) and J.B. Priestley's *English Journey* (1934). The Westralian River Avon runs through Northam and Toodyay. The landscape is tamed and productive, historic and picturesque. The bush mum plays her part. The Western Australian Historical Society had been founded in 1926. This photograph, too, celebrates the centenary of European settlement in Western Australia.

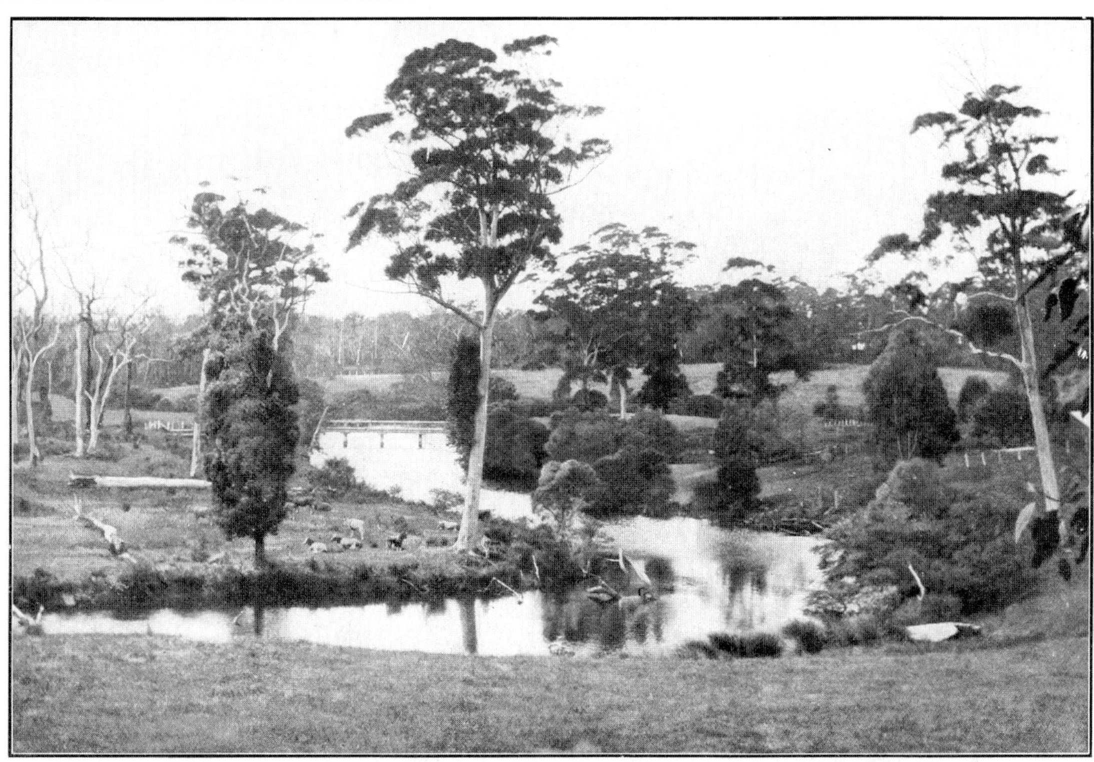

A Picturesque Scene on the Denmark River,
in the South-West.

Photo. N. G. Tyler.

William Wordsworth at work in Western Australia's south-west: 'Open unto the fields, and to the sky:/All bright and glittering in the smokeless air . . . Ne'er say I, never felt, a calm so deep/The river glideth at his own sweet will'. Arcadian London; sylvan Denmark.

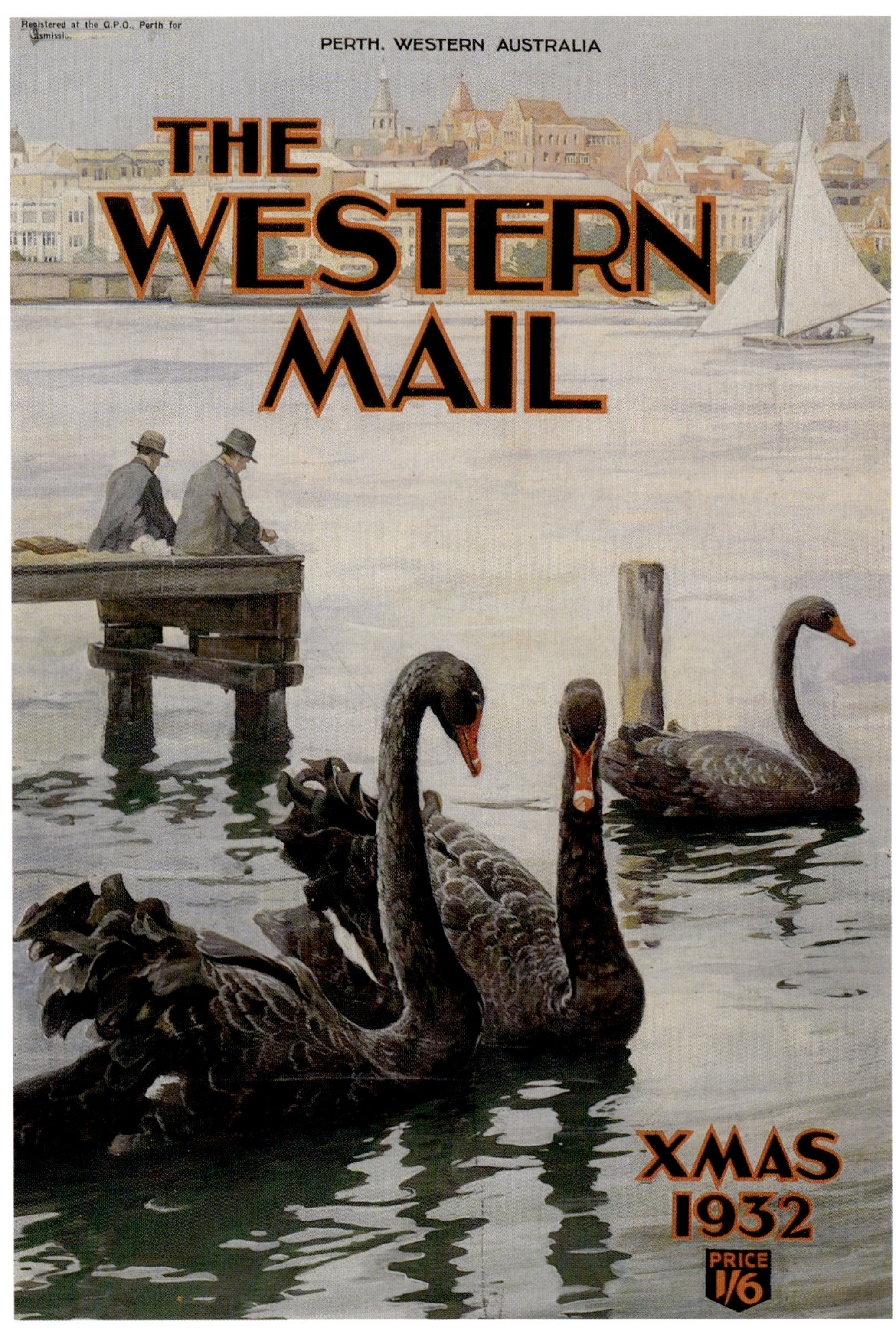

Unhurried, tranquil and arcadian, the new world's Perth floats on the gentle waters of the Swan.
Amy's image validates the immigrant experience and reconciles nature and civilisation. Perth is a
garden city whose little heart is lying still. The Great Depression is at its fiercest.

AMY HEAP

Amy Elizabeth Heap came from an old and large South Lancashire family. She was born at 63 Bradford Street, in the city of Bolton in the sub-district of Songe with Hanlgh, on 6 February 1874. Her father, James, was a wine merchant; other male members of branches of the family were clergymen and schoolmasters, with one, the Rev. T. Hargreaves Heap, also a minor painter. Amy was educated at Bolton and later trained at an art school in nearby Manchester. From Manchester and London she later sat for examinations to become an art teacher. She was twenty-one years of age when in November 1895 she received an 'Art Class Teacher's Certificate' from the grandly titled Department of Science and Art of the Committee of Her Majesty's Most Honourable Privy Council on Education. In order to gain her Certificate Amy submitted a sheet on geometrical problems, an outline of ornament, a shaded drawing from a group of models, and a shaded drawing from a piece of ornament. She also passed the Department's exams in Science, Perspective, Drawing in Outline from the Cast, and Drawing in Light and Shade.

Two years later, in November 1897, Amy passed the Department's 'Certificate for Art Instruction' in drawing. This time she submitted a perspective problem in words and then worked in ink. She also prepared a sheet of diagrams showing the applications of the principles on which Foliated Design was constructed. She did a figure sheet. But most importantly, she drew a sheet of foliage drawn in outline from a freely growing plant, and a study in colour of a 'growing plant from nature', as the Certificate records. In addition she produced three related designs of the plant 'to fill agreeably a square, a

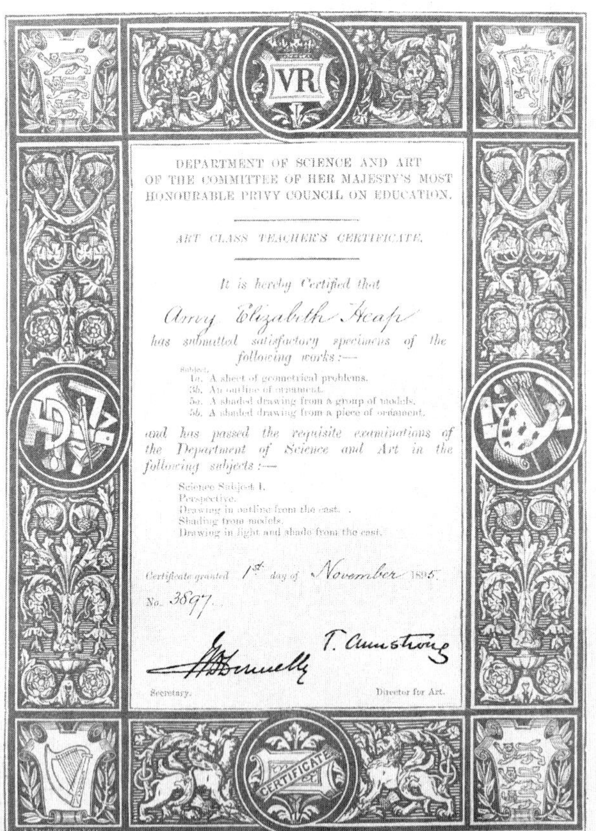

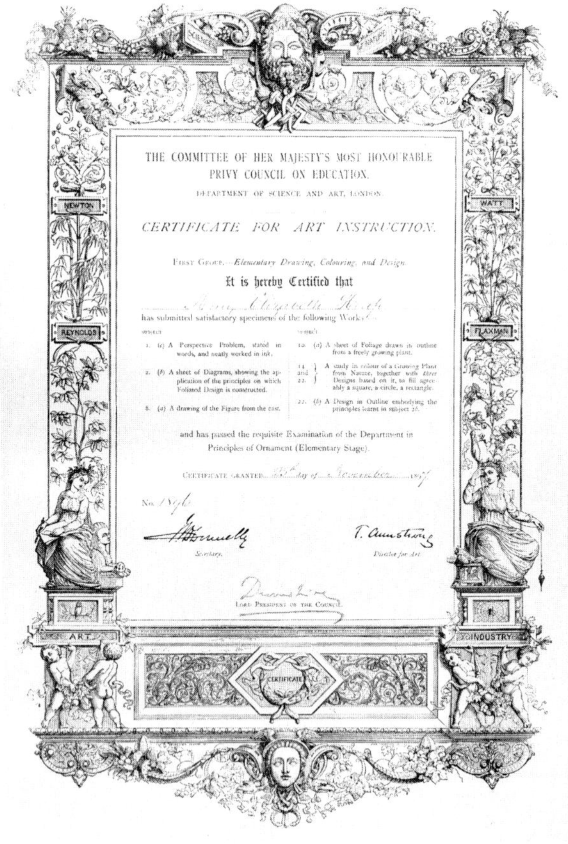

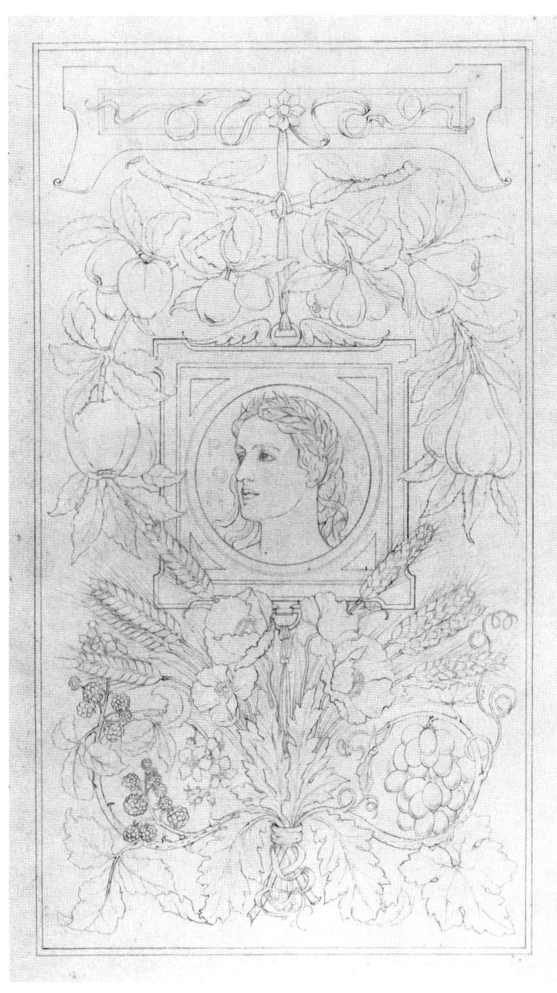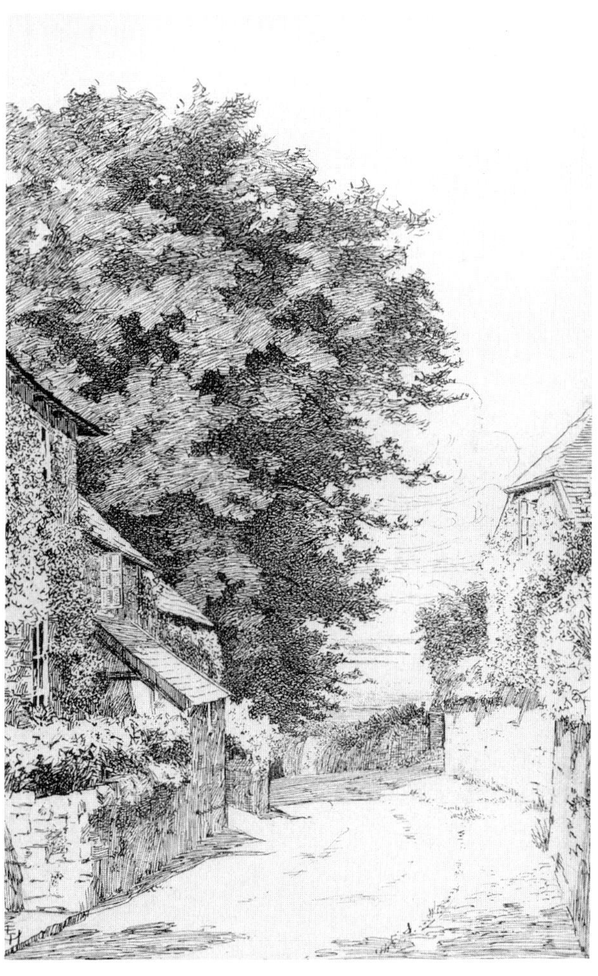

Emigrant Amy presents her English credentials, including art certificates, a specimen of 'works'
required by the Committee of Her Majesty's Most Honourable Privy Council on Education,
Department of Science and Art, London, and a drawing of an early painting trip
to Cornwall or Devon.

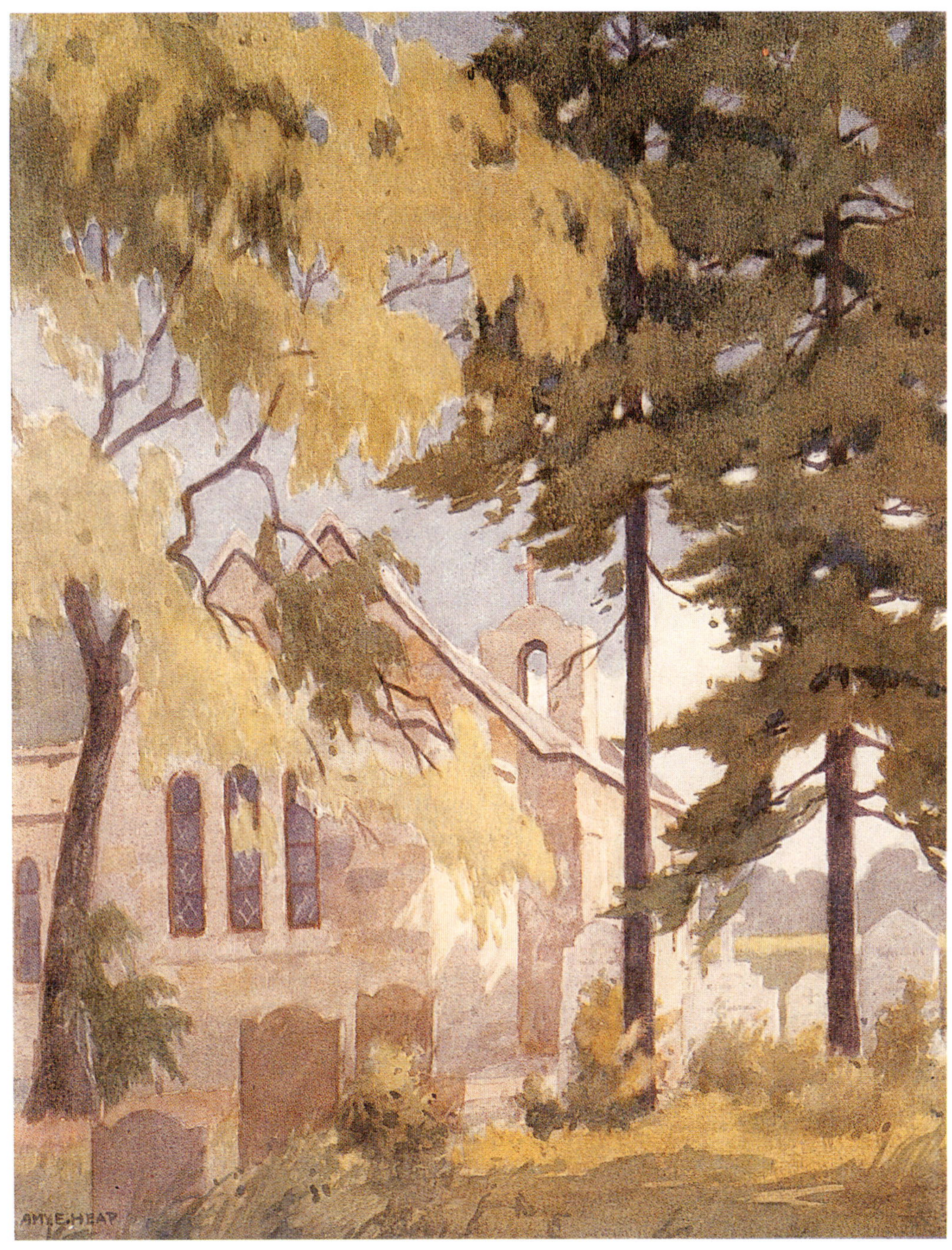

St Mary's Church, Busselton, 1934. Amy was drawn to the old Anglican churches of Western Australia from York to Albany. She also painted the Monastery at New Norcia. Reprinted in the *Western Mail* 1936. Her caption is 'Here are the graves of many West Australian Pioneers'.

circle, a rectangle'. She passed the exam on the principles of ornament, and emerged as an artist and teacher, especially of watercolour and pen and ink. Two extant drawings seem to have formed part of her folio for the London exams.

Over the next decade Amy's career is seen through a glass darkly. She certainly travelled in the south-west of England on sketching tours; and it is likely that she taught art classes, although her parents were comfortably off and by then could be described as being of independent means.

Yet in 1909 Amy, her brother, and her sister Ethel, decided to migrate to Australia, perhaps under the Western Australian Government's assisted passage scheme, but more likely in response to the general 'Land of Opportunities' publicity campaign in Britain. The years 1910 and 1911 brought the greatest number of migrants to Western Australia between 1903 and 1919. Amy and Ethel were among them, arriving in 1910 and living first in 'a home in the bush' at Freshwater Bay in Claremont, and later, more permanently, at Darlington.

From 1912 to 1925 she exhibited irregularly with the West Australian Society of Arts. She also exhibited even less continuously with the newly formed Perth Society of Artists, from 1933 to 1944. Her first exhibited watercolour was of the Quayside, St Ives, in Cornwall. Many young artists, particularly women, visited the artists' colonies in Cornwall, sometimes to attend classes given by well-known painters such as Stanhope Forbes, sometimes merely to sketch the attractive scenery of the area. In a way Amy's choice of painting for exhibition in Western Australia was a presentation of her

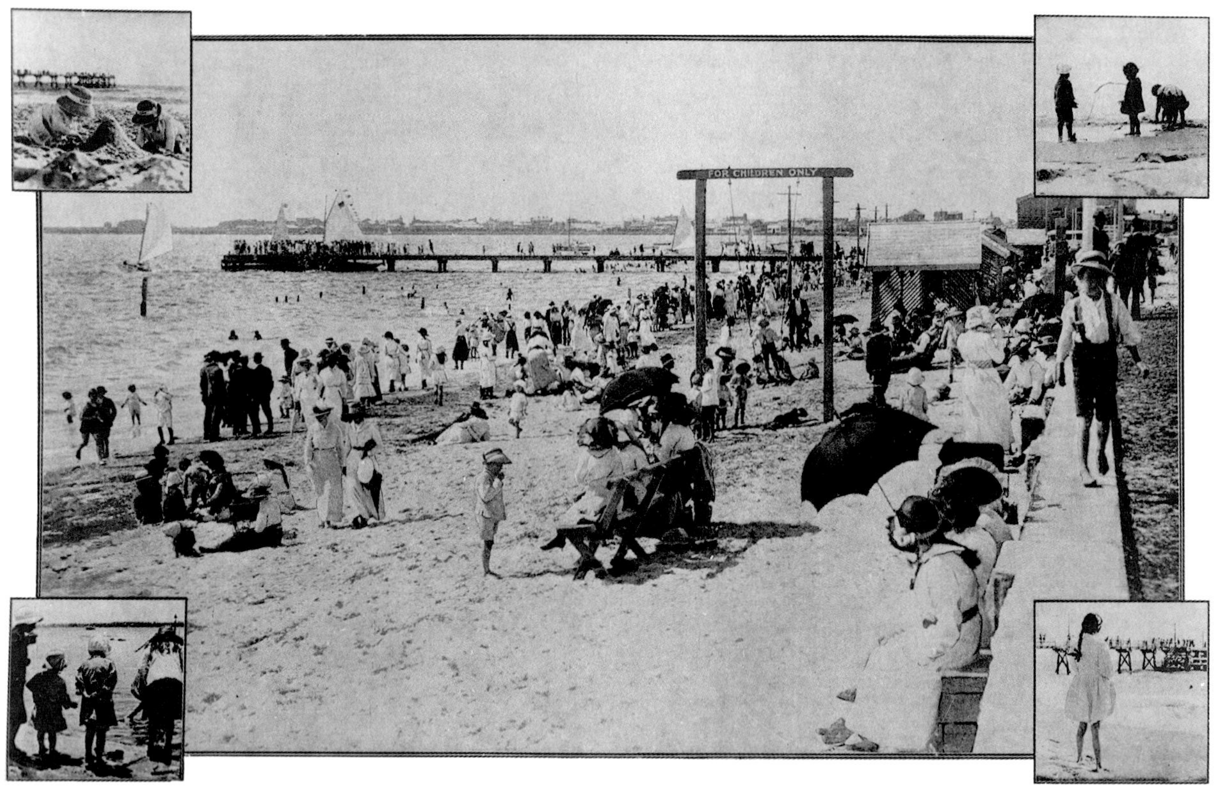

The pier is a central motif in English beach paintings. It is classless and pleasure-laden. It represents a family ideal, magnified here by Amy Heap's border photographs. Amy loved Rottnest and Albany among Western Australian resorts. These images are of South Beach, Fremantle, in 1918.

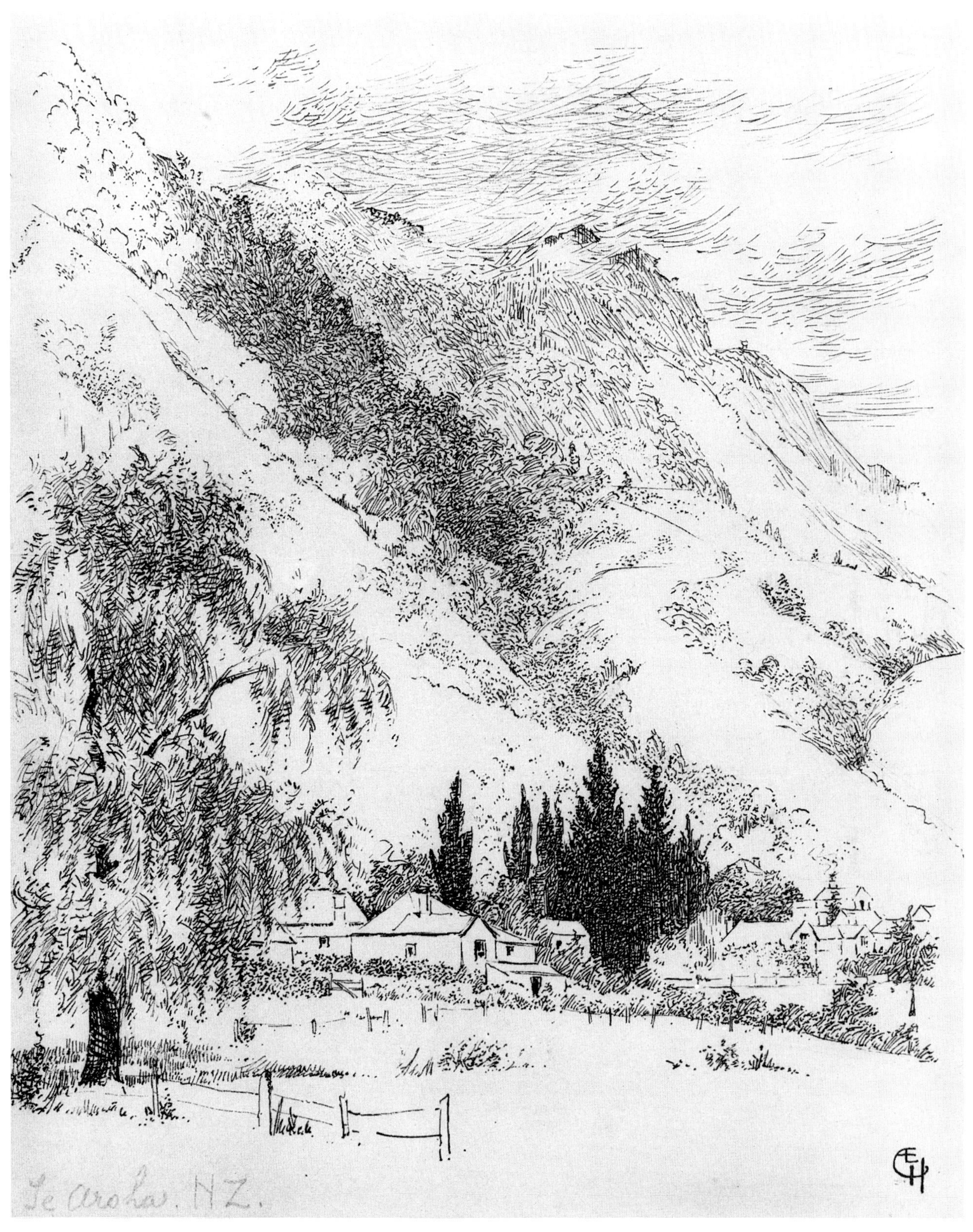

Te Aroha, New Zealand. Amy loved to travel to mountainous regions, whether in New Zealand or Tasmania. The comfortable tamed landscape, green and unpolluted, merges naturally into the wilderness.

artistic credentials.

In 1912 Amy also exhibited other works in several mediums. She had travelled to York, that most historic and English of country towns in Western Australia, and her drawing was simply called 'College St. York'. Other drawings were of Freshwater Bay and 'The Old Camp, Claremont'. The last named was Heap's first attempt to link the Westralian past and present in a spirit of harmony and beauty. Amy also exhibited covers for a table, a duchesse and a cushion, as well as a teacosy and an embroidered bag. This needlework seems to have been designed by Amy and probably executed by her, although her sister Ethel worked a portfolio cover, also exhibited. Decorated boxes were also sold. The prices asked for drawings and artefacts varied from one pound five shillings to two pounds twelve shillings and sixpence.

The following year, 1913, Amy again exhibited with the West Australian Society of Arts. From the value put on the items, it seems that they were watercolours rather than just pen and ink drawings: 'Interior of Old Church, York' — four pounds; 'The Homestead' — three pounds. Only 'The Cottage', priced at three pounds was a drawing. The titles are evocative: 'old', 'cottage', 'homestead'. Amy looked for the picturesque and historical in her new surrounds.

In 1916 she was well enough known and respected for one of her drawings — 'Bengaberring Farm' — to be included in the anthology edited by Walter Murdoch called *The Westralia Gift Book*. Among other contributors were Henri van Raalte, Alfred Chandler, William Siebenhaar and George Pitt Morison. W.C. Thomas's story 'When

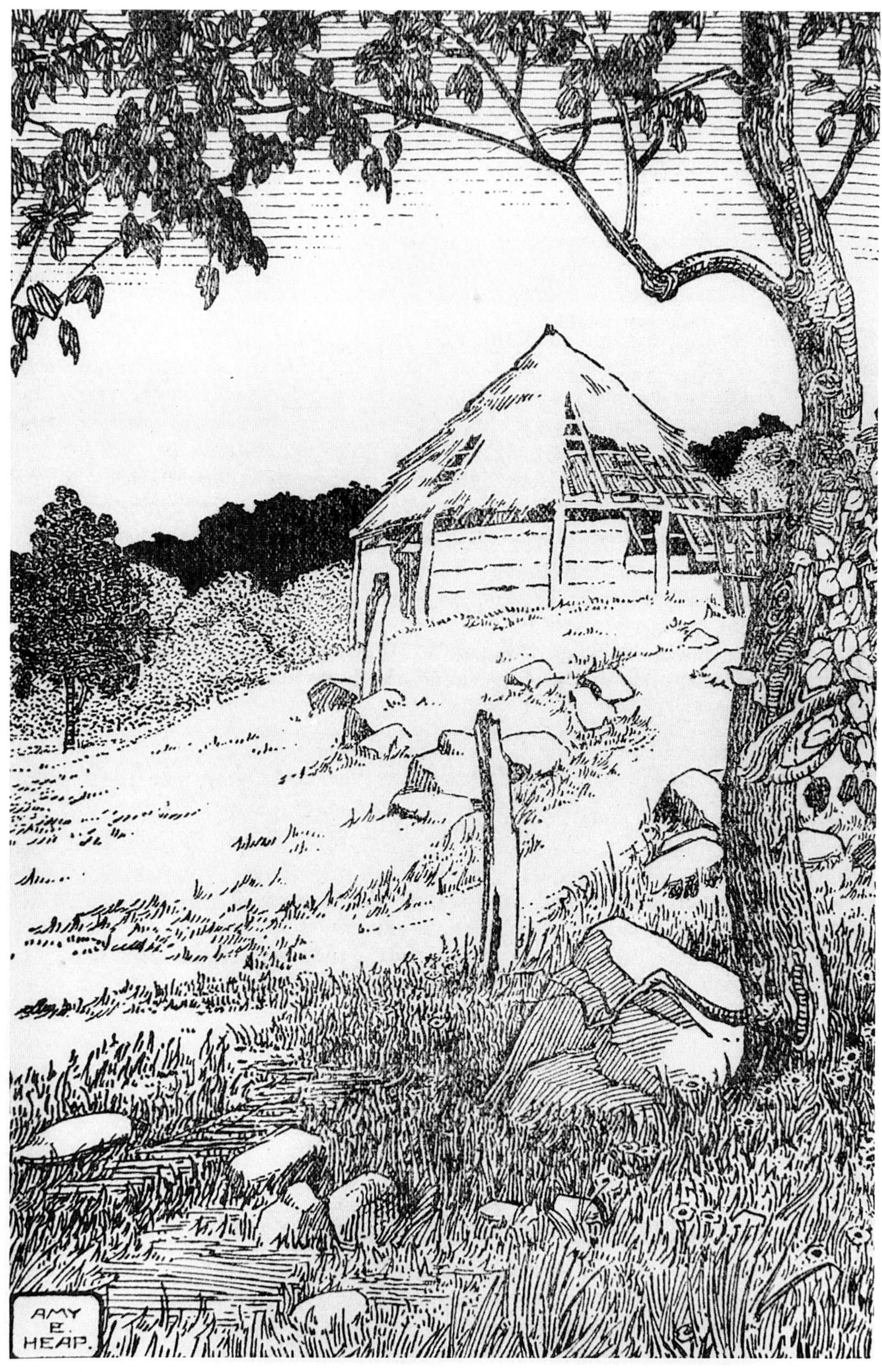

One of Amy's earliest known published Western Australian drawings — 'Farm at Bengaberring'. It was commissioned by Walter Murdoch, editor of *The Westralia Gift Book*, 1916. Bengaberring is near Goomalling in the wheat belt. Many of these properties were opened up under Sir John Forrest's Homestead Act of 1893 and after the construction of the goldfields pipeline in 1903.

the Mill Awakens', set in the idyllic south-west of Western Australia, is closest in feeling to Heap's drawing. The themes of the book were patriotism (the recipients of the sales of the book were the YMCA and the Retired Nurses Fund), the beauty of nature, and the importance of community in a time of great human stress from outside. Rural contentment in a Westralian Eden was the antidote to, or antithesis of, war. It was a theme which Heap would bring to complete fulfilment in the interwar years.

Some time during the Great War Amy Heap was invited by the proprietors of Western Australian Newspapers Ltd, which published the *West Australian*, the *Western Mail* and the *Daily News*, to join the staff as a photographer/artist. It may have been her skill as a photographer which first won her employment. In the 1918 Christmas issue of the *Western Mail* Amy combined with E.L. Mitchell, the principal photographer, on two decorative pages of beach and fishing scenes. Heap's photos were used as corner/border decorations for Mitchell's large centred photographs. However, it seems clear that Charles Harper may have been an early purchaser of Amy's watercolours, and her employment at the *West* may have been instigated by him as proprietor.

From 1922 Heap began to contribute drawings to the *Western Mail*. Her London training in ornament stood her in good stead, for she was asked to provide border drawings for photos, poems, articles and short stories. Amy's keen sense of design and skill in execution mark many pages of the Christmas issues of the *Western Mail* right through to the late 1930s. Indeed she took over the border drawing role from the *West*'s principal artist since 1903, Stanway Tapp. In the 1923 issue of the *Western Mail* she decorated C.N. Carter's poem 'Fairy Gifts' and contributed side drawings — of Australian bush pixies — to a large photograph of Meelup Beach, taken probably by Fred Flood. Interestingly, no photographs by Heap seem to have been ever reproduced again, although it is known that she remained a keen photographer.

In the early and mid-1920s the Christmas issue of the *Western Mail* carried colour reproductions of original paintings by Archibald B. Webb, the noted art teacher. Stanway Tapp, too, contributed original paintings, but mostly he printed colour-tinted photographs, as did the vibrant Len Cutten.

Nineteen twenty-five seems to have been a crucial year for Amy Heap. In that year she produced a major series of drawings on the theme of 'The Pioneer's Progress', illustrating evocatively four photographs of farm development. She also did numerous decorative drawings for a series of photographs comparing and contrasting Perth in 1890 and in 1925, including Arcadian scenes from Kings Park. Here she found a subject matter compatible with her nostalgia for rural England, so dominant in her British sketches. It was an approach, a theme, a sentiment, she would never lose. And it was compatible in spirit with discussions about the formation of the Western Australian Historical Society in the same year.

The following year, 1926, the *Western Mail* published the first of Amy's two-colour drawings. These included a strikingly ornate loose-leaf calendar for 1927; and a notable drawing of a boy on the weathered old steps of Thomson's Bay on Rottnest Island. She had first exhibited this in 1925. She visited Rottnest on several occasions, sometimes in the company of the photographer Fred Flood. Neither noted the island's use as an Aboriginal prison; both gloried in it as a place of rest, a place of goodwill and a place of high spirits, as well as a place of great natural beauty.

By 1928 Heap and Flood dominated the Christmas issue of the *Western Mail* in its visual imagery. Indeed they often combined to produce stunning effects for Westralian scenes. And in 1929, Western Australia's Centenary Year, Amy's brilliant watercolour 'Nuytsia Floribunda', or 'Christmas Tree in Bloom', complete with an attractive landscape and homely scene with a girl under a parasol, was the front cover of the *Western Mail* annual. Heap contributed all four watercolours in the issue.

In 1933 Amy's work was included in Glascock's celebrated anthology, *Jarrah Leaves*. Like *The Westralia Gift Book* of 1916, *Jarrah Leaves* appeared at a time of community and personal difficulties and struggle, the period known in popular memory as the Great Depression. It was designed as an affirmation of the worth of rural values and community goodwill. Heap contributed two evocative scenes, bringing together the enduring and transcendent strengths of rural life and English law: 'The Old Barn, Manjimup', and 'Old Supreme Court, Perth'.

It was in 1933 or 1934 that Amy Heap retired from West Australian Newspapers and went to live at Albany. Her colleagues recall that she did not move with them to their new quarters, Newspaper House, on the south side of St George's Terrace, in 1934. Thereafter, for several years, Amy was only an occasional contributor to the newspaper's annual. By 1940, with the advent of the use of full-colour ('natural

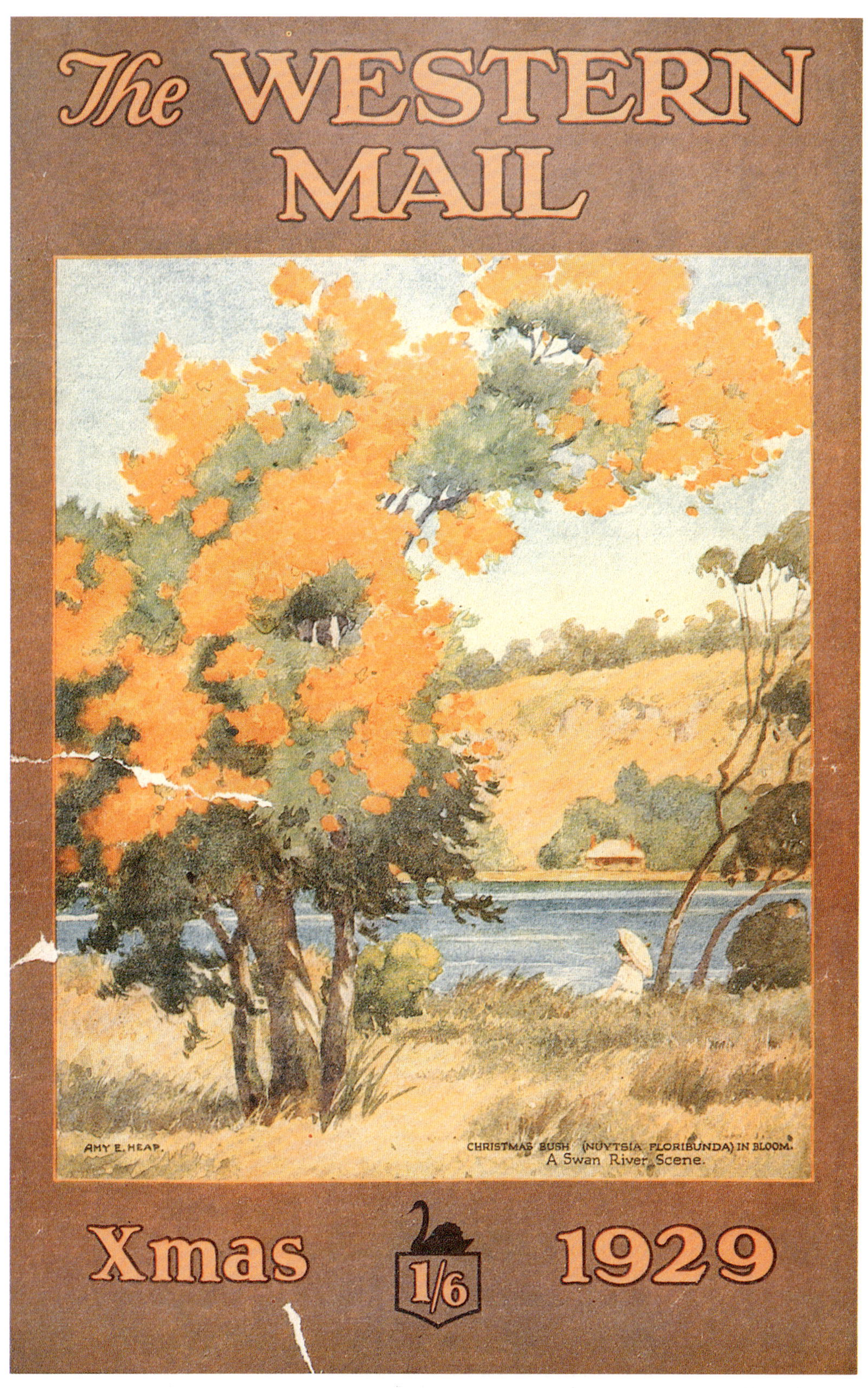

Amy Heap as the poetess of the urban pastoral. Living for a time at Freshwater Bay, Amy later exhibited several watercolours of the Bay. She returned to the area to paint 'Nuytsia Floribunda: Christmas Tree in Bloom on the Swan River' for the cover of the *Western Mail* 1929. Mosman heights form the backdrop for the twin beauties of nature and art.

colour') photography, her skills were no longer required. Flood made a relatively easy transition to colour photography. But that art did not need border pen drawings, and few original paintings were thereafter reproduced.

Amy Heap retired from Darlington to Albany. In her lifetime she was an inveterate traveller. By 1923 she had been to Tasmania and New Zealand, drawing always. In 1938 she visited England, returning home to Manchester where she showed paintings and drawings in a mixed exhibition. Back in retirement in Denman Road, Albany, living with her sister Ethel, Amy painted many local scenes. Some of these watercolours were purchased years later by Sir Claude Hotchin, then developing the great collection for the benefit of the people of Western Australia. He donated Amy's paintings to the Albany Town Council where they hang to this day. In her old age Amy made several donations of jewellery to the Western Australian Art Gallery. These included an old brooch which belonged to her grandmother: 'It is oval in shape 3″ x 2″ with a scroll design in gold framing it, and the central panel has six curls of hair beautifully arranged on a white porcelain with fine gold lines.' Interestingly, Amy sent the brooch first to Dr Battye (2 July 1952) who passed it on to Laurie Thomas, the Director of the Art Gallery. Thomas would have despaired of Amy's watercolours and drawings, for he was a 'modernist' man. But he accepted the brooch and silver boxes happily enough.

Amy Heap is remembered as aristocratic in bearing, manner and speech; and very, very English. One of her former colleagues at the *Western Mail* described her affectionately as a 'Dresden china' sort of person, small but very impressive. At

Denman Rd.
Albany.
5ᵗ Aug 1952.

LT/SH

The Director.
Art Gallery
Perth.

Dear Sir
   Thank you for your letter of the 30ᵗ July.
I am sending by the same post (registered) a small parcel containing the brooch + have also enclosed three little silver boxes, which I think would be used for scent or smelling salts, also an old quaint Sampler 1741. These were exhibited some years ago in the Antique Exhibition in Perth.
I would like to donate these also to the Museum in the Art Gallery if they would be acceptable to you.
   Yours faithfully
   (Miss) Amy E. Heap.

Amy offers the family heritage to the Museum and Art Gallery of Western Australia, 1952.

Newspaper House she was always referred to as 'Miss Heap'. Her handwriting, even in old age, was precise, neat and self-confident. Her private life remains that. Her friendship with artists like Muriel Southern is beyond recall, as is her household world. She was an independent person, driving a motor car from early on; and she joined the Australian Journalists Association B Division for photographers/artists. A brilliant observer of land and people in her adopted country, she was known in her lifetime as a 'specialist in embellishment'. She died on 17 April 1956.

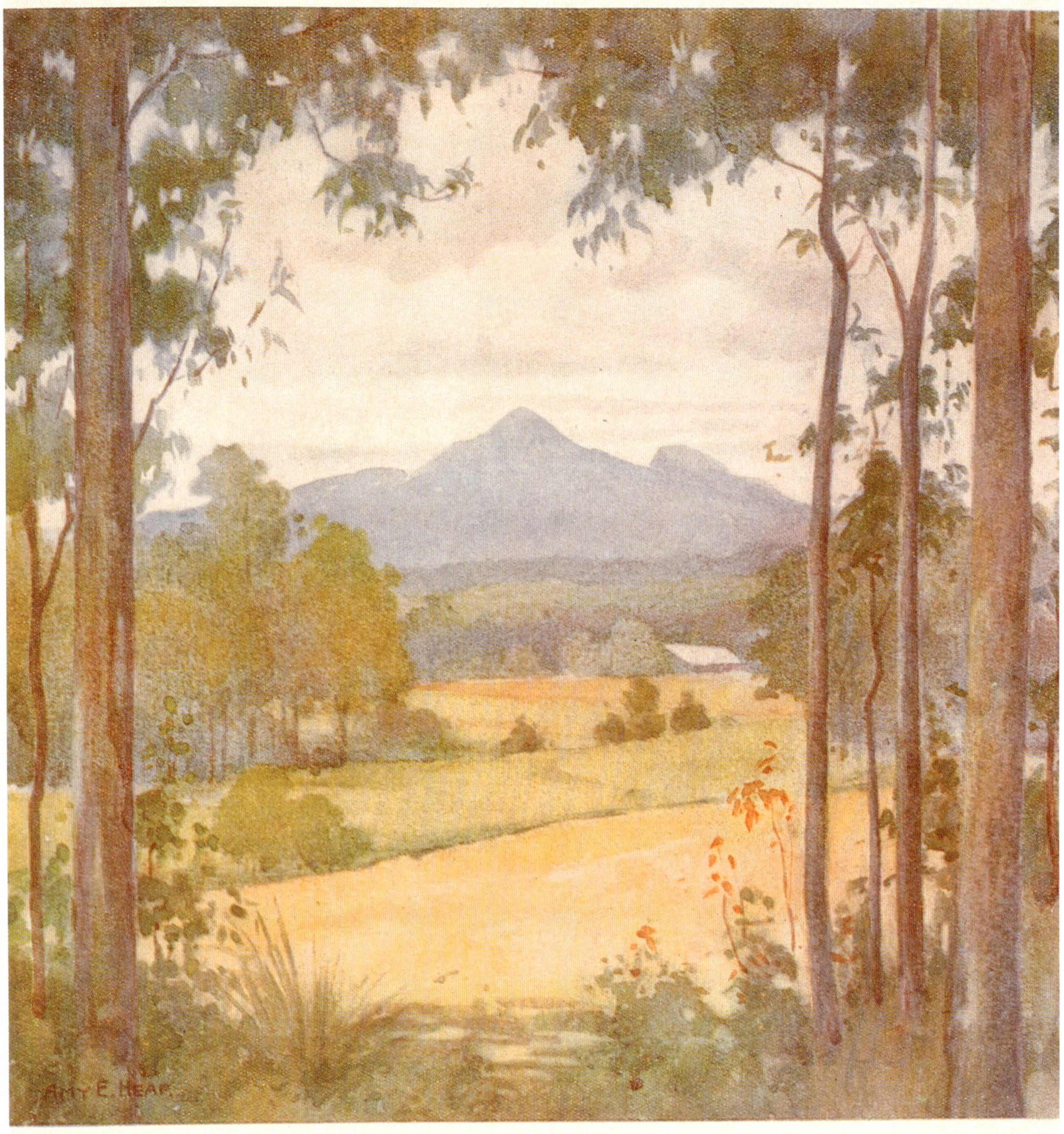

A Glimpse of the Stirling Ranges.

Nature had a religious power for Amy. In Western Australia the Stirling Ranges came closest to the mountains of New Zealand, Tasmania, and parts of England. A glimpse at the Stirling Ranges is transformed by image and caption: 'I will lift up mine eyes unto the hills', lines from Psalm 121 so well known to Amy and her viewers that they do not need 'from whence cometh my help. My help cometh from the Lord, which made heaven and earth'. Did Amy put her trust in God's protection? Her images suggest so.

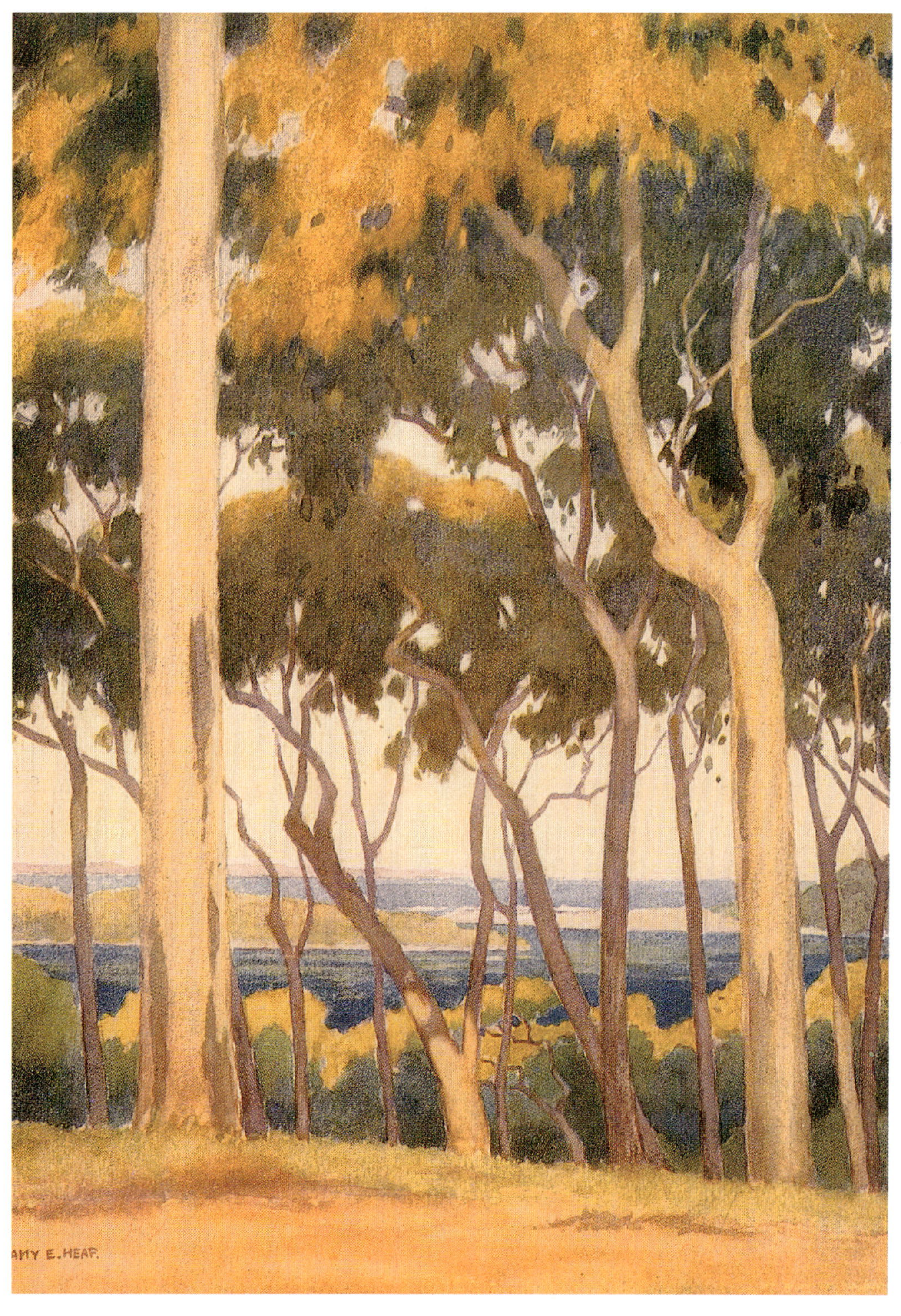

Inlet at Augusta, 1936. In retirement at Albany Amy painted many local scenes such as Middleton Beach and the inlet at Augusta to the west.

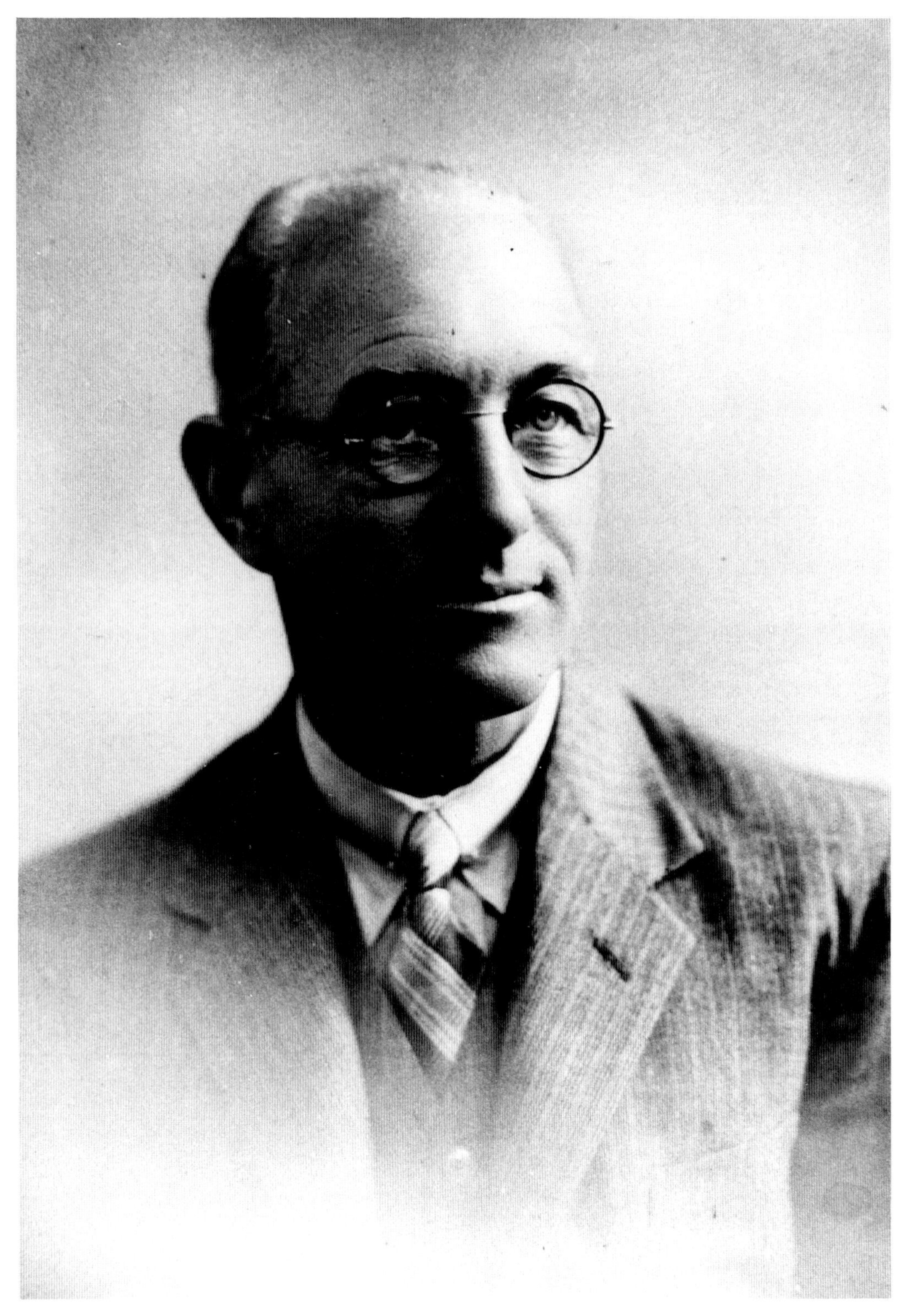

Fred Flood, photographed c.1920.

FRED FLOOD

Frederick William Flood was born at St Paul's Deptford, near Greenwich, in London, on 19 August 1881. His parents, Frederick and Jessie, lived at 29 Camplin Street, Hatcham. Frederick senior worked nearby as an auctioneer's clerk. Young Frederick grew up in a working-class household in a working-class suburb with some lower middle-class employment prospects. Fred took early employment as a copying clerk, copying being a skill still valued highly in late Victorian England before the general use of the typewriter. Indeed by the early 1900s Fred seems to have found employment outside his suburb, for family memory has him being placed second in an international copy-plate writing competition. He may have had some technical training in one of the many schools for the industrial arts, for he seems also to have worked as a commercial artist and designer.

On Christmas Day 1904, Fred married Kate Sillitoe. Both were aged twenty-three years. At this time Fred seems to have been boarding at lodgings at 28a Daphne Street, Wandsworth, in South London, not far from his birthplace. Kate, whose father was a mat weaver, was possibly a fellow lodger, her occupation being a shop assistant. They were married in the Anglican church of St James, Wandsworth, with Fred's sister Daisy in attendance.

In 1912 Fred and Kate, with three children, migrated to Australia, only two years after Amy Heap. Fred came on the government's assisted passage scheme. Perhaps the move was prompted by poor employment/income prospects, for manual copying was no longer as prized for industrial and commercial uses. Fred may also have been

Writing is almost as important as speaking

F. W. Flood,

December 1952.

A late example of Fred Flood's copy-plate writing (1952).

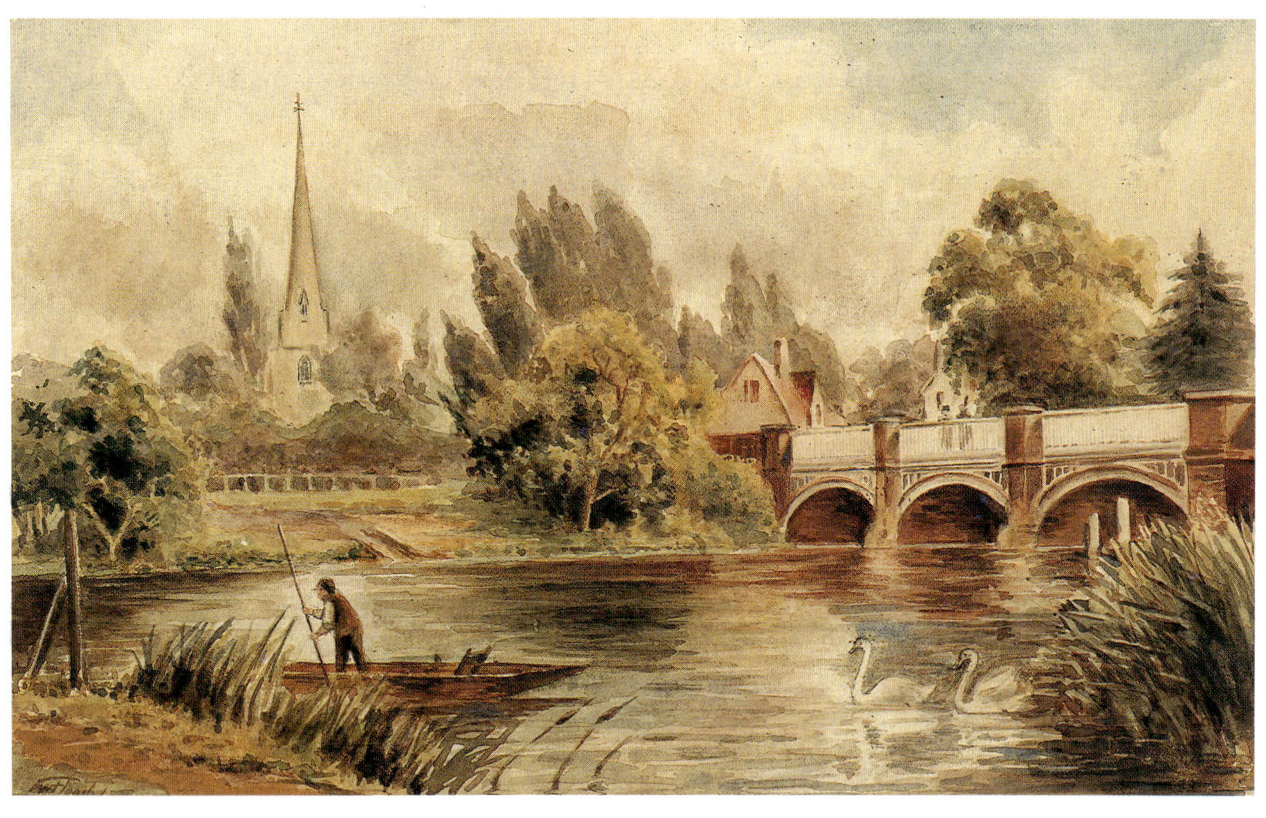

'Weybridge-on-Thames', a watercolour by Fred Flood in 1910. Rural contentment was a theme which was to dominate Flood's work in Australia.

influenced by his wife's sister Lillian who had migrated a little earlier to Perth in Western Australia. They did in fact meet in Perth, but only briefly as Lillian and her family decided to move on to New Zealand. Fred and Kate opted to stay on in Western Australia. Indeed, unlike Amy Heap, he never revisited England.

The first few years in Western Australia were not easy for the Flood family. Fred gained employment in Perth in the real estate and surveying firm of Daniel Kenny. Kenny, who had made a fortune from the practice of medicine, including insurance cases, had throughout the goldrush boom invested in suburban land — from Mosman Park to Bassendean and beyond. Flood's job was, in part at least, merely to measure building sites.

It was Fred's copy-plate work which was to give his career a lift. He was discovered and then commissioned by the Western Australian State Education Department to prepare writing copybooks for schoolchildren. Generations of Western Australian schoolchildren learnt to write in Fred's English lettering; indeed it seems that his copybooks were not fully replaced until the 1960s.

Flood's big break came in February 1919, when West Australian Newspapers Ltd employed him as an artist in their process-engraving department. He received four pounds ten shillings per week, enough to assist him to raise his family in their Peel Street, Jolimont, home to the west of the city.

Fred Flood's early work for West Australian Newspapers involved preparing the artwork for advertisements. To collect the rough copy he would ride a push-bike

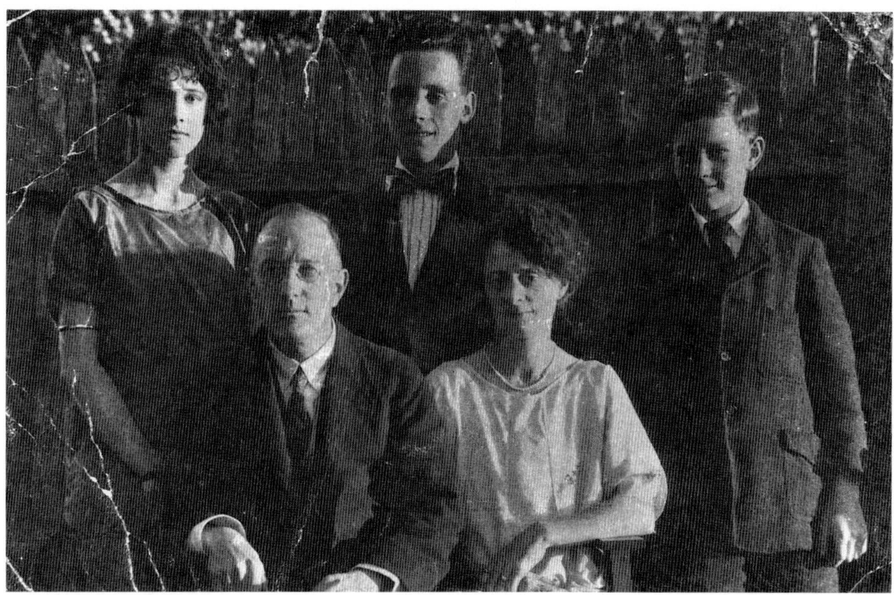

Fred and Kate Flood with children Wally, Len and Kate, c.1923. Taken at their Jolimont home in bushland west of the city of Perth.

around central Perth. The artwork was demanding, and Fred found that the intense concentration required was weakening his eyes. While in England he had developed an interest in photography, and he had practised it on a part-time basis since arriving in Perth. One of his earliest photographs was of the decaying, but historic, Perry homestead, near present day Perry Lakes. The photo dates from 1916. It was a link with old Western Australia and the Australian landscape that Flood was to develop strongly in the coming years.

From the early 1920s Fred was taken away from the formal artwork within West Australian Newspapers and allowed to practise his skills as a photographer. He became in fact the company's second full-time photographer. As such he was provided with cameras and, equally important, a motor car. From then until his retirement in the 1950s, Fred Flood took thousands of photographs of Western Australian scenes and people. Many plates and prints remain in his family's hands; and hundreds were published in the *Western Mail*, and in the *West Australian* as it developed a news photograph section. His finest work was for the Christmas issues of the *Western Mail*, from about 1920 through to the late 1940s.

In the early 1920s Flood moved from Jolimont to 285 Nicholson Road, Shenton Park, then a developing suburb. In 1934 he moved to a new house overlooking Dyson's Swamp where the Aborigines had once camped. The swamp was later drained and renamed Shenton Park Lake. Fred's eldest son, Wally, inherited his father's artwork flair and established in the district a major sign-writing firm; a younger son, Len, joined

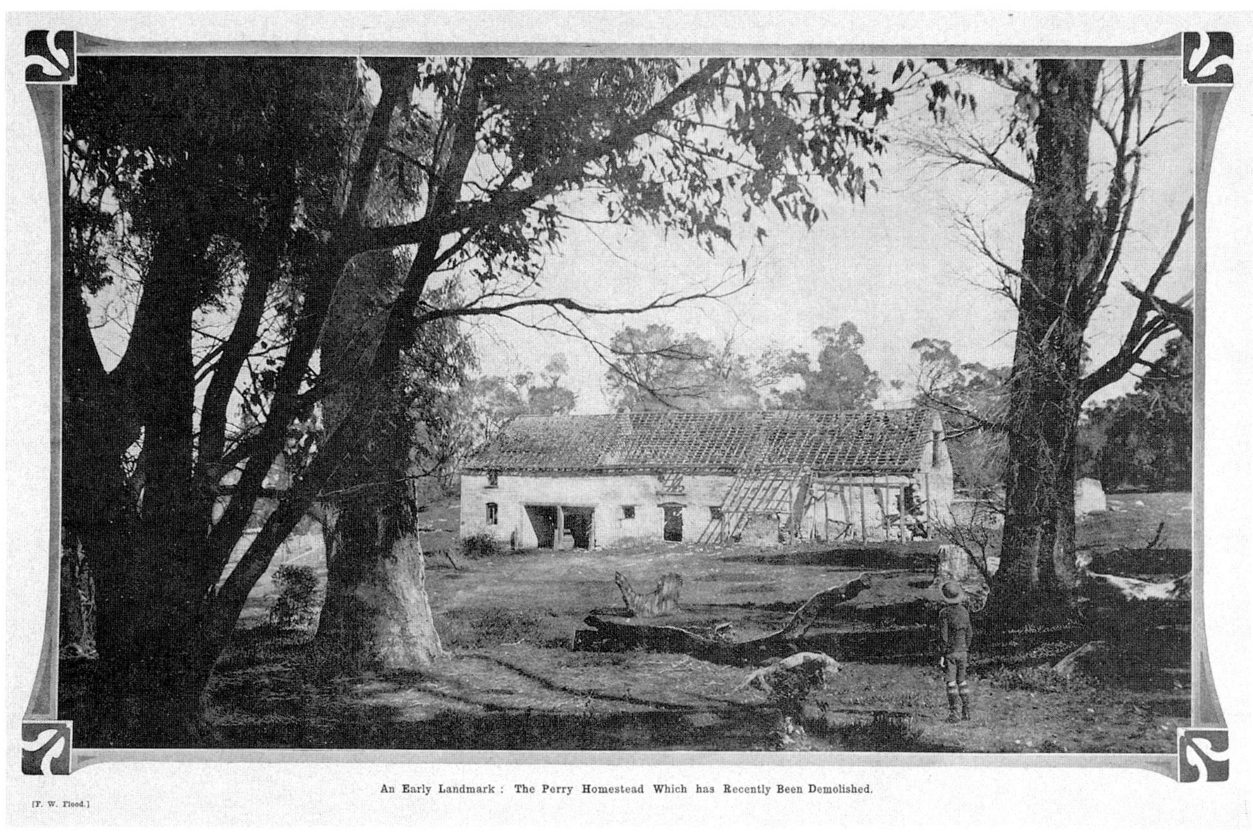

An Early Landmark : The Perry Homestead Which has Recently Been Demolished.

'An Early Landmark: the Perry Homestead'. Joseph Perry began his career in the 1860s by tending others' cattle out near what is today called Perry Lakes. As his money accumulated he bought blocks of land in the city of Perth. He also built a homestead near the lakes. Perry died in 1920; the homestead was demolished between 1921 and 1923. Fred Flood was a sympathetic and acute observer of the passing of pioneer life and its relics.

The other observer in the picture is Fred's son Wally.

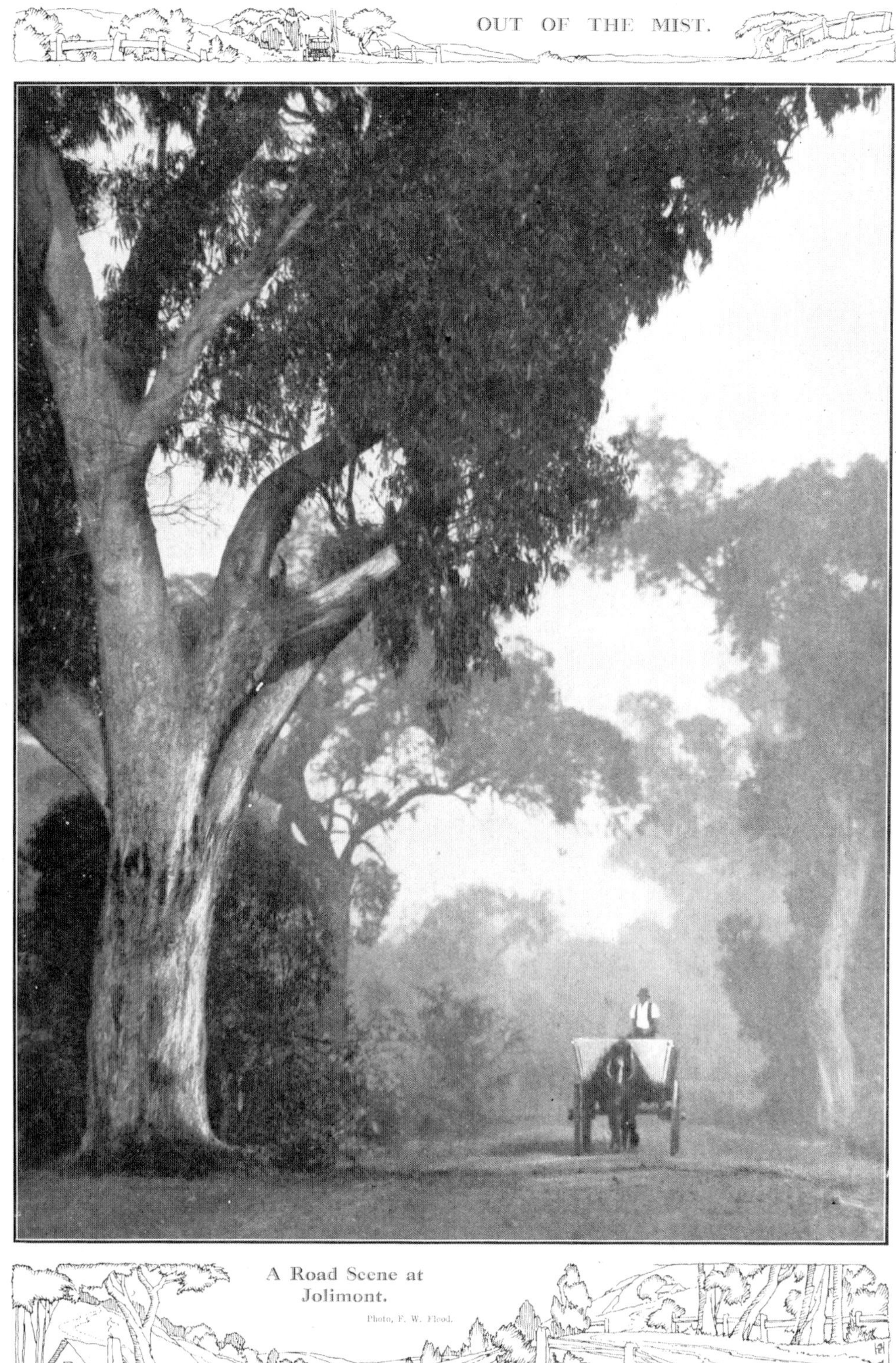

A Road Scene at
Jolimont.

Photo, F. W. Flood.

'Out of the Mist. A Road Scene at Jolimont'. Flood took many photographs in the Jolimont area, including flood scenes. As there was no electricity or gas in Jolimont the Flood family would hire a horse and cart to collect timber from the adjacent bush for heating and cooking.

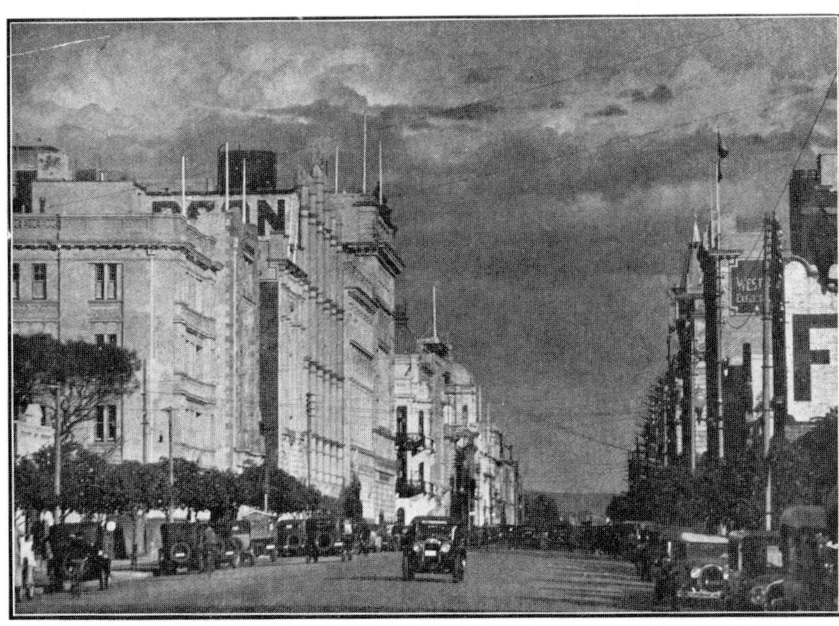
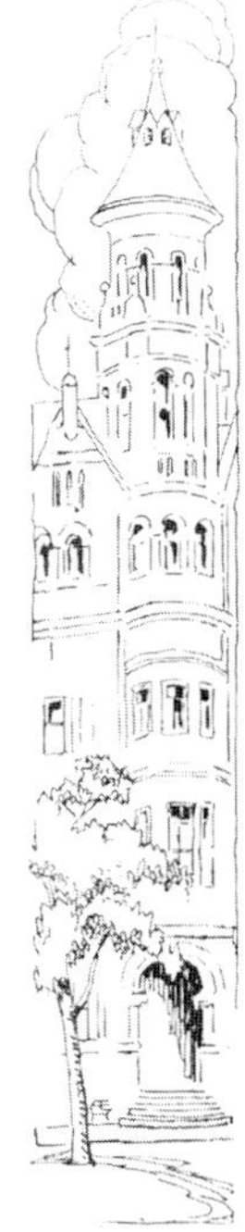

The Passing Storm.

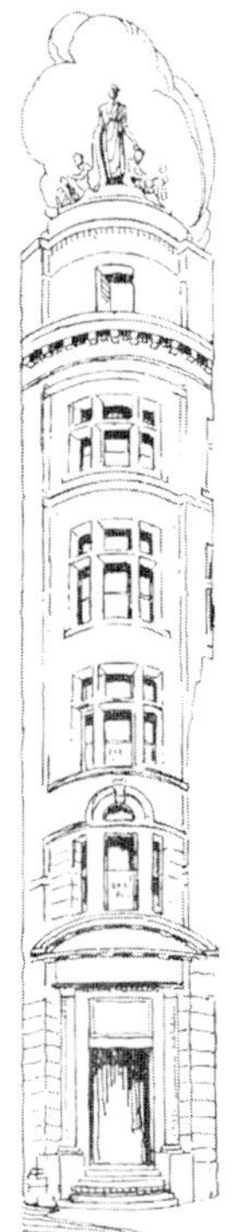
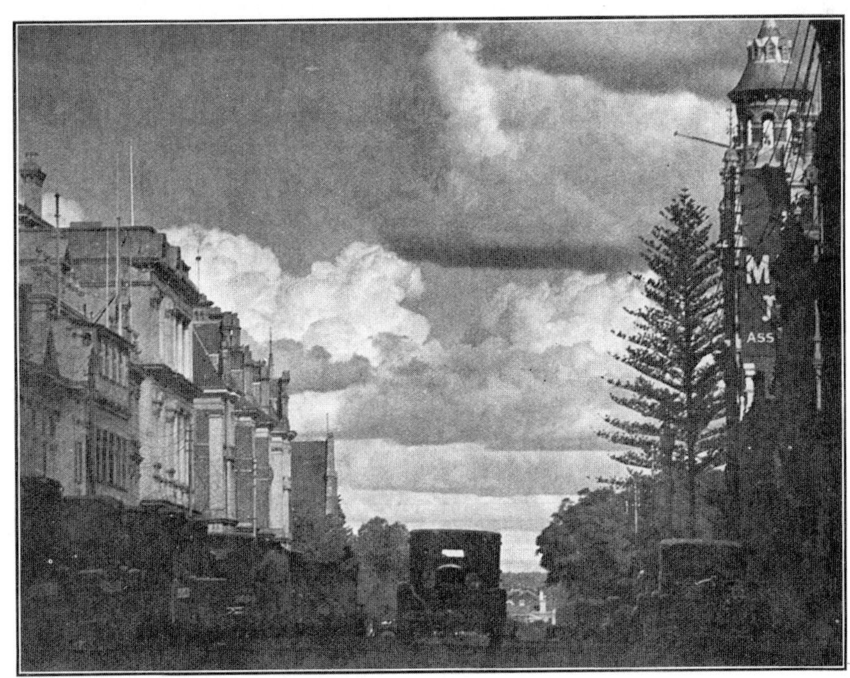

"After Clouds Fair Weather."

St George's Terrace: 'The Passing Storm' and 'After Clouds Fair Weather'. Flood worked at Newspaper House in 'the terrace' and was well placed to explore momentary effects such as these.

the *West Australian* as a lino machinist.

Fred Flood's family believe that he had some art training in England. Fred painted watercolours. Only a few have survived from his Westralian years. Unlike Amy Heap he was not known in Perth in 'professional' art circles, and he does not appear to have been a regular exhibitor with either the Perth Society of Artists or the Western Australian Society of Arts. Nevertheless, works such as his landscape paintings reveal him to be a competent watercolourist in a romantic vein. Many presentation scrolls to worthy and eminent persons in Perth were designed and executed by Fred Flood. He was also well known as a miniaturist, his specialty being the Lords Prayer on a threepence. Flood died on 30 June 1965, aged eighty-three years.

Fred Flood, or 'Floodie' as colleagues like Clem Ambler called him, was a small, precise sort of man, and a meticulous worker. Unlike one of his later colleagues, Fred Ford, who worked quickly and intuitively as a news photographer as well as a scenic one, Flood spent a long time 'composing' his scenes and waiting on light effects. He was a leading member of Western Australia's first photography club, named after an eminent local etcher Henri van Raalte, and is remembered as a fine exponent of art photography, and for winning prizes in competitions, as far afield as Paris.

It is hard to imagine the photography of Fred Flood as avant-garde. But his early Western Australian work shows clear signs of having been influenced by the photographic art movement known from 1892 as pictorialism: soft focus images and, as the 1908 'Salon des Refuses' exhibition catalogue puts it, 'the gradual and keener

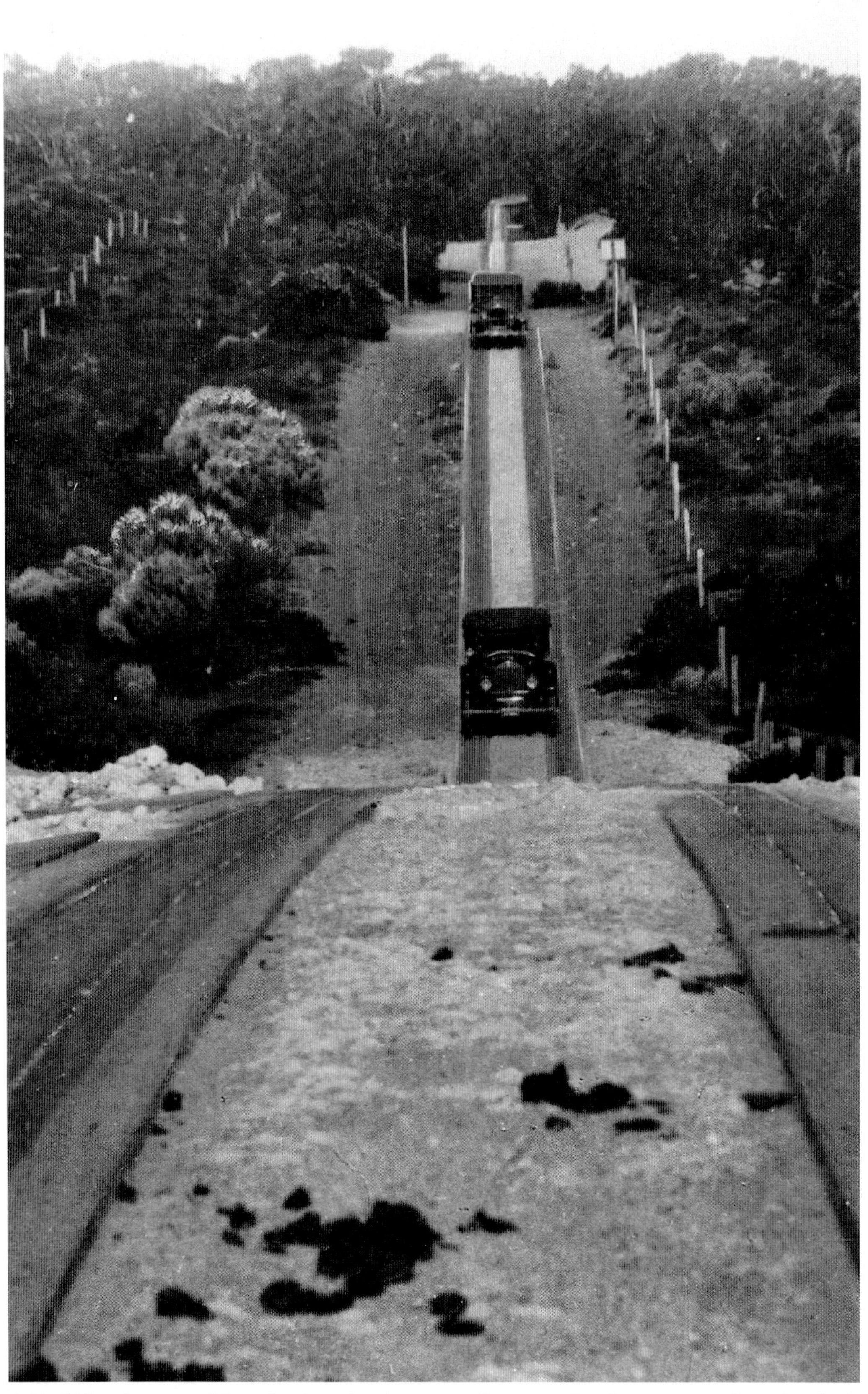

A Fred Flood image of the suburban development of interwar Perth: cars move along the Plank Road west to City Beach.

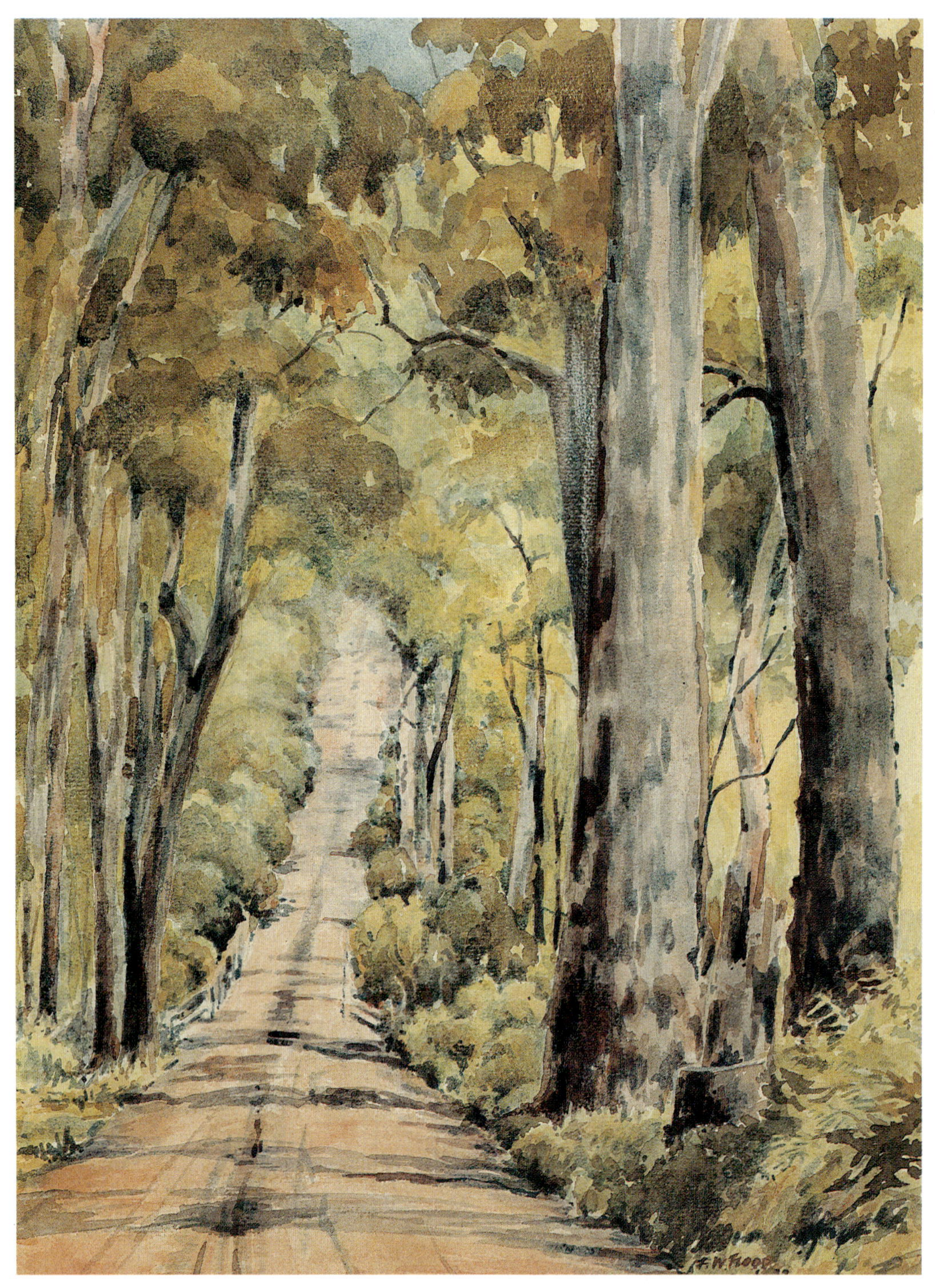

'A Country Road'. Flood did not exhibit his watercolours; sometimes he used his skill to tint black and white photographs and to touch-up colour photographs. This is a characteristic painting done for private and family pleasure. Flood loved travelling by car in Western Australia, perhaps as a reaction to the cramped London of his youth. He took delight in reaching the end of roads, as with the famous Plank Road out to City Beach, constructed when Flood lived nearby in Jolimont; he liked roads shaded by great trees; and he enjoyed landscape vistas from the edge of high roads.

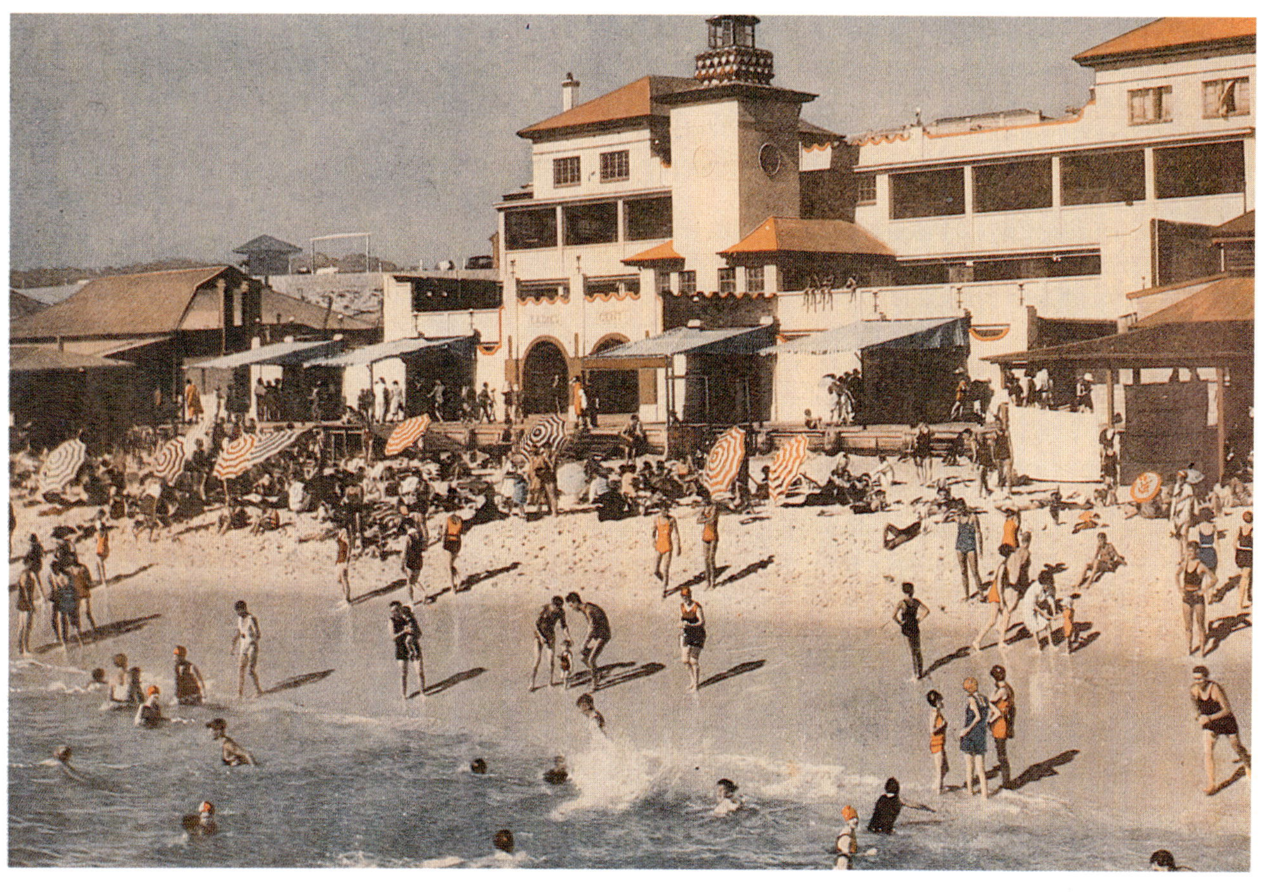

The Flood family sailed boats in the river. Fred often visited the beaches of Perth, usually with camera in hand.

perception and expression of nature and beauty apart from more temporary art crazes and artistic shibboleths'. As an art movement in Britain, pictorialism seems to have lost its avant-garde status by the Great War; but because it was introduced later in Australia its effects were longer lasting. Flood probably 'brought' pictorialism into Western Australia.

Critics would describe work like Flood's as the 'mist and vapour school' or the 'English twilight school'. Some Australian photographers wanted to develop an 'Australian Sunshine School', analogous to the high-keyed paintings of the Heidelberg School of Tom Roberts and Arthur Streeton; but such made little headway until after the Great War, and even then Fred Flood remained relatively immune to its influence, with the exception of beach scenes. The pictorialists in all Australian States 'generally restricted themselves to subject matter that was already popular in other art mediums — ethereal women, wayward children, rural scenes, romantic back streets'. Flood was light on the ethereal women; but the rest he photographed plentifully.

In the literature on pictorialism, there is frequent use of the word 'conservative', often with a class overtone, as in 'the conservative and professional middle classes'. Flood was a working-class boy; but he had middle-class aspirations which he could reach through his technical and professional skills. In his articulation of his values, he found the pictorial language of beauty and truth in nature, and organic holism with human interest tenderly expressed, a perfect vehicle. In short he could 'deliver the world golden', even the Westralian world.

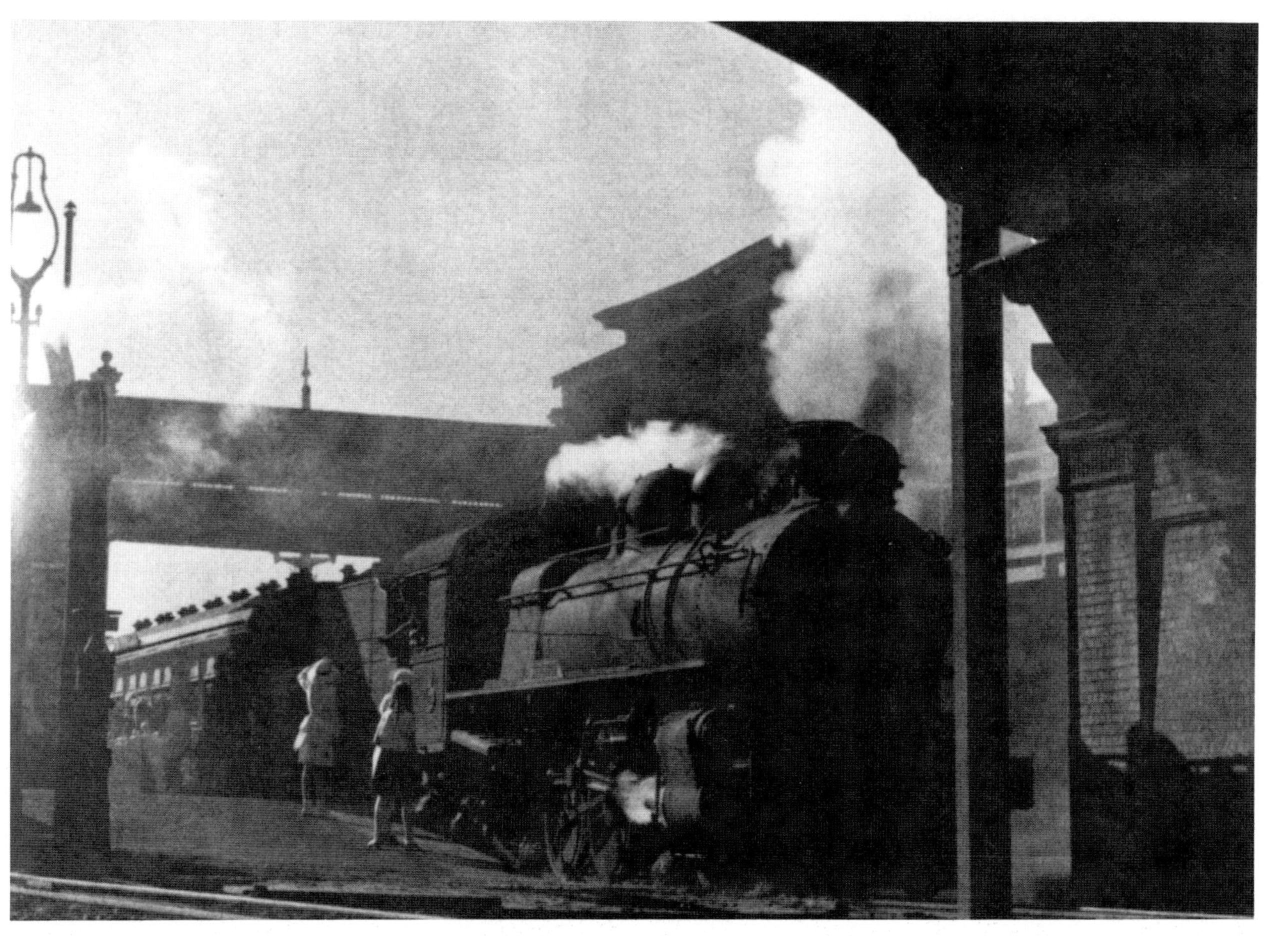

Like impressionist painters such as Claude Monet, Flood was interested in the effects of steam in railway stations. The train is a symbol of modernity and urbanization, but Flood transforms train and station into a timeless feature of fascination for the young, in this case replacing the horse. The photo is titled 'The Westland express leaving Perth central railway station for the eastern states'.

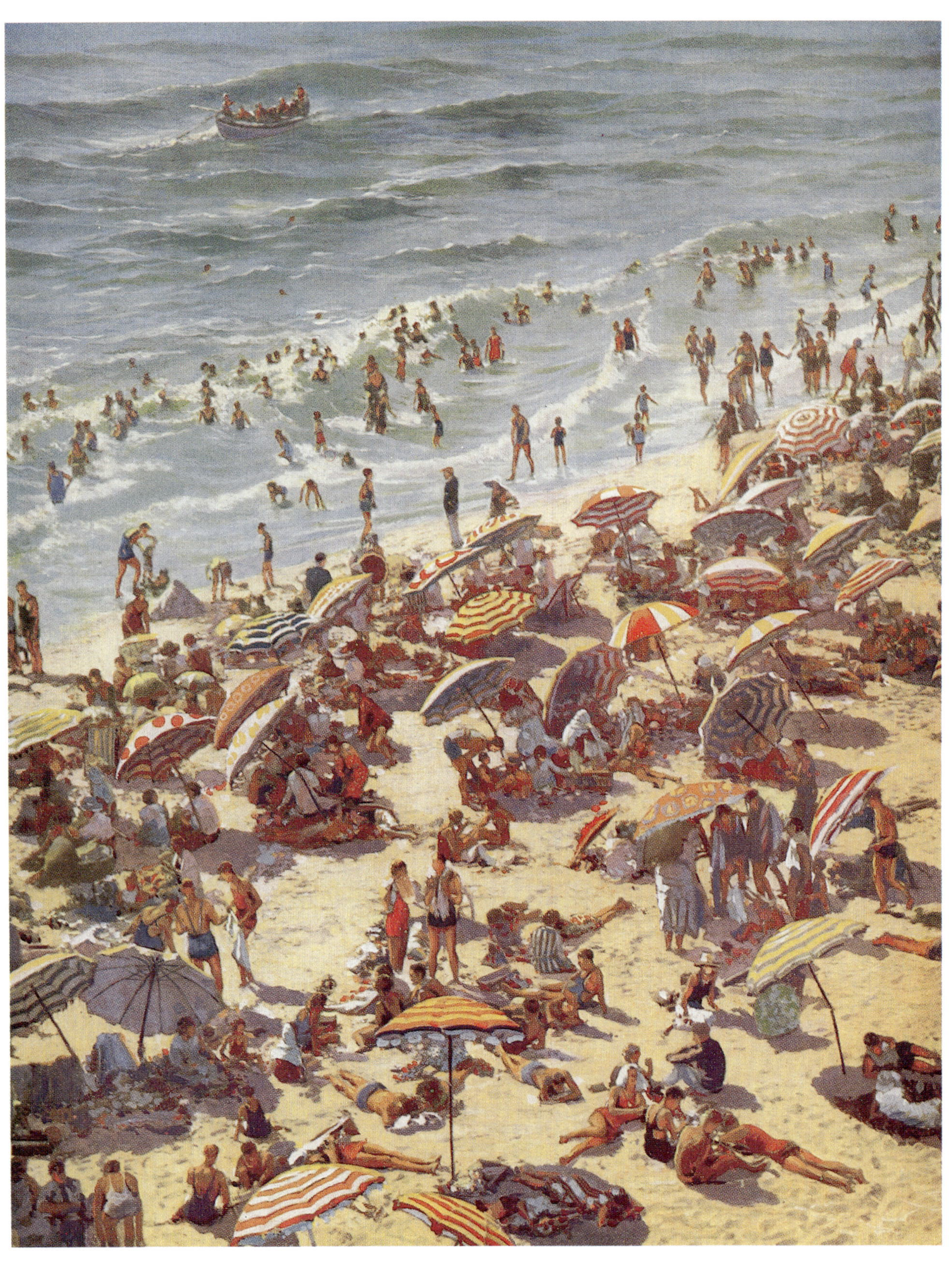

'The Lido of the West: A Sunday Afternoon in summer at Ocean Beach in Cottesloe'
(Fred Flood photograph, coloured by Len Cutten), 1935.

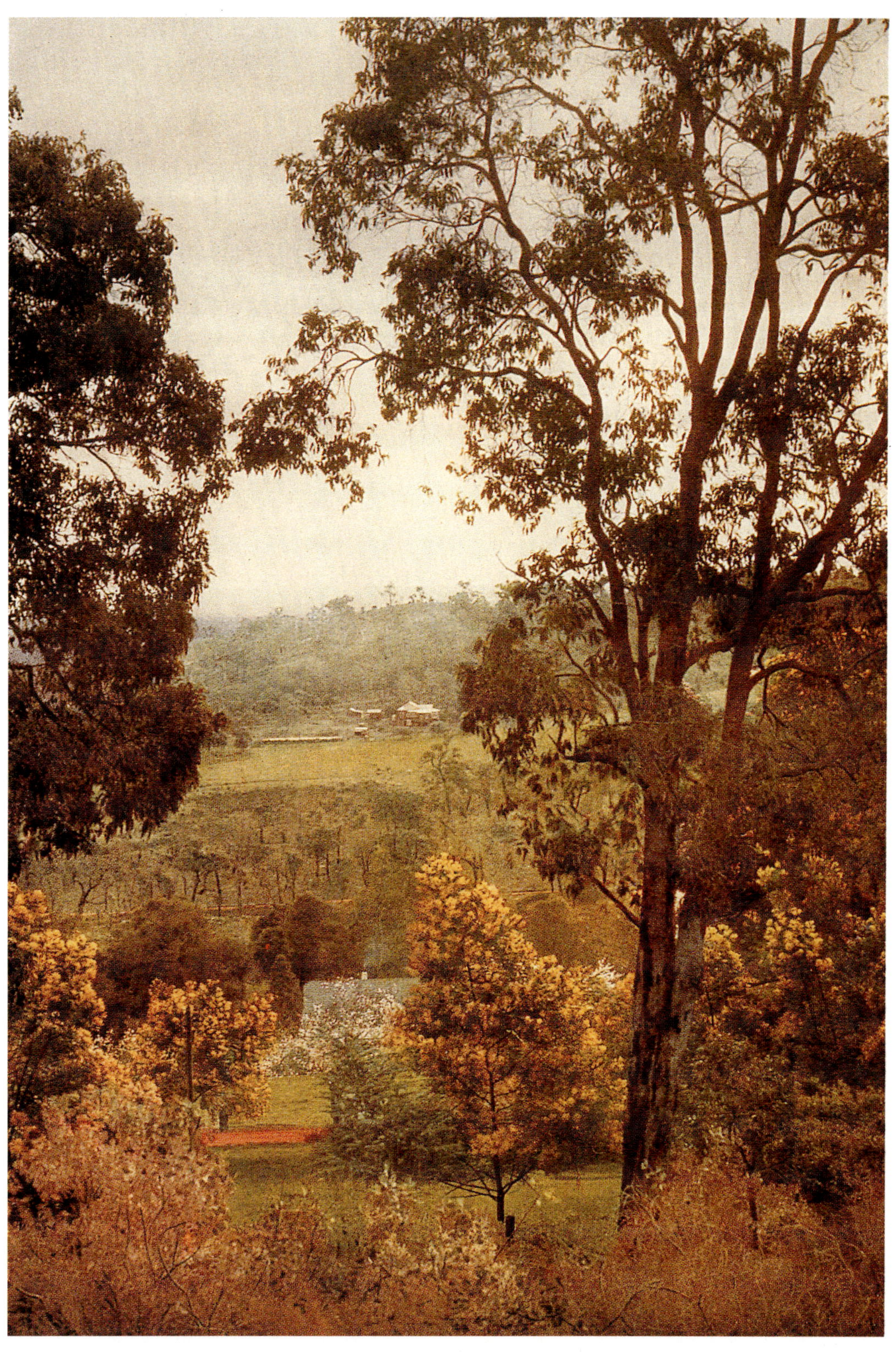

Natural coloured photography was used in the *Western Mail* from 1936. Flood experimented with it and the *Mail* published his efforts until the early 1950s. This spring natural colour photograph of a valley in the Darling Ranges catches perfectly Flood's sustaining vision of the country to which he had emigrated so long before, that profound combination of Englishness and Australianness which he continued to celebrate in the autumn of his and the *Western Mail*'s life.

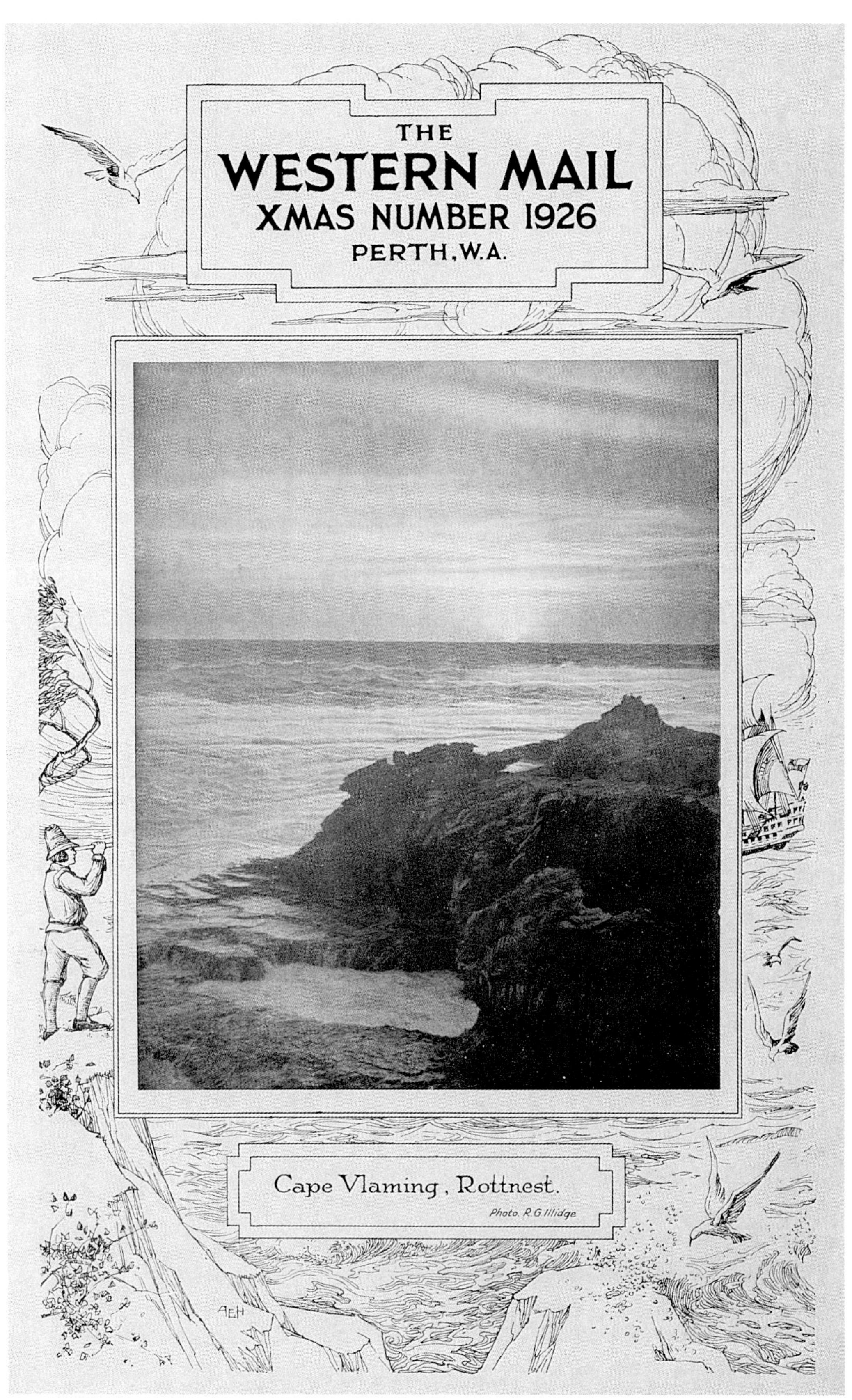

Here was one beginning for the European history of Western Australia. Amy returns the Dutchman Willem de Vlamingh and his 1697 ship to the cape which bears his name.

THE IMAGES

AMY HEAP

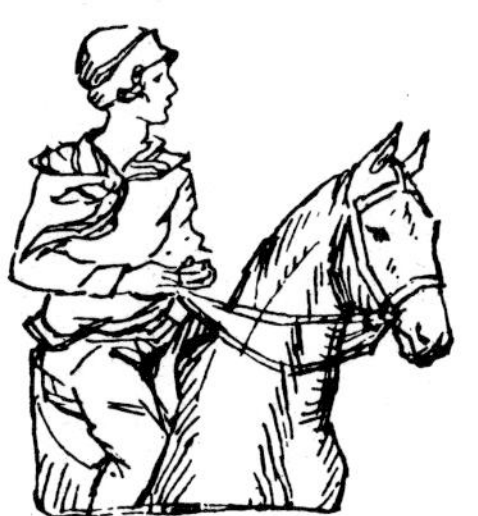

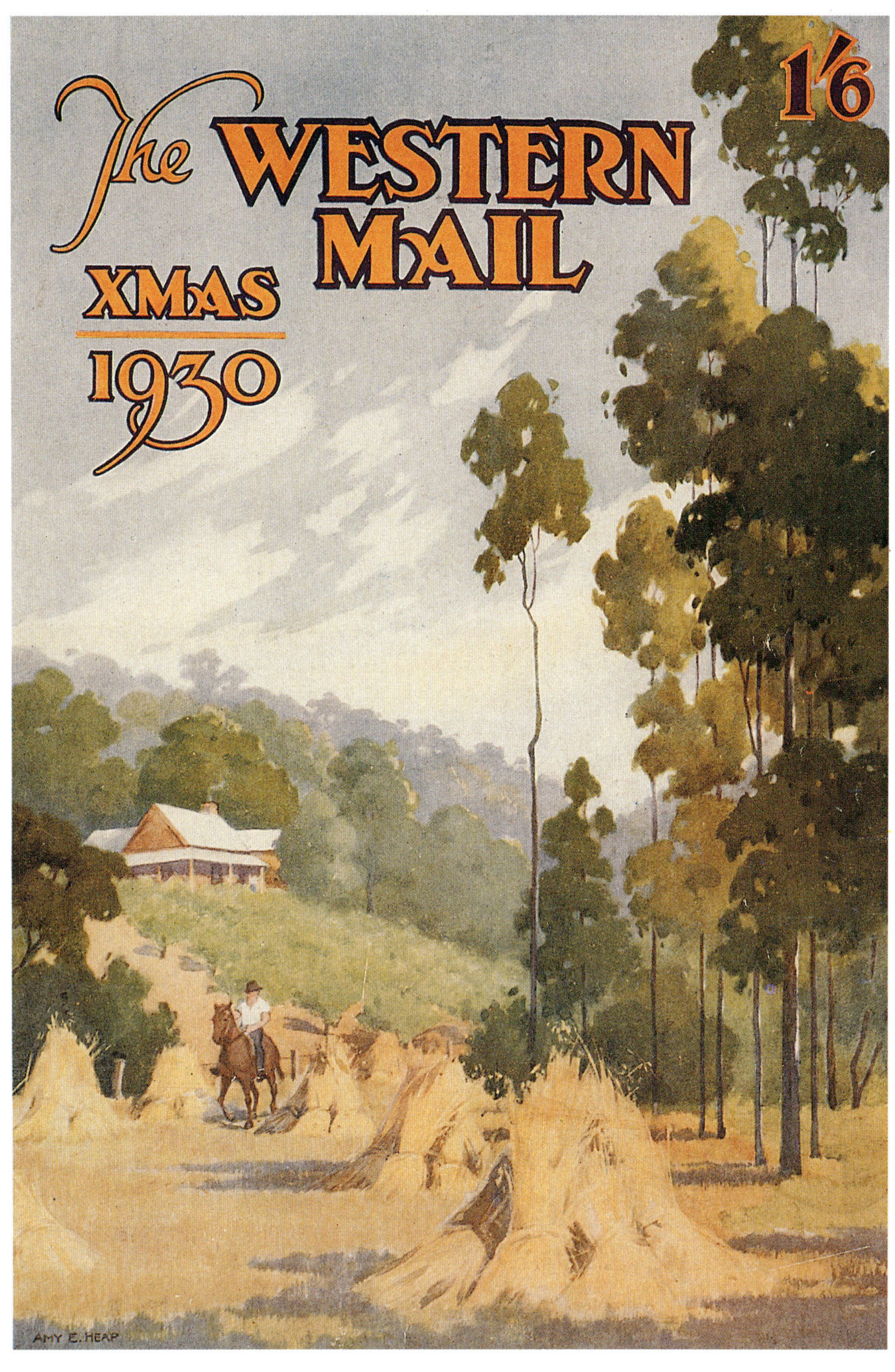

The Westralian land is bountiful and beautiful, forever bathed in sunlight, even as wool and wheat prices drop and rural labourers join the unemployed.

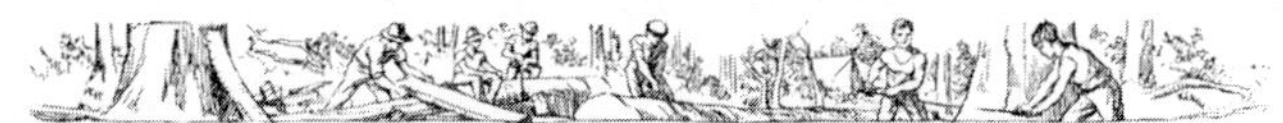

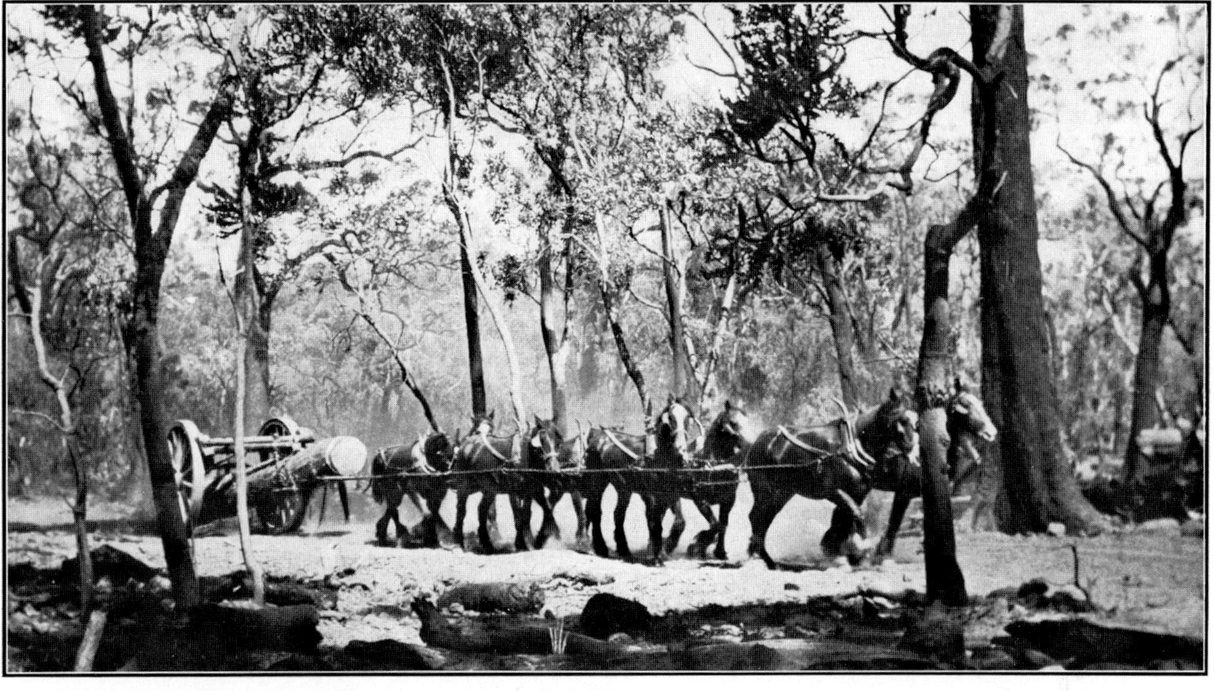

Log Transport in the Bush.

The prize-winning Snapshot in the Action Division of the Photographic Competition associated with the Christmas Number of "The Western Mail."

Photo, Mrs. A. G. Spencer.

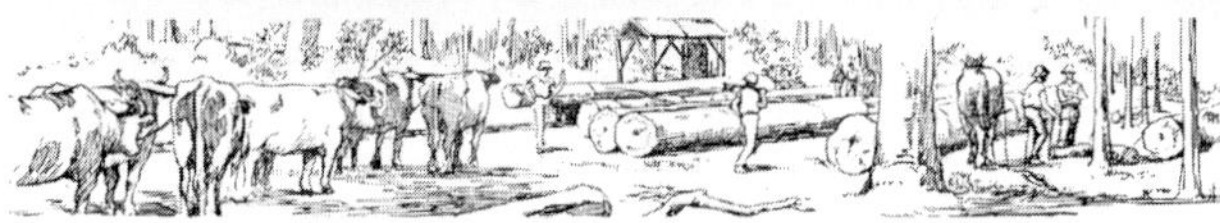

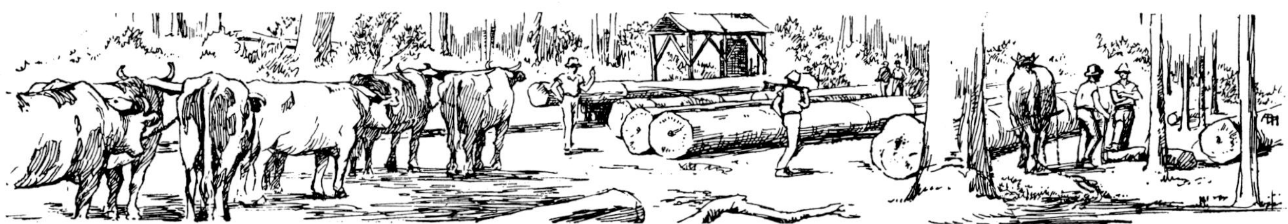

And when Europeans came they brought oxen and horses and axes with which to hew a new Jerusalem from the forests of South West Australia. In 'The Haulers', Amy captures the dignity of labouring men and beasts unencumbered by company boardroom concerns about investment and profit, industrial relations and workers compensation.

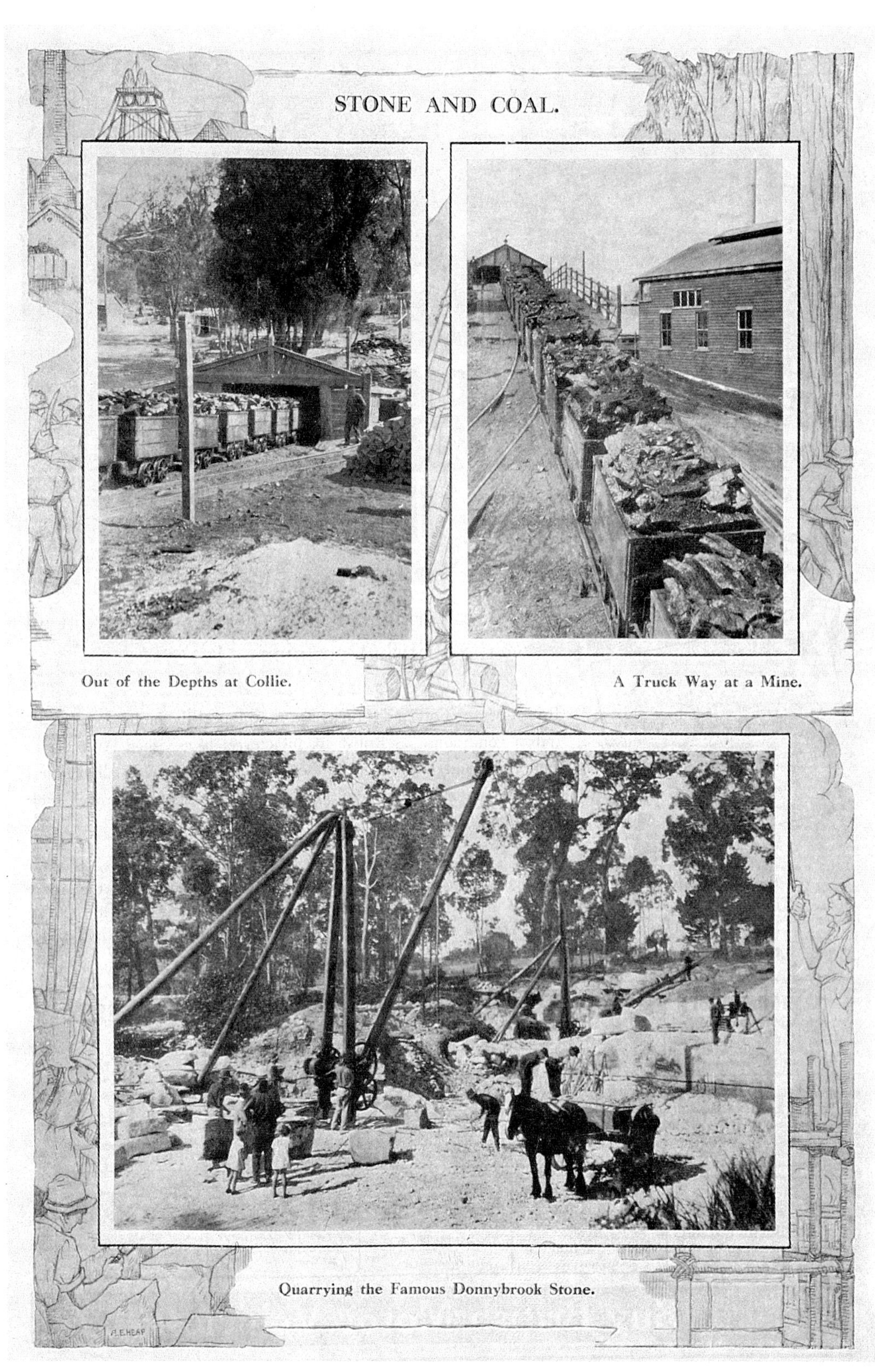

Out of the Depths at Collie.

A Truck Way at a Mine.

Quarrying the Famous Donnybrook Stone.

Donnybrook stone and Collie coal, so central to interwar industry and commercial building.
Amy enhances the human face of development.

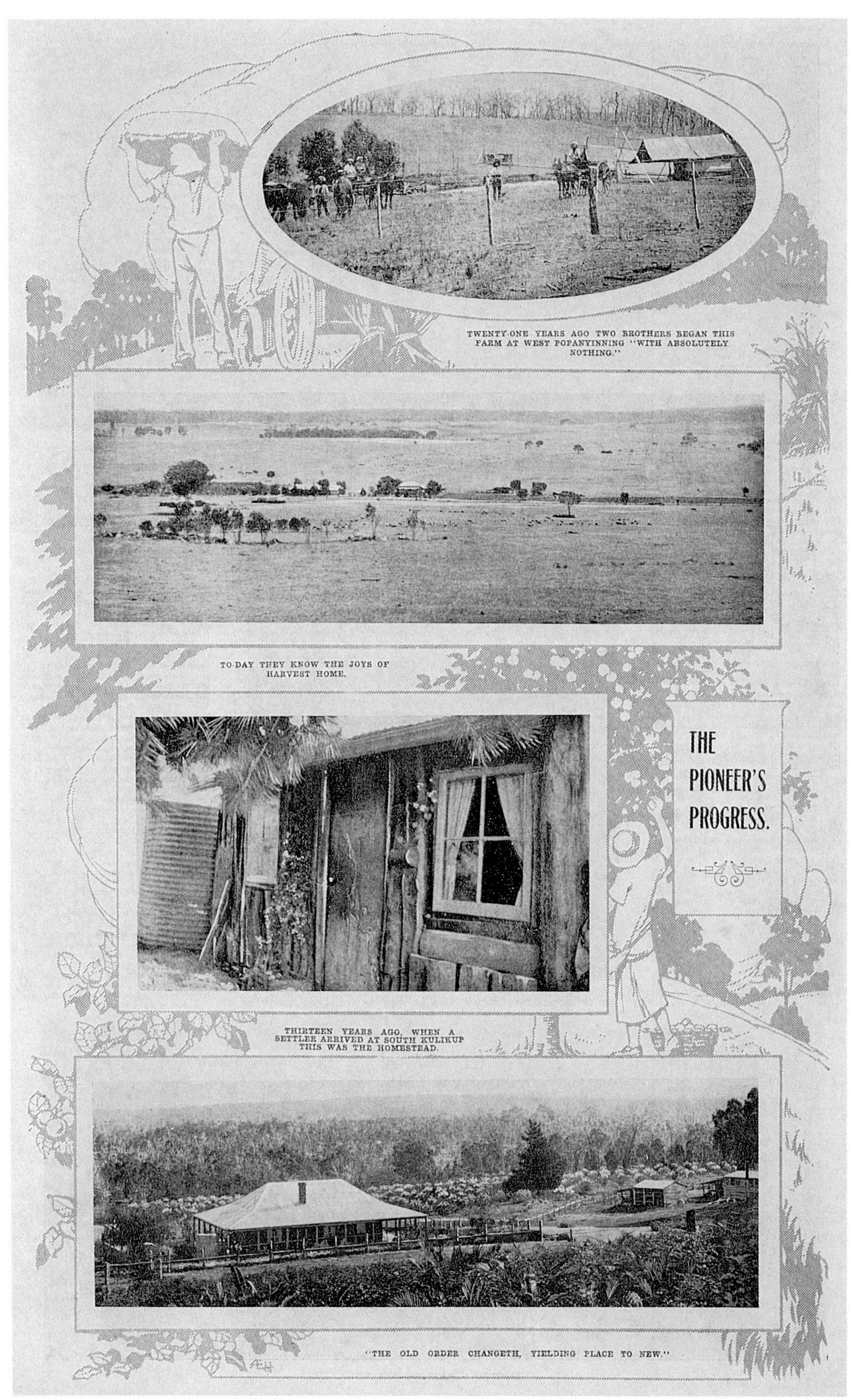

TWENTY-ONE YEARS AGO TWO BROTHERS BEGAN THIS
FARM AT WEST POPANYINNING "WITH ABSOLUTELY
NOTHING."

TO-DAY THEY KNOW THE JOYS OF
HARVEST HOME.

THIRTEEN YEARS AGO, WHEN A
SETTLER ARRIVED AT SOUTH KULIKUP
THIS WAS THE HOMESTEAD.

"THE OLD ORDER CHANGETH, YIELDING PLACE TO NEW."

The idea of Empire progress was central to interwar imagery. Behind today's wheat belt prosperity lie the trials and tribulations of the pioneers. Amy elaborates the theme by showing the strength of farming men and the role of decorative but working farming women. Blossoms, fruit and grain provide the good life as, in Lord Alfred Tennyson's words, 'The old order changeth, yielding place to new'.

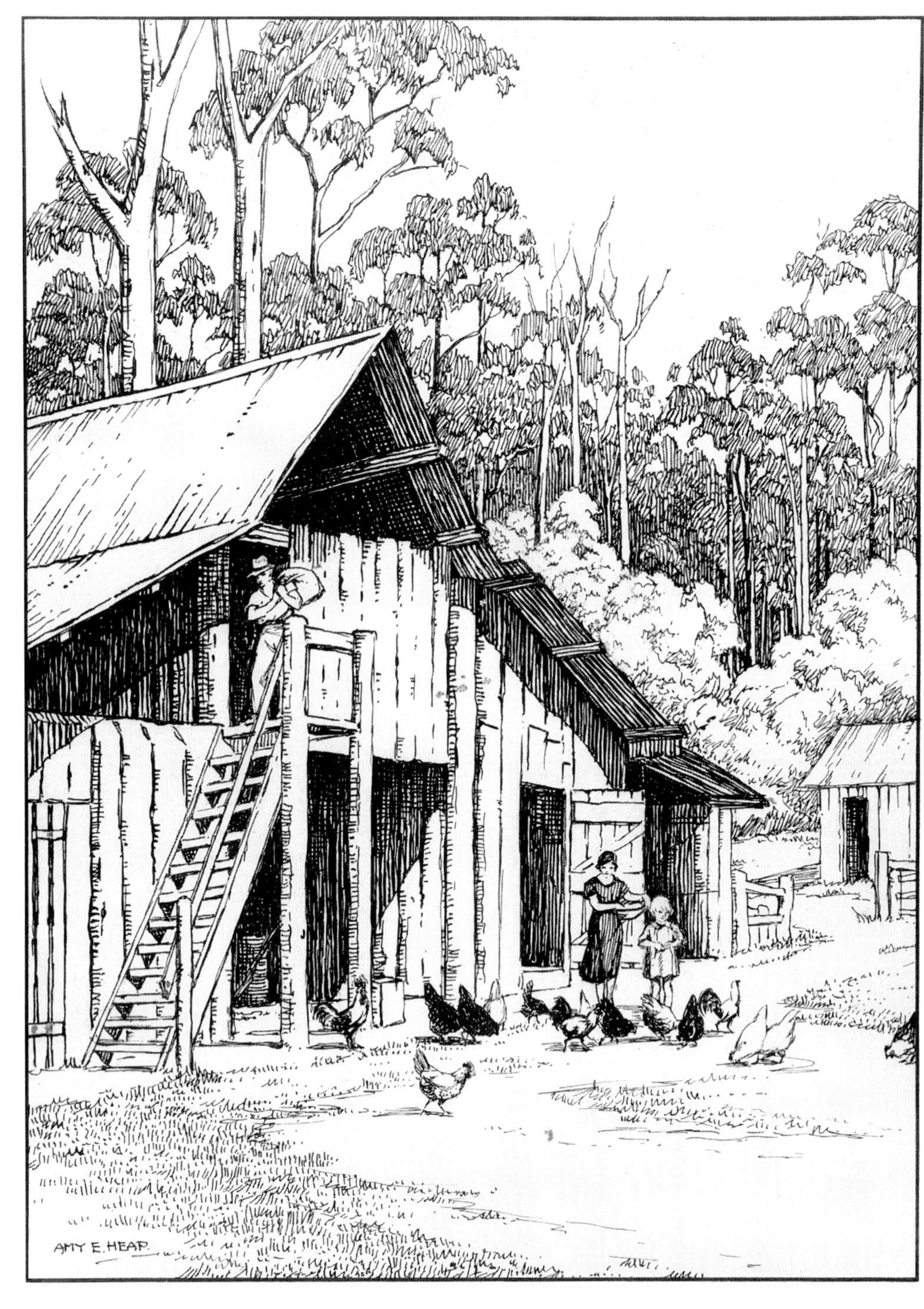

With a child to help now, the pioneer theme is continued in Amy's drawing 'The Old Barn,
Manjimup', printed as an illustration in John L. Glascock's popular
1933 anthology *Jarrah Leaves*.

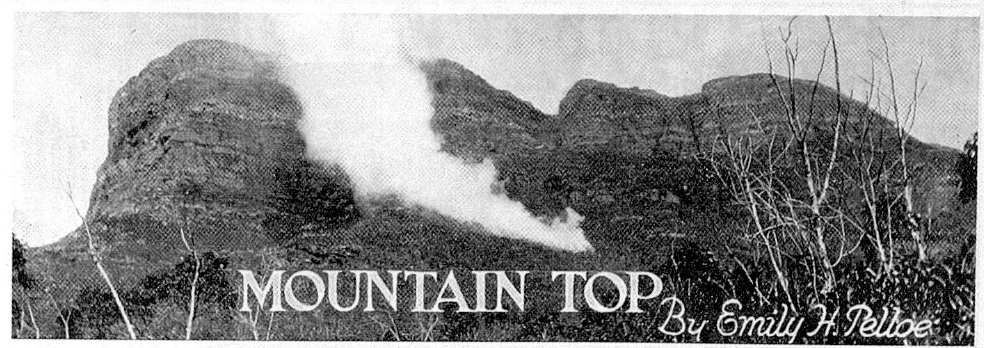

MOUNTAIN TOP

By Emily H. Pelloe

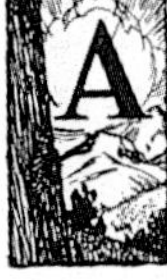

A SMALL cairn of stones marks the topmost point of Bluff Knoll, king peak of the Stirling Range. Upon it in dazzling spring sunshine, exhilarated after the arduous climb by the wine-like fillip of the rarefied air, Ruth Parry stood erect and unafraid. Hers was the first feminine foot to scale the giddy heights of riven crags, split by some titanic influence in remote ages, where, through enormous fissures in great granite boulders, storm winds howl and shriek in demoniac din.

But Ruth was no picturesque spirit of the mountain-top, posed as on a painted pinnacle with airy draperies floating, cloud-like, about her form. Though inwardly thrilled with responsive ecstasy by the peerless panorama of peaks and plain, outwardly Ruth was an incongruous figure. Acquaintance with the clothes-destroying difficulties of lesser peaks had influenced her choice of attire when the long desired chance to attempt ascent of Bluff Knoll materialised. Garbed in unfeminine blue dungaree overalls, old heavy-soled shoes and an ancient felt hat, Ruth when leaving the camp by the creek in the foothills with Kitty Morrow from Perth, her brother Ben, and Stephen Blair, naturalist and writer, had winced at the contrast between her ugly practical outfit and the smart elegance of the town visitor's finely pleated skirt of beige and jade-flecked tweed, with a Fair Isle cardigan covering a tailored jumper of gleaming ivory crepe de chine, the whole surmounted by a chic little jade-ribboned visca hat.

Ruth surveyed delightedly the glorious expanse of the Salt River plains nearly 4,000 feet below; the towering peaks melting to westward in colourful perspective beyond the rugged loveliness of triple-crested, queenly Toolbrunup, scrub-covered Warrangup—a flower paradise specially beloved by Ruth—with razor-backed Mondurup and the twin-peaked Abbey conspicuous in the distance; or the granite solidity of Pyongorup with the domes of Isongorup and Ellen's Peak deeply purple to the east. She picked out easily the tree-clumps clustering round Maradup, the home she shared with Ben, her only brother. The mallee and yate scrub, where pure merinos grazed, was a vast undulating stretch of soft grey greens and amethyst shadows.

Incidents of the climb flashed in kaleidoscopic jumble through Ruth's thoughts. Where were Ben and Kitty now, she wondered? Were they still at the fallen log by the cascade that seemed so far away at the head of the little creek half way up the almost perpendicular flower-gemmed gorge, where ascent though difficult, was possible? A thousand feet of strenuous climbing had proved to Ruth the advantage of her ungainly but substantial attire, proof against the thorny spikes of shoulder-high prickly undergrowth and destructive rasp of shingle slips and sharp-edged rocks. Kitty Morrow, as grimy through contact with burnt boughs and perspiration streaks as the others, had railed with vexation at this condition, the spoliation of her carefully considered toilette, torn and tousled by passage through almost impenetrable scrub, and ruin of expensive shoes and stockings. Her ill-tempered whimperings had palpably irritated Stephen Blair, clad like Ruth and Ben, in dungaree, and impatiently eager to reach the summit in good time. When Kitty had slipped, wrenching an ankle painfully, and sunk upon the log, half-sobbingly protesting her inability to go on, Stephen had suggested her remaining there with Ruth, while Ben and he climbed on. But Ruth had refused—absolutely, point blank—to miss the ascent she had dreamed of almost since babyhood. So Ben had volunteered to stay with Kitty and take her back to the camp later on. The whole arrangement, apparently, had infuriated Stephen.

Ruth's cheeks burned beneath their grubbiness at thought of Stephen's indignant back as he had climbed on, ever well ahead of her, sometimes waiting with unconcealed irritation at the delay of her comparatively slow progress, but never once holding out a helping hand in difficult or dangerous places. Yet his ill humour had melted somewhat as they reached the top of a ridge from which the ocean could be seen, with the Porongorups, like pigmy hills, bristling the plains between. Ruth's cry of delight had roused Stephen from intensive study of a low-growing acacia covered closely with spikes of fluffy pale gold bloom. All around were great clumps of Southern Cross. The tough stalks, on which swung the starlike cross-clusters of white flowers, had made effective hand-hold in the gorge when mallee growth was left behind. On their right the great split crest had loomed, towering above the steeply precipitous strata-streaked granite face of Bluff Knoll Though the day was still, gusts of air had rustled through a narrow cavernous opening with a noise as though a million newspapers were being rattled. The mist which all the way to the head of the gorge had enveloped the actual mountain top had suddenly vanished, and the splendour of the spectacle had moved her almost to tears.

Ruth's appreciation of the beauty familiar to the man apparently had made her company worth while, and from then until the actual summit was reached, Stephen had talked freely or listened smilingly to her exclamations of genuine delight. The thousands of nodding yellow darwinias had seemed to her like golden bells that surely must, when storms raged about Bluff Knoll, peal out delicate melody in rippling echo to crash of thunder.

Ruth, standing on the summit, forgot the ache of muscles strained by the strenuous four-hour climb as she gazed down, picking out the spot three miles from the foot of the gorge where Stephen Blair had camped for a month in springtime for six years, just ten miles from Maradup. She reviewed the friendship that had grown between Ben and herself during that time, and the quiet thoughtful young man who came yearly to collect natural history specimens and observe the wonders of Nature upon and about the Stirling Range. She had never been really alone with him before, and now here she was on the top of the world—or so it seemed—and

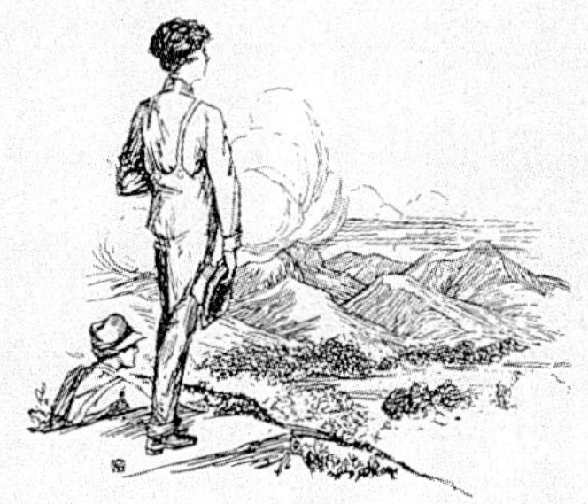

Standing on the summit, Ruth forgot the ache of muscles strained by the strenuous four-hour climb as she gazed down.

somewhere down, far down the mountain side, he had left the girl with whom she jealously supposed him to be in love. It was not until he had asked her to invite Kitty Morrow down from Perth to enable the city girl to make the desired ascent of Bluff Knoll that Ruth know how much she cared for Stephen. Though realisation that she had grown fond of a man who regarded her only as a kind and useful friend was bitter truth for Ruth, her native commonsense and joyously sane disposition banished foolishly-sentimental longing.

Stephen, calmly munching what Ruth called an "iron ration" lunch—hard boiled eggs and slices of bread and cheese, with occasional sips of water from the screw-on top of a military flask—was seated on a stone beside the cairn—great loose-blossomed, puff-like flower-heads of rose pink isopogon all around him.

"Have lunch now, Ruth," he suggested kindly.

"Yes, and then I must lean over and look down," she replied, shuddering slightly at the prospect.

Her lunch eaten, Ruth lay flat upon the rock and drew herself slowly forward until she could just peep out over the edge of the sheer two thousand feet drop. Slightly giddy, she clung tightly to a small shrub, scarcely realising that her sedate companion was holding her very firmly by the ankles. She wriggled carefully back to the cairn, awed to speechless wonder by the terrifying abyss . .

"Wait here and rest," said Stephen. "I want to gather up a few specimens."

Ruth thought ruefully of Kitty, unfairly contrasting the blonde, shingled, powdered, lip-sticked, assertive loveliness, and slim silhouette of the city stranger with the countrified object she imagined herself to be, overlooking the fact that a healthy complexion needing no cosmetics, long thick brown hair arranged always with Madonna-like simplicity, thoughtful grey eyes, sweet expression, unaffected naturalness, and a tall, lithely-muscular figure were equally attractive. Yet there had been moments, she pondered, at Stephen's camp down below on the foothills where they had stayed the night, when he had visibly recoiled from Kitty—when they were watching the sun set behind the mountains, for instance, with big Bluff Knoll loftily stupendous before them as they sat, gazing in silent wonder at the magnificence of the mountain's mighty bulk against the orange and rose-streaked sky, ruddy mists floating about the wedge-like crest, and the fading light blurring the long shadows of trees and rocks in purple haze. Stephen, breaking the silence, had solemnly recited William Sharp's lovely lines:

"Across the boulder'd majesty,
Of the great hills, the passing day
Drifts like a wind-borne cloud away,
Far off beyond the western sky.
And while a purple glory spreads
With straits of gold and brilliant reds,
An azure veil, translucent, strange,
Dreamlike, steals over each dim range."

Trivialities would then have seemed to Ruth to strike a jarring note on a veritable symphony of silence. Yet Kitty, with a laugh had cried "Bravo, but let's be cheerful!" and springing up, had done some Charleston steps on top of a flat rock.

"Come along, we must get back to camp," Stephen had said sharply. "We have to start at dawn, remember."

And then, crossing the wattle and spyridium-fringed creek, he had whispered to Ruth: "I wish you could have seen the cloud-fleece form on Bluff Knoll. It was just coming up. But distractions like the Charleston would have quite spoiled its effect."

How he loved the Stirlings, thought Ruth. But so did she, and it was joy to be with him on the top of Bluff Knoll. Thus she mused till Stephen returned with his collecting bag and pockets bulging with botanical and geological treasures.

"Now for a quick look round, and then down," he said. "Down to civilisation and—the Charleston."

They walked to the slightly sloping acreage of rock-strewn hill-top that runs back from Bluff Knoll's highest point. At a great square-angled mass of stone they stopped. "I call this Abraham's Altar," said Stephen, and seemed inclined to linger near it.

"Ruth," he said suddenly. "I have always liked you. To-day has taught me that I love you. You are so strong, so brave, and somehow, so understanding." He took her in his arms. "Tell me you will share all my climbs, my work, my life—everything —with me, always."

"But—er—what about Kitty?' stammered Ruth, "I thought it was her you loved and wanted to go climbing with. You were always against my attempting Bluff Knoll before she came down here, you know."

"Ruth, she is nothing to me. You are everything. My sister has been doing her damndest—excuse me, dear—to marry me to Kitty, and thought her pretended interest in the mountains—our mountains, Ruth, yours and mine—would win me. In Perth I almost loved Kitty. But thank God, I have found out in time that her apparent enthusiasm for the things I live for was a sham. She is mentally unable to comprehend the majesty of mountains even were she physically capable of climbing them. Ruth dear, you have known me now for years. You have been a dear friend. You must be my wife. Will you?"

In the great silence of the mountain-top, Ruth's half-breathed sigh of acquiescence was all-sufficient for Stephen.

"Come," he said, gladly. "Let us go down now —down to life and love."

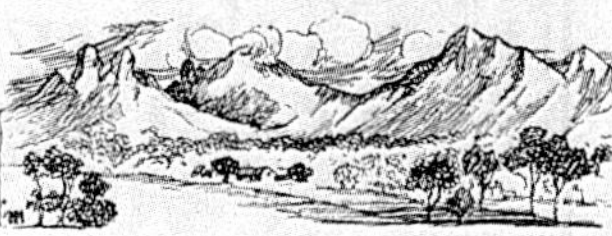

Above the hills and dales rose the 'Mountain Top', hard to find in Western Australia; but at least there was Bluff Knoll, 'king peak of the Stirling Ranges'. Amy's leisured lady and gentleman, seen often in interwar images of the Lake District, here counterpoint Emily Pelloe's gripping story of love on the heights.

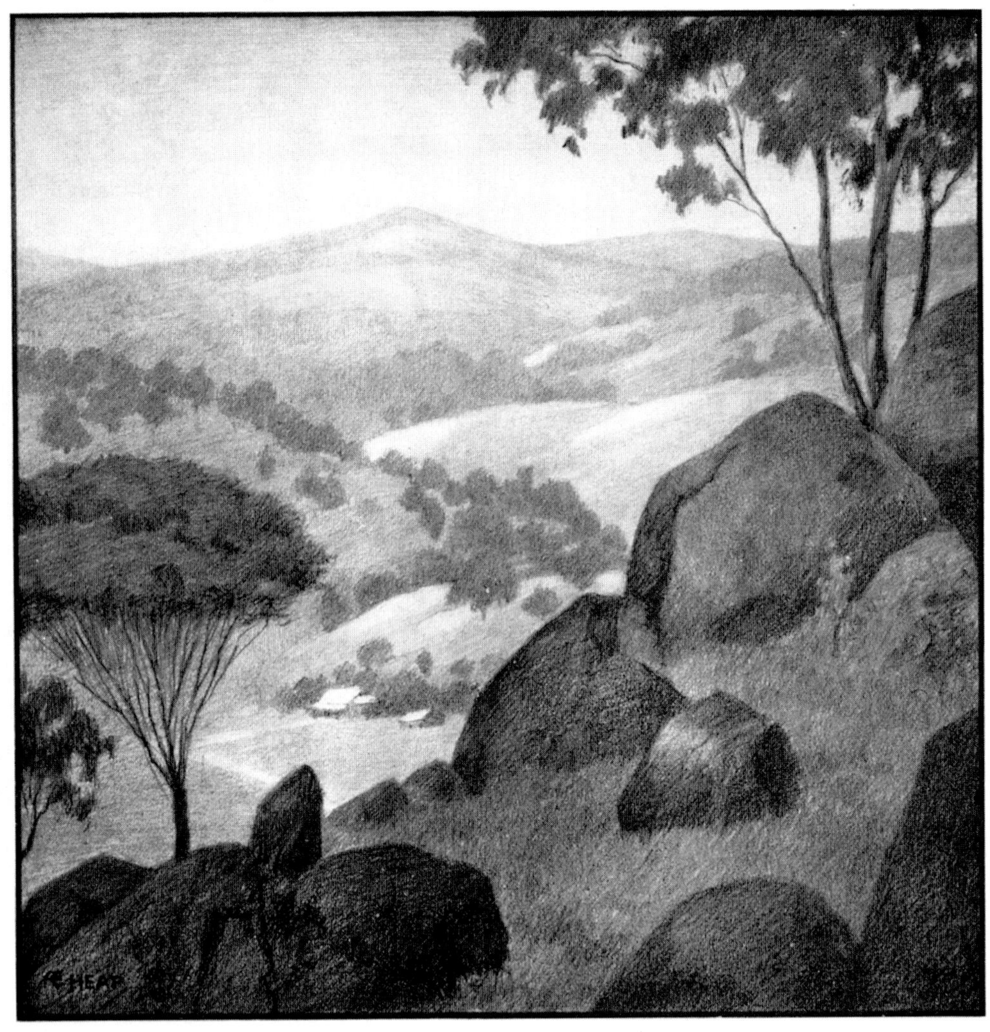

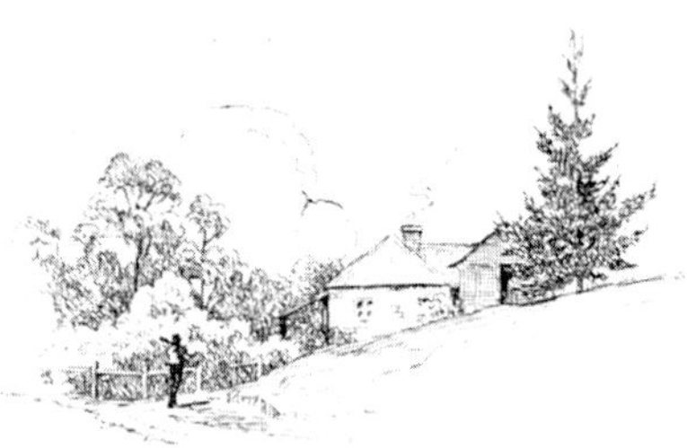

Jimperting Valley, Toodyay.

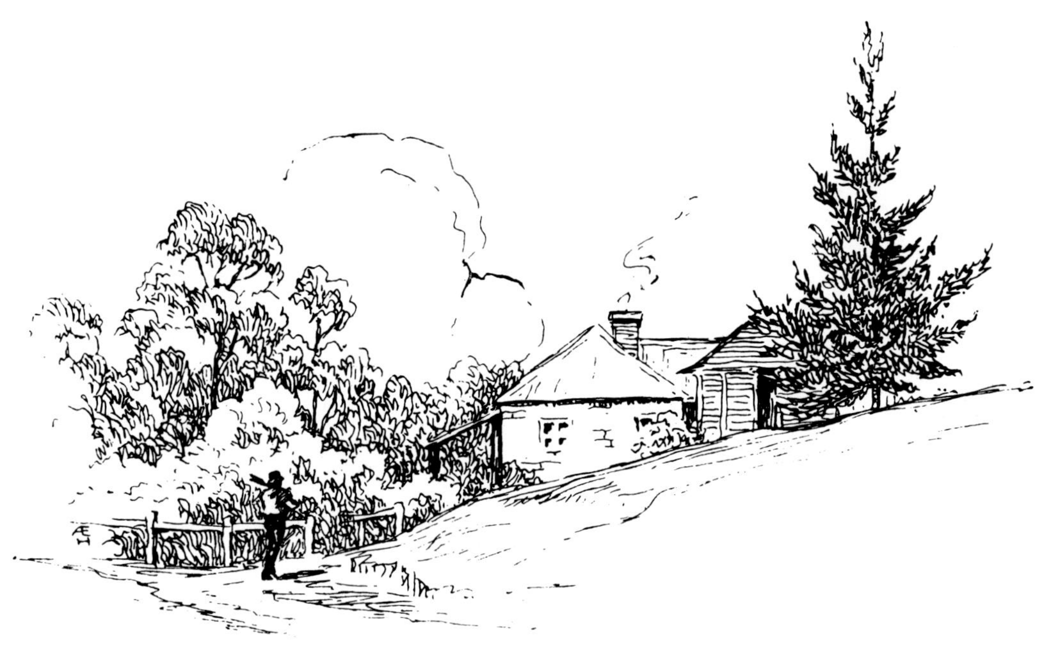

In the long settled Avon Valley, as at Jimperting, near Toodyay, near where convicts had once been based, the land has taken on an arcadian convictless English feel, strengthened in Amy's main and border drawings by the title 'Over Hill, Over Dale' from Shakespeare's *Midsummer Night's Dream* (Act II Scene i line 2). It could have been 'O'er vales and hills' from Wordsworth's 'I Wandered Lonely as a Cloud'.

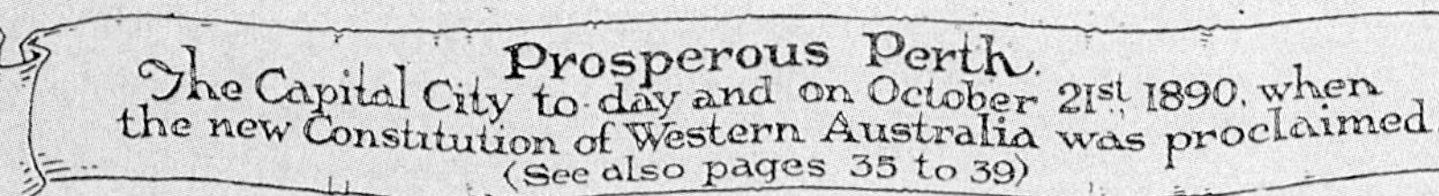

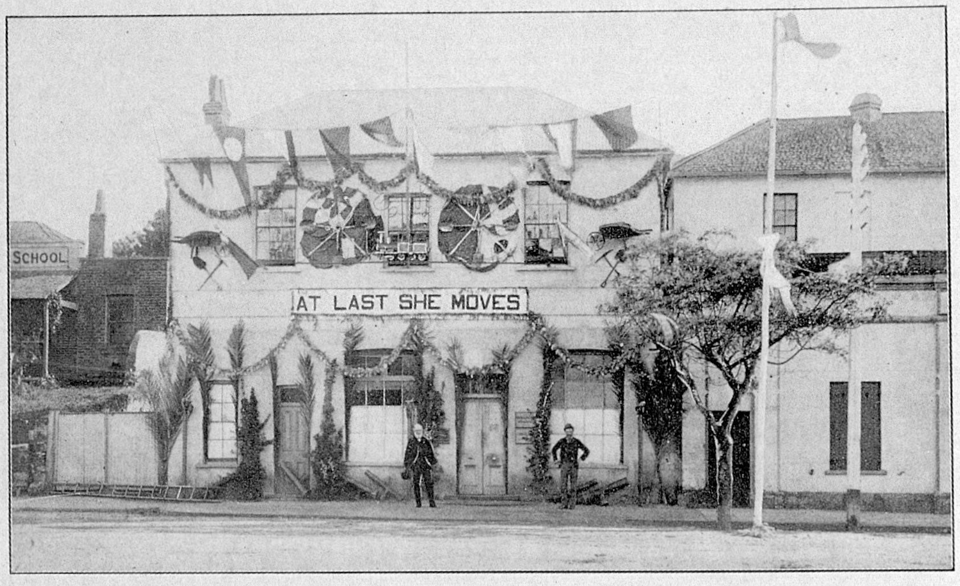

Above : The offices of the Midland Railway Company, St. George's-terrace, 1890.
Below : On the same site to-day rises Forrest Chambers.

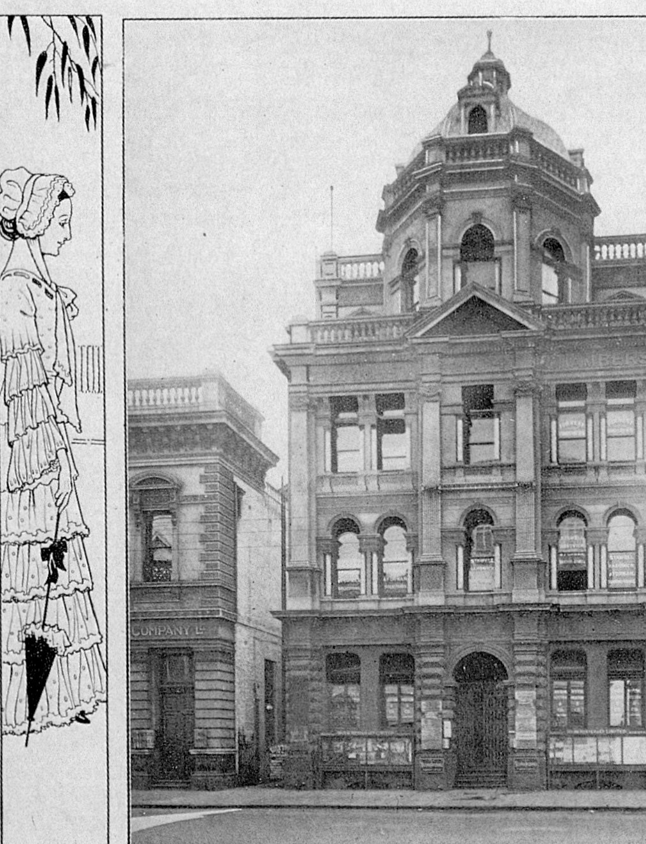
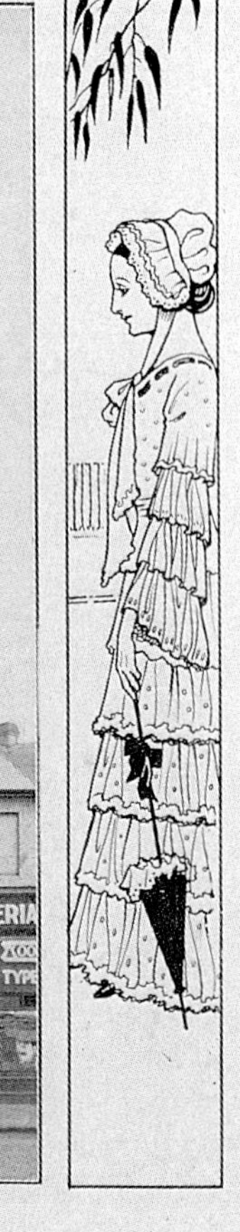

And Perth prospers as the country develops. Here Mr Keane's quaint 1890 offices have literally
'moved' and become Forrest Chambers. Amy's womenfolk look on resignedly.

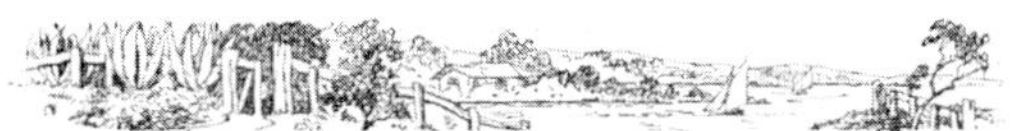

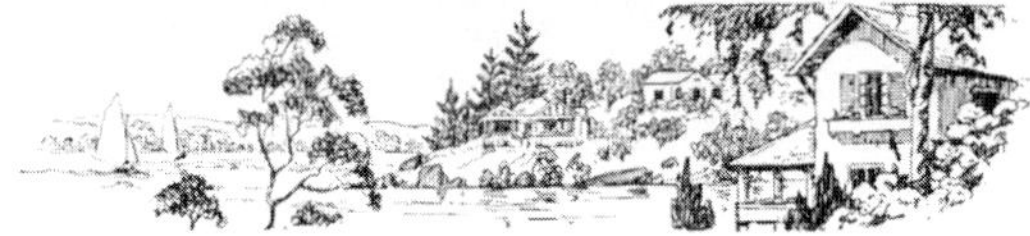

Keane's Point, Peppermint Grove.

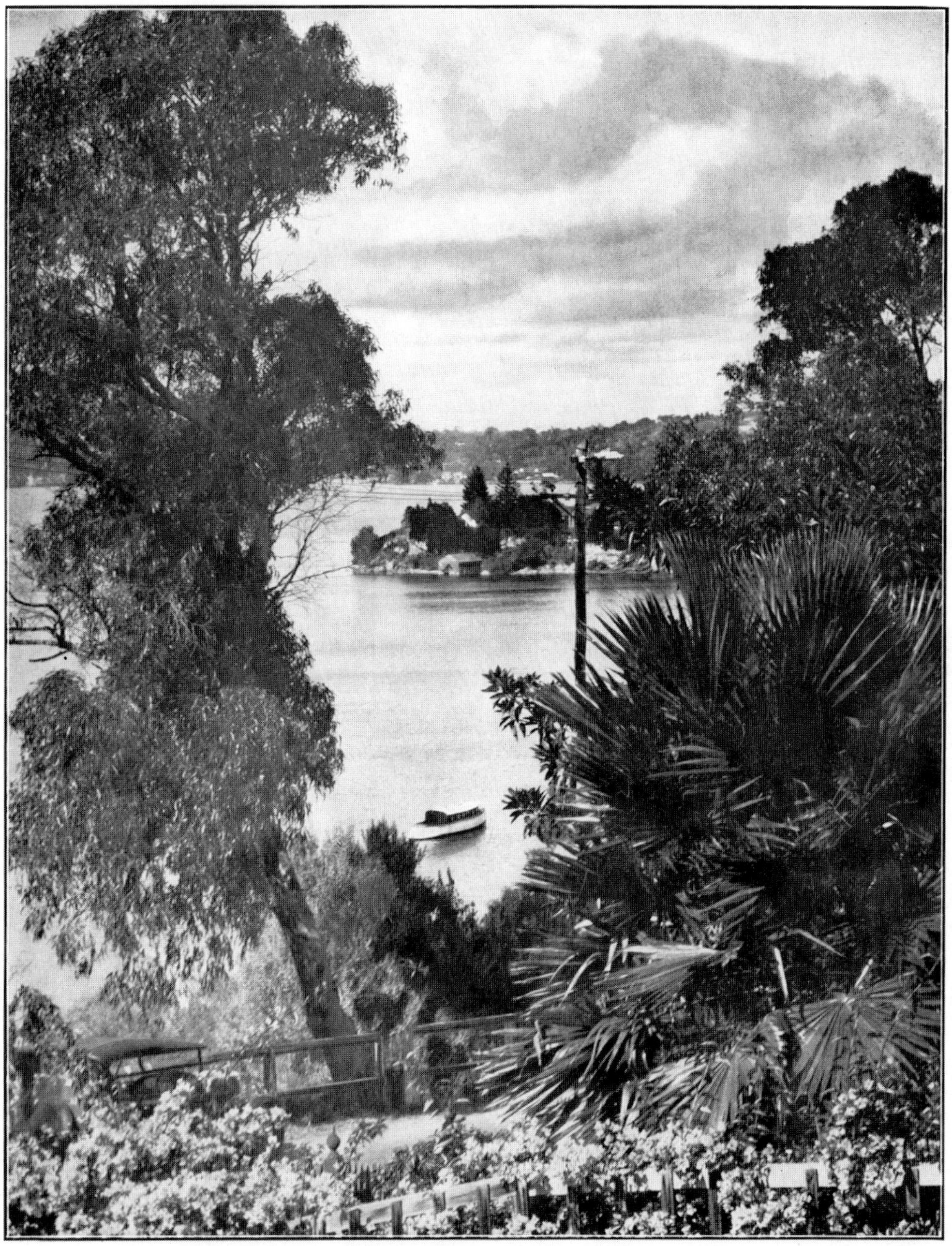

Photo, F. E. Ford.

In her imagery Amy did not venture into the working class suburbs of Bassendean and Victoria Park; instead she dwelt in the beautiful places, like Keane's Point, Peppermint Grove, where the houses were grand and river views superb.

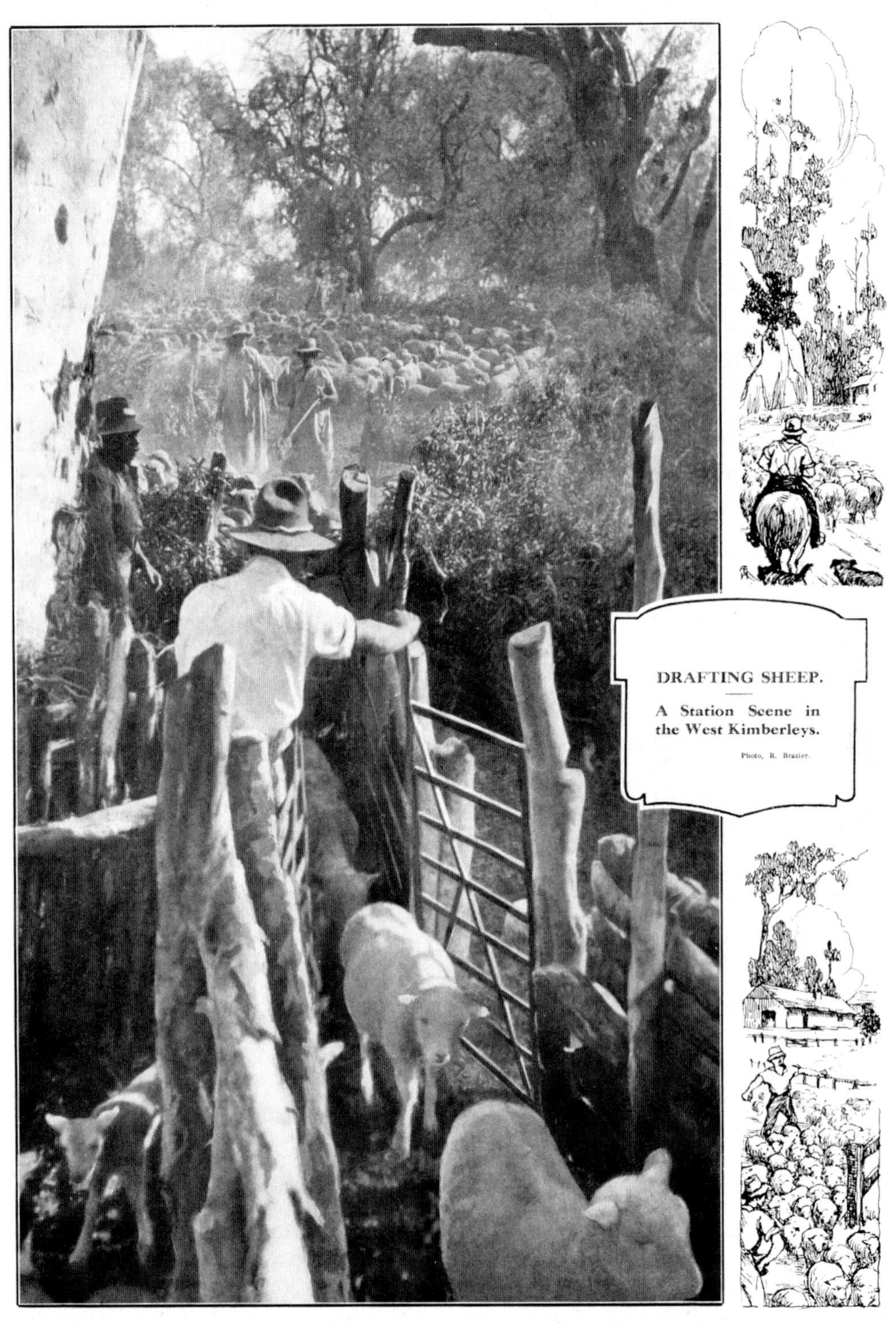

DRAFTING SHEEP.

A Station Scene in the West Kimberleys.

Photo, R. Brazier.

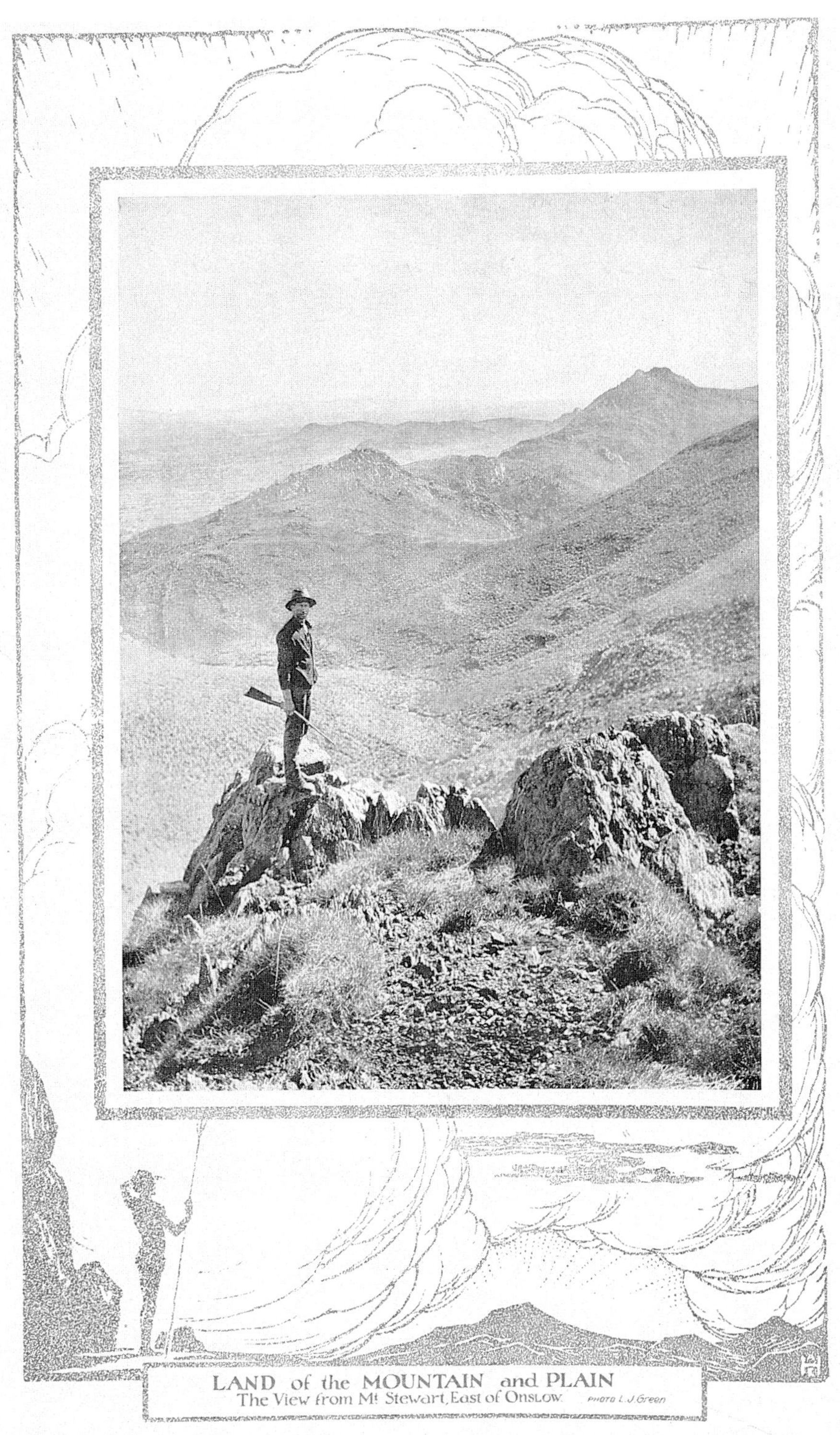

Some of the owners of the grand homes of Peppermint Grove lived off the profits of the northern sheep and cattle industry. Amy is disconcerted by the imagery of the photographs she must decorate. She bypasses the presence of Aboriginal labouring women and quietly restores the Anglo-Imperial base of development. Yet two years earlier she had taken courage in her hands and aimed a spear straight at the European gunman who now dominates mountain and plain. Perhaps in 1928 knowledge of the 1926 massacre of Aborigines on Marndoc Reserve and the subsequent Royal Commission directed her pen; perhaps by 1930 such knowledge was less troubling.

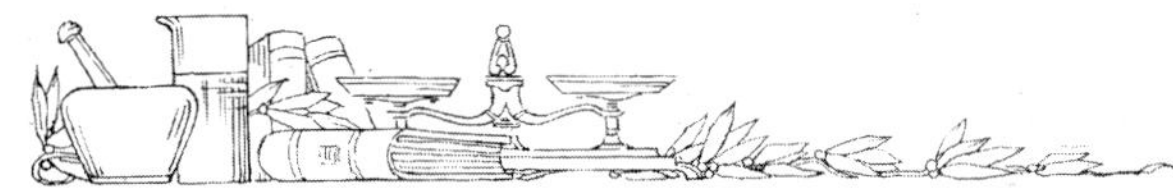

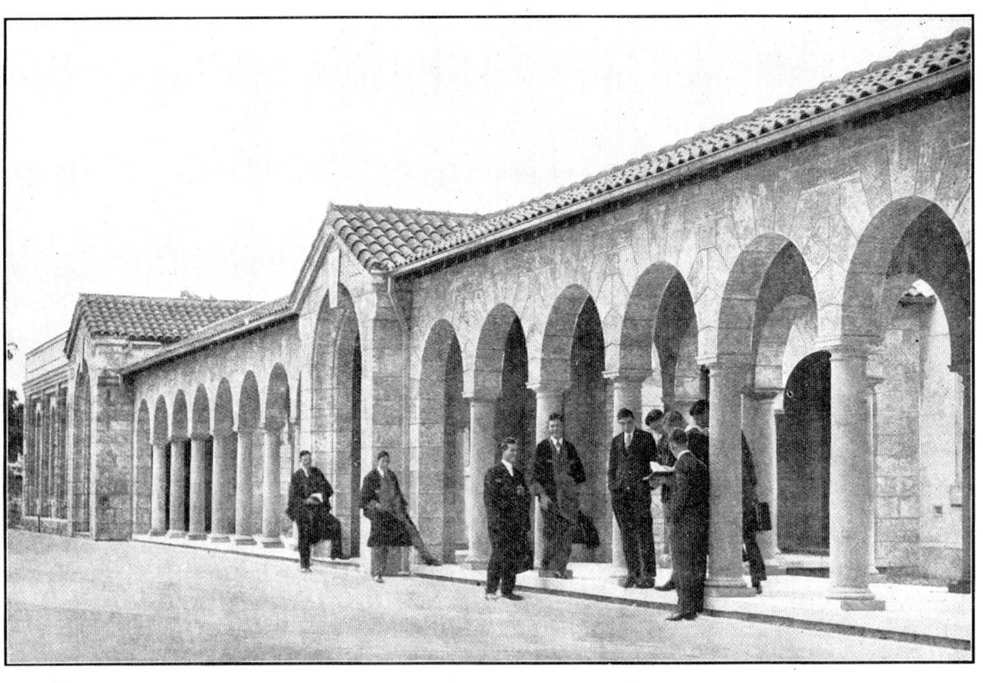

The cloisters on the west side of the Guild of
Undergraduates' block.

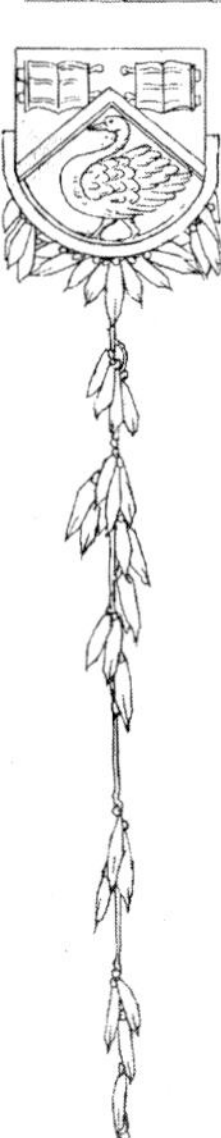

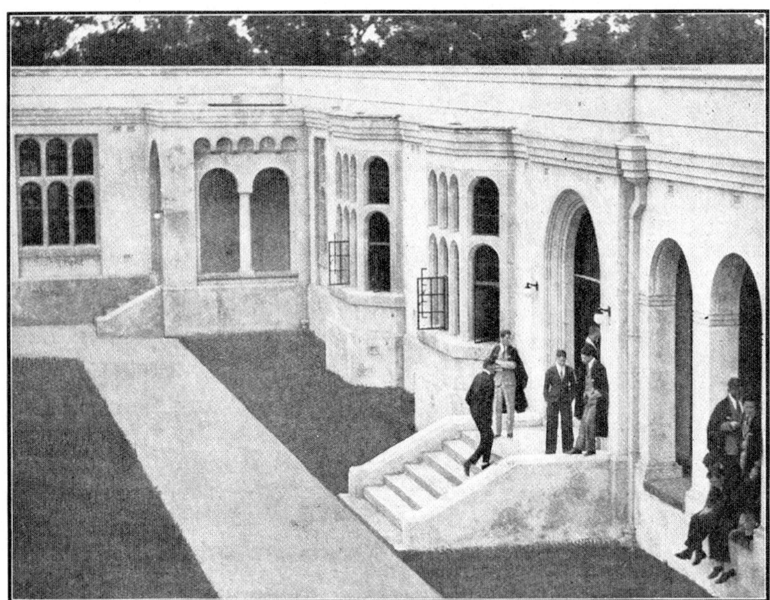

The eastern face of the
same building.

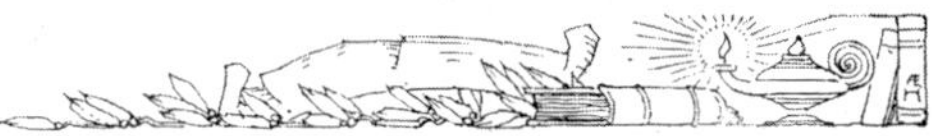

Staff photos.

Amy was more at ease embellishing photographs of the 'new university' buildings at Crawley in
1931. Here she draws directly on comparable images from her English art instruction portfolios
— the civilizing images of books and cloisters, mottos, and the lamp of learning.

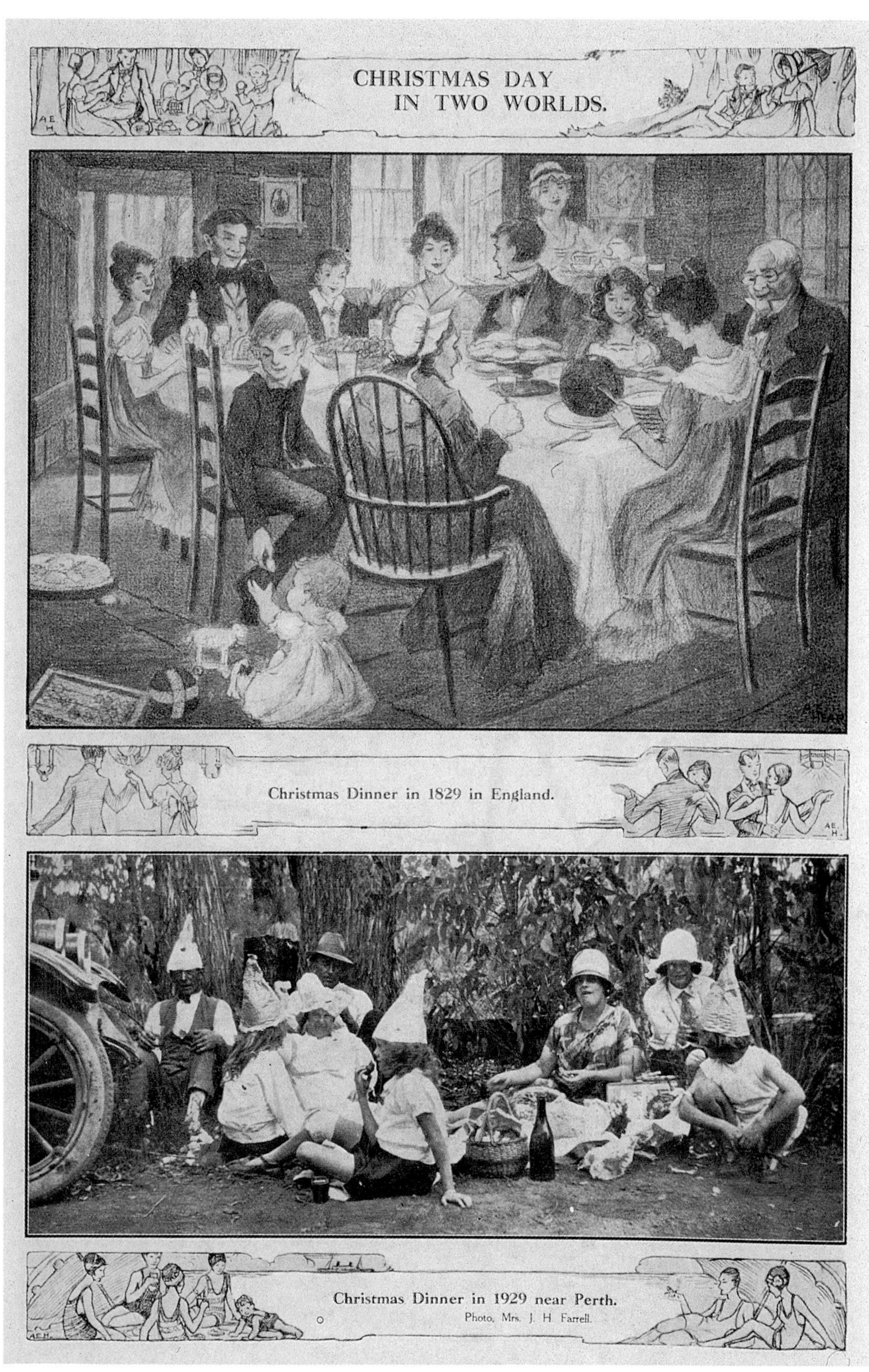

Amy had a keen eye to both the beauty and crudity of the Australian festive season. Here she juxtaposes one of her own drawings of middle class England indoors at Christmas dinner in 1829 with Amy Farrell's lively photograph of a bush-park Christmas dinner near Perth in 1929. Amy's border drawing of languorous and beautiful Perth beach bathing belles counterpoints the muscularity of the people in Farrell's photo.

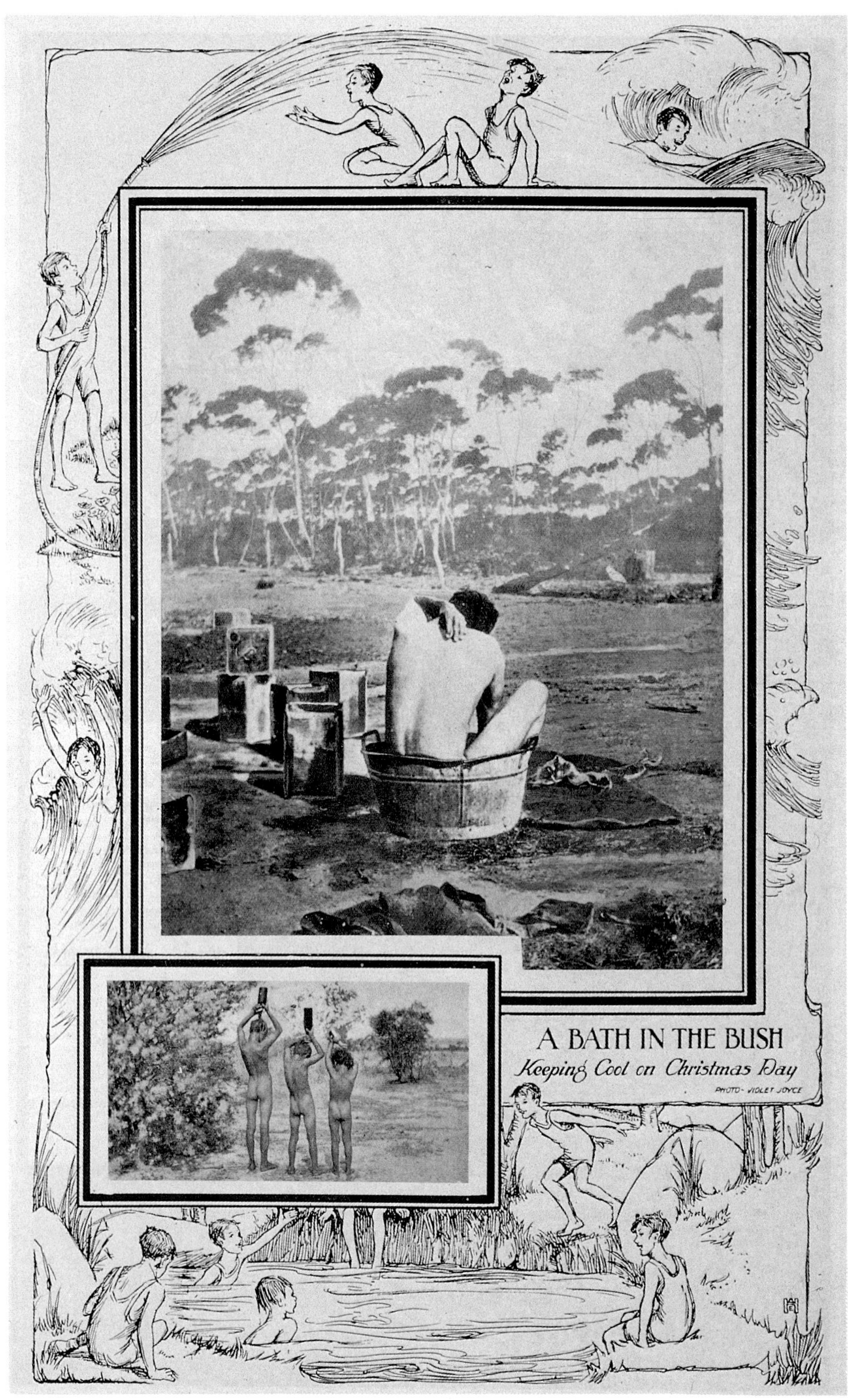

Still on the Christmas theme, Amy takes a mildly humourous bush situation and transforms it into a children's summer idyll, a sort of Swallows and Amazons in Western Australia.

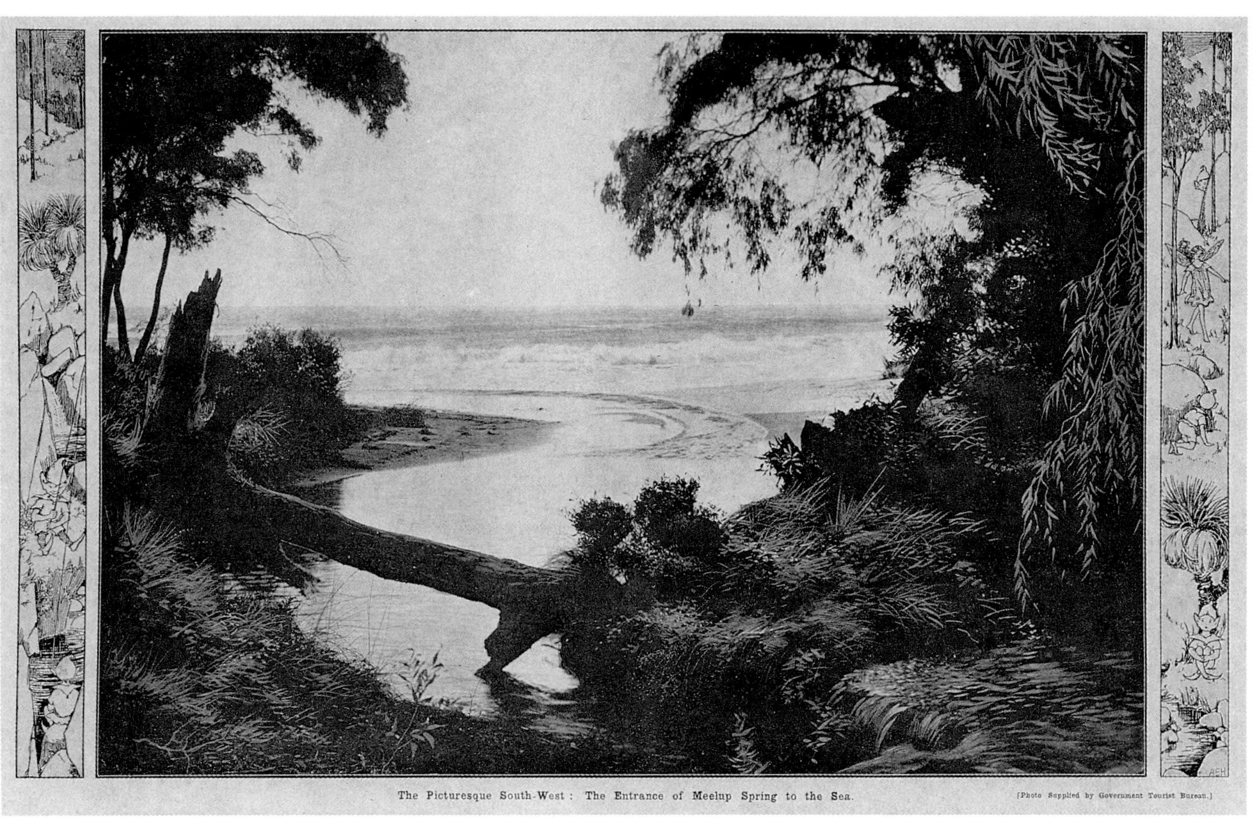

The Picturesque South-West : The Entrance of Meelup Spring to the Sea.   [Photo Supplied by Government Tourist Bureau.]

Across the continent the artist Frederick McCubbin had found fairies in the Australian bush
and even in suburban backyards; and Amy too knew of the fantasy of the fairy in all our lives.
Here in the bush adjoining dark, beautiful, and mysterious Meelup Spring,
Amy's child fairies and elves swing and play.

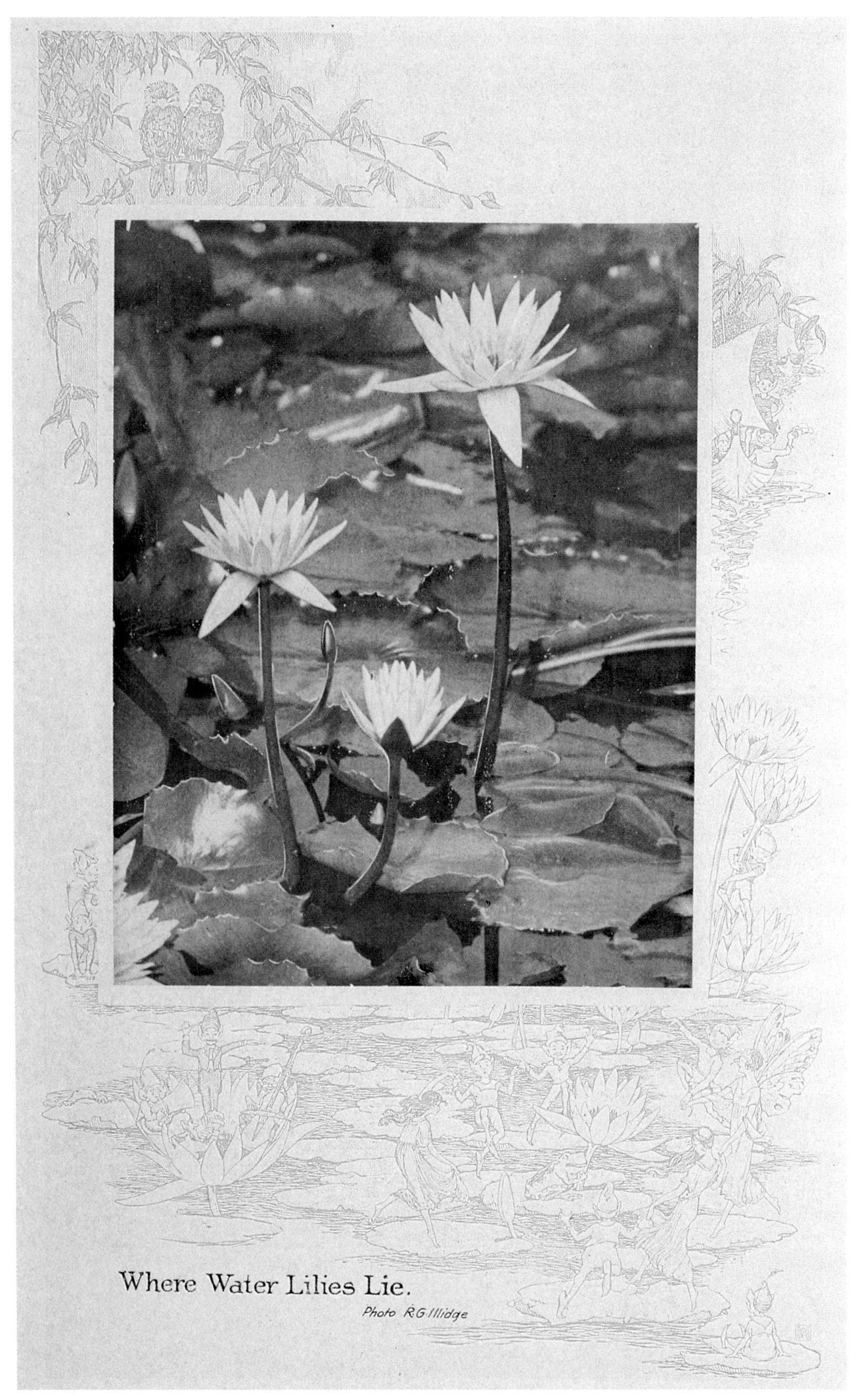

Cicely Mary Barker's popular Flower Fairy books are no more beautiful than Amy Heap's fairy drawings from the 1920s. Amy's cavorting water lily fairies are watched over by what may be young kookaburras: 'Where there are flowers, there fairies are'.

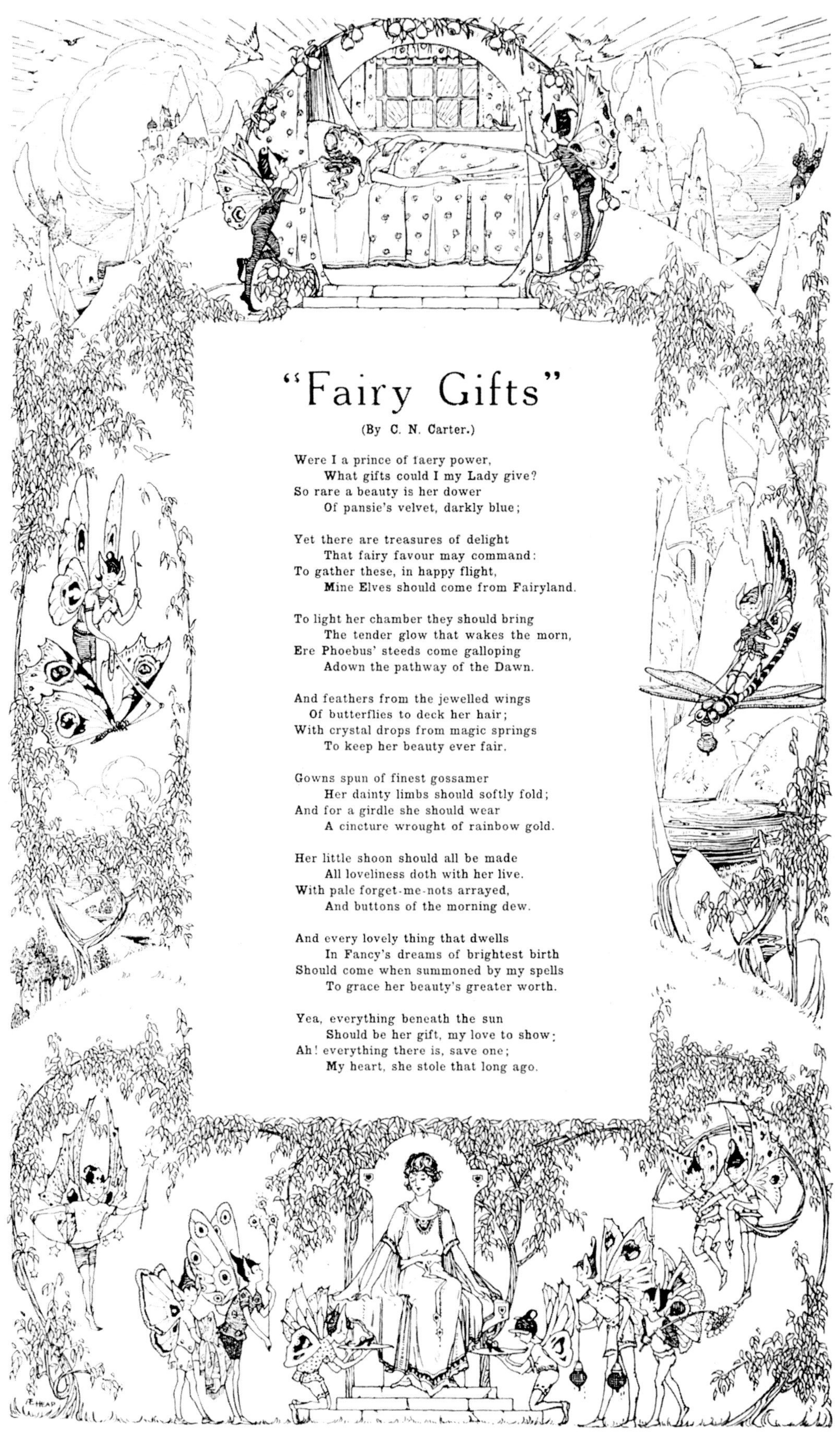

"Fairy Gifts"

(By C. N. Carter.)

Were I a prince of faery power,
    What gifts could I my Lady give?
So rare a beauty is her dower
    Of pansie's velvet, darkly blue;

Yet there are treasures of delight
    That fairy favour may command:
To gather these, in happy flight,
    Mine Elves should come from Fairyland.

To light her chamber they should bring
    The tender glow that wakes the morn,
Ere Phoebus' steeds come galloping
    Adown the pathway of the Dawn.

And feathers from the jewelled wings
    Of butterflies to deck her hair;
With crystal drops from magic springs
    To keep her beauty ever fair.

Gowns spun of finest gossamer
    Her dainty limbs should softly fold;
And for a girdle she should wear
    A cincture wrought of rainbow gold.

Her little shoon should all be made
    All loveliness doth with her live.
With pale forget-me-nots arrayed,
    And buttons of the morning dew.

And every lovely thing that dwells
    In Fancy's dreams of brightest birth
Should come when summoned by my spells
    To grace her beauty's greater worth.

Yea, everything beneath the sun
    Should be her gift, my love to show;
Ah! everything there is, save one;
    My heart, she stole that long ago.

THE LOST CHILD
BY ERNESTINE HILL

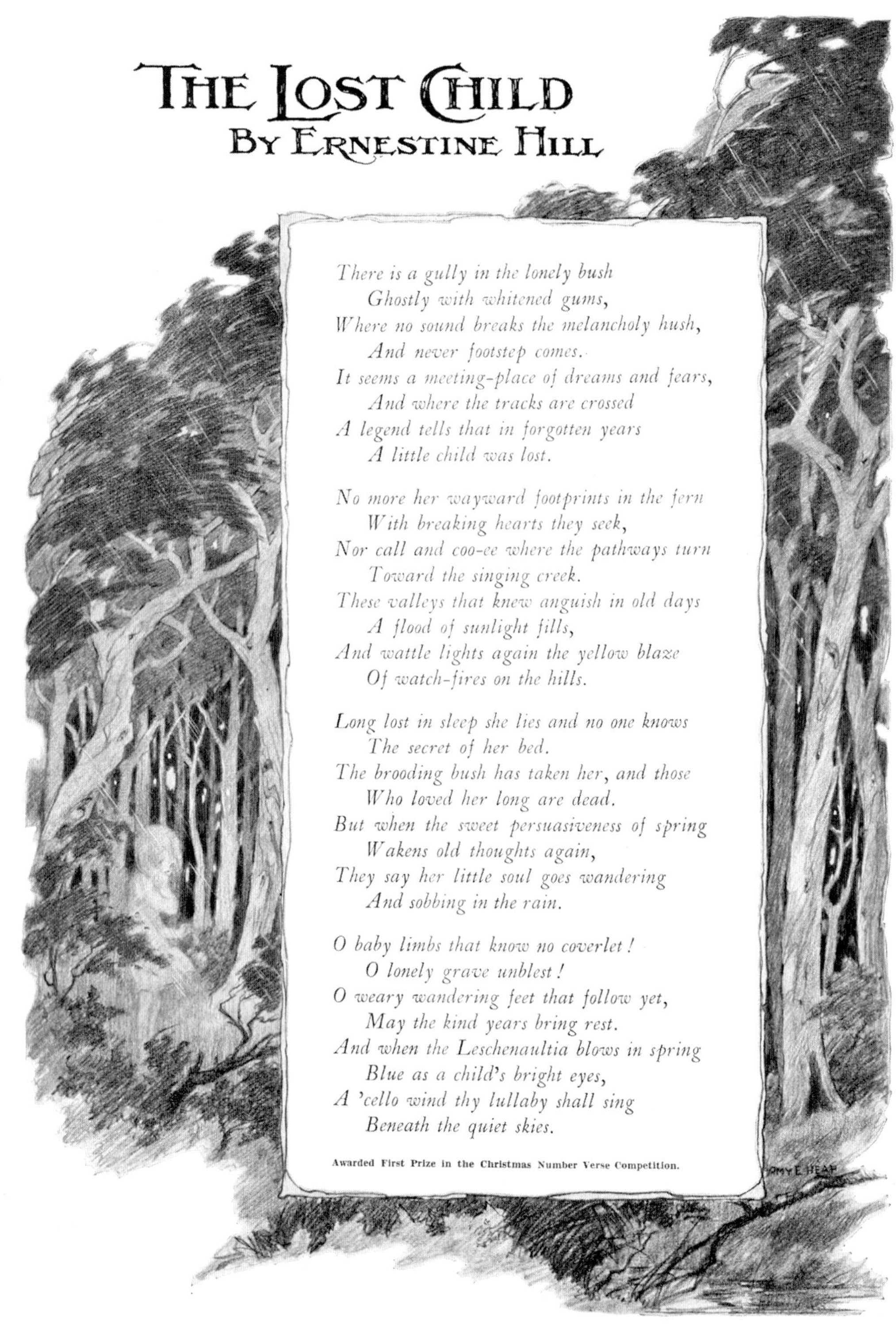

'The Lost Child' in the Australian bush had been immortalized by Frederick McCubbin in the 1880s, but it was a theme and an experience which lay deep in the psyche of European families in bush and city. Amy complements Ernestine Hill's poem with a threatening tentacled bush which envelopes the wraith-like elfin figure of the lost girl.

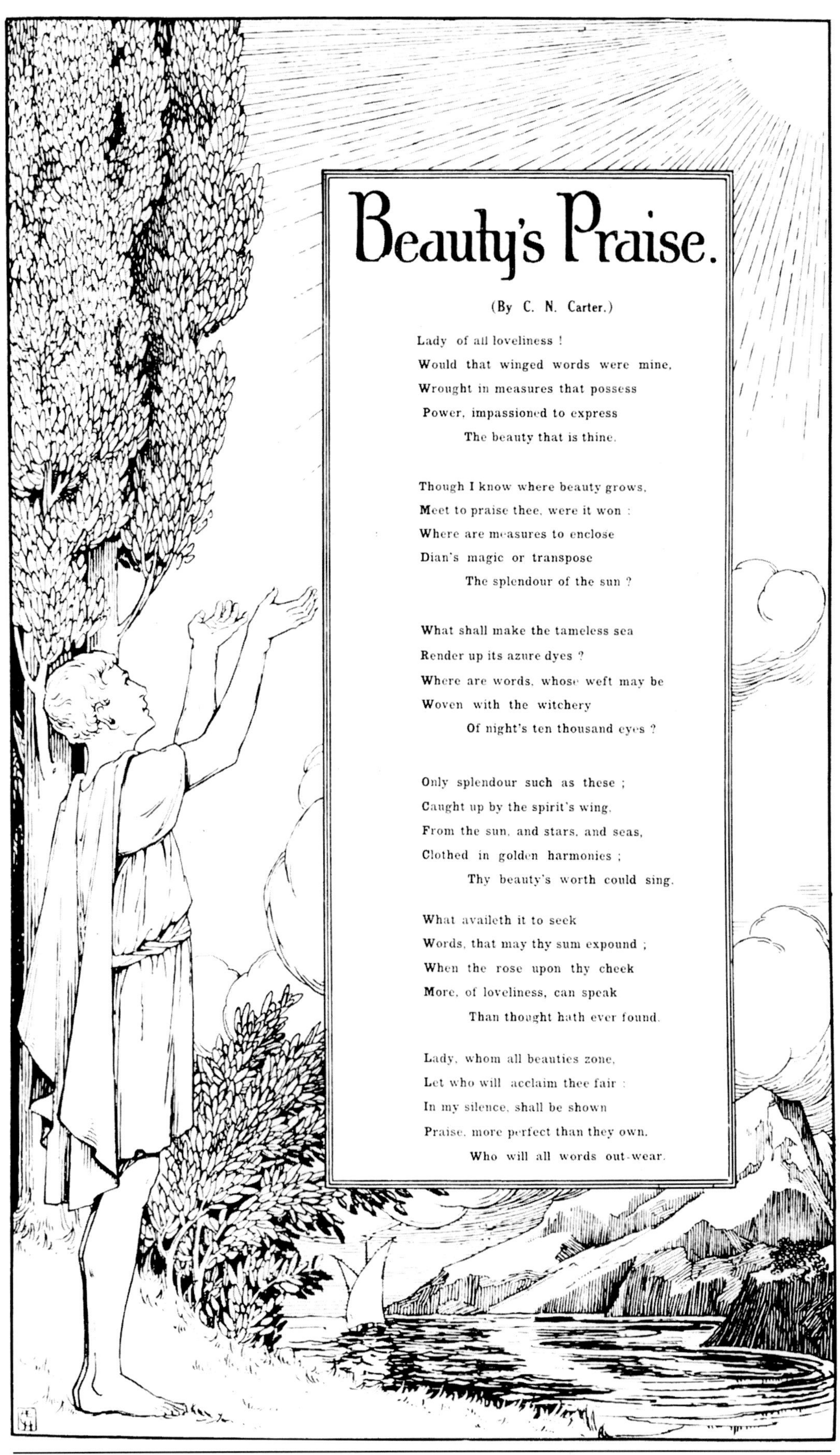

Beauty's Praise.

(By C. N. Carter.)

Lady of all loveliness !
Would that winged words were mine,
Wrought in measures that possess
Power, impassioned to express
    The beauty that is thine.

Though I know where beauty grows,
Meet to praise thee, were it won :
Where are measures to enclose
Dian's magic or transpose
    The splendour of the sun ?

What shall make the tameless sea
Render up its azure dyes ?
Where are words, whose weft may be
Woven with the witchery
    Of night's ten thousand eyes ?

Only splendour such as these ;
Caught up by the spirit's wing,
From the sun, and stars, and seas,
Clothed in golden harmonies ;
    Thy beauty's worth could sing.

What availeth it to seek
Words, that may thy sum expound ;
When the rose upon thy cheek
More, of loveliness, can speak
    Than thought hath ever found.

Lady, whom all beauties zone,
Let who will acclaim thee fair :
In my silence, shall be shown
Praise, more perfect than they own.
    Who will all words out-wear.

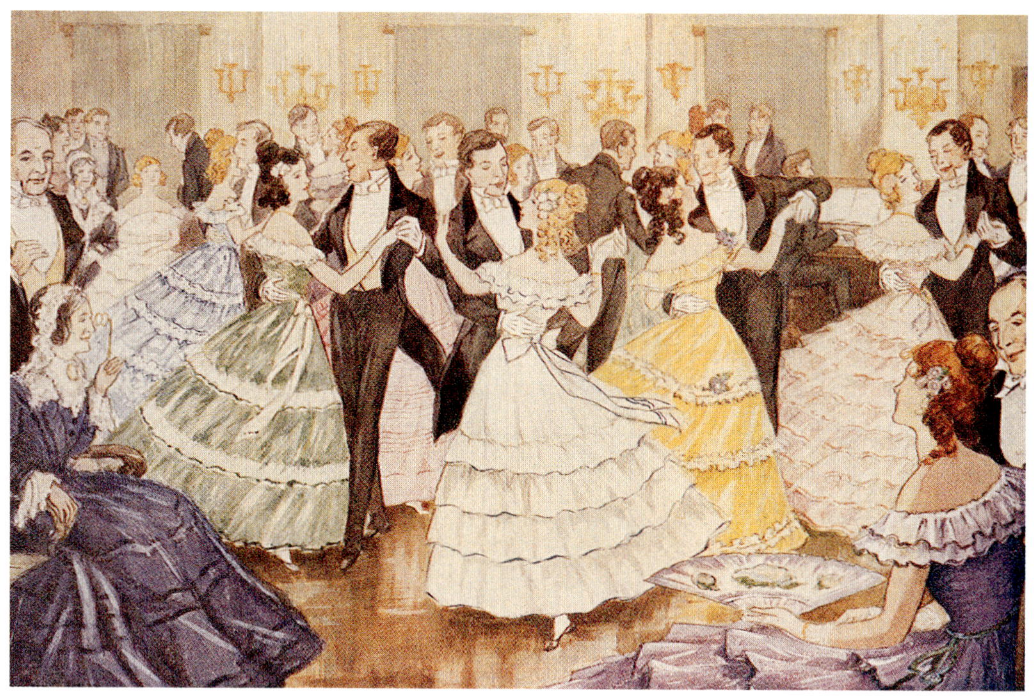

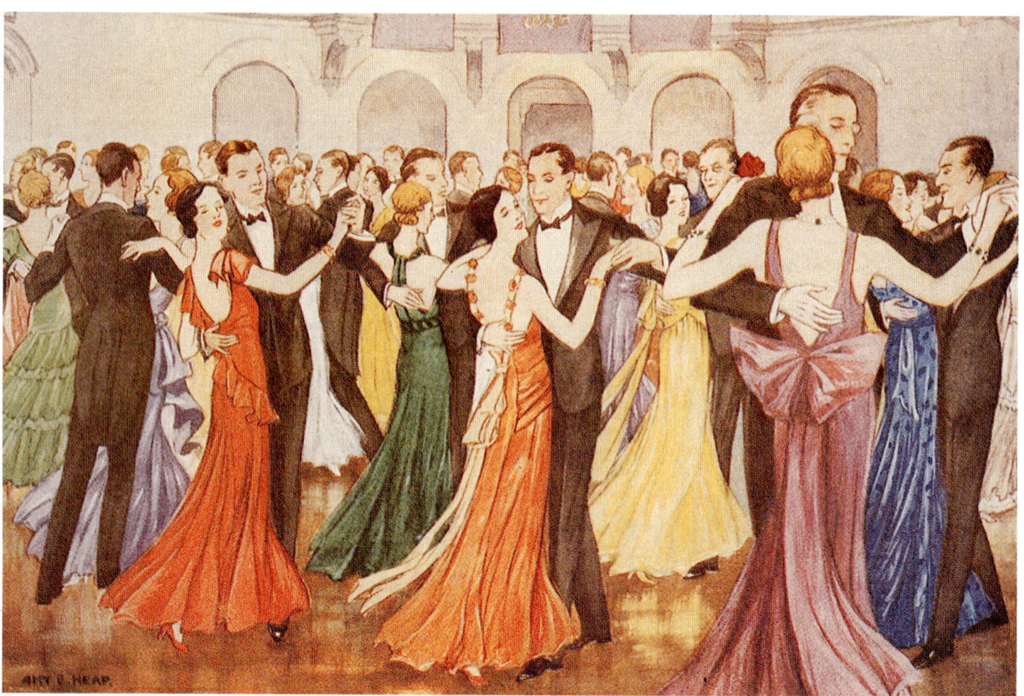

The beauty of dance and elegant dancers could also be praised, as Amy does historically for Balls at Government House in 1833 and 1933.

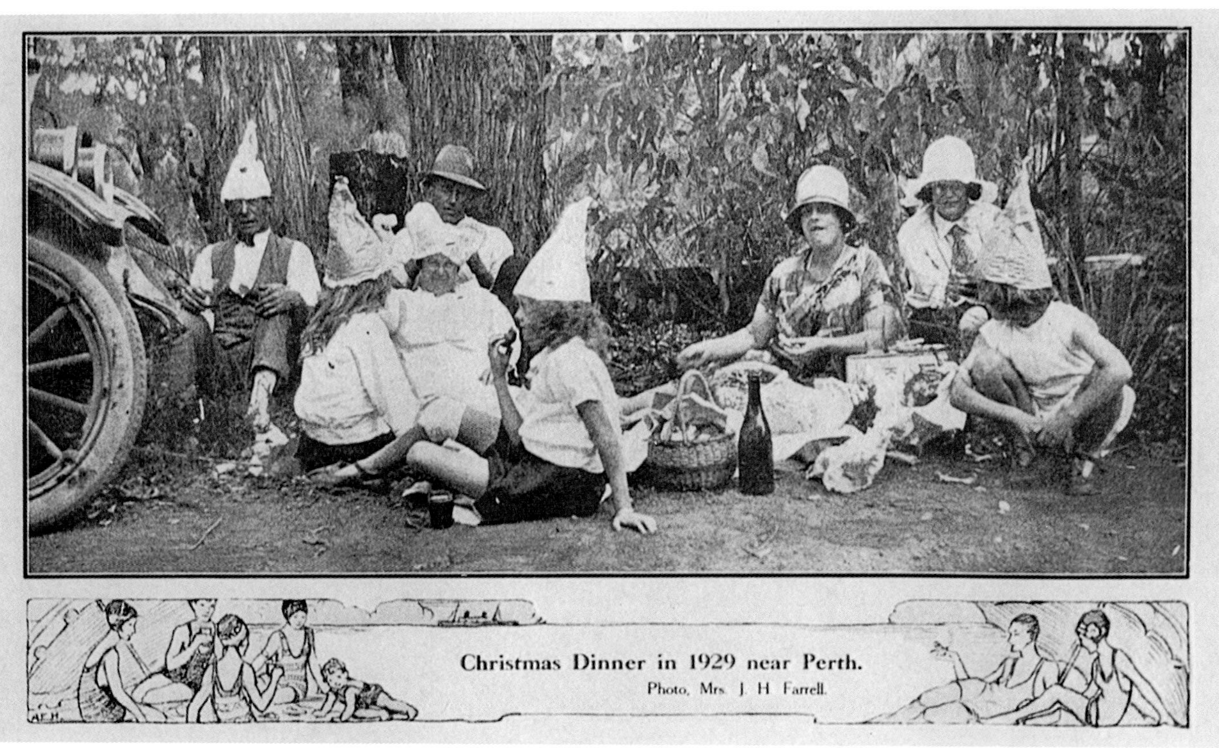

Christmas Dinner in 1929 near Perth.

Photo, Mrs. J. H. Farrell.

Amy loved the youthful hedonism of Perth, perhaps especially as contrasted with the dour Bolton of her own youth. Here in Christmas 1929, she surrounds a pleasant picnic scene with images of bounty and beach. Contented parents and children in Perth are worlds away from the crash on Wall Street.

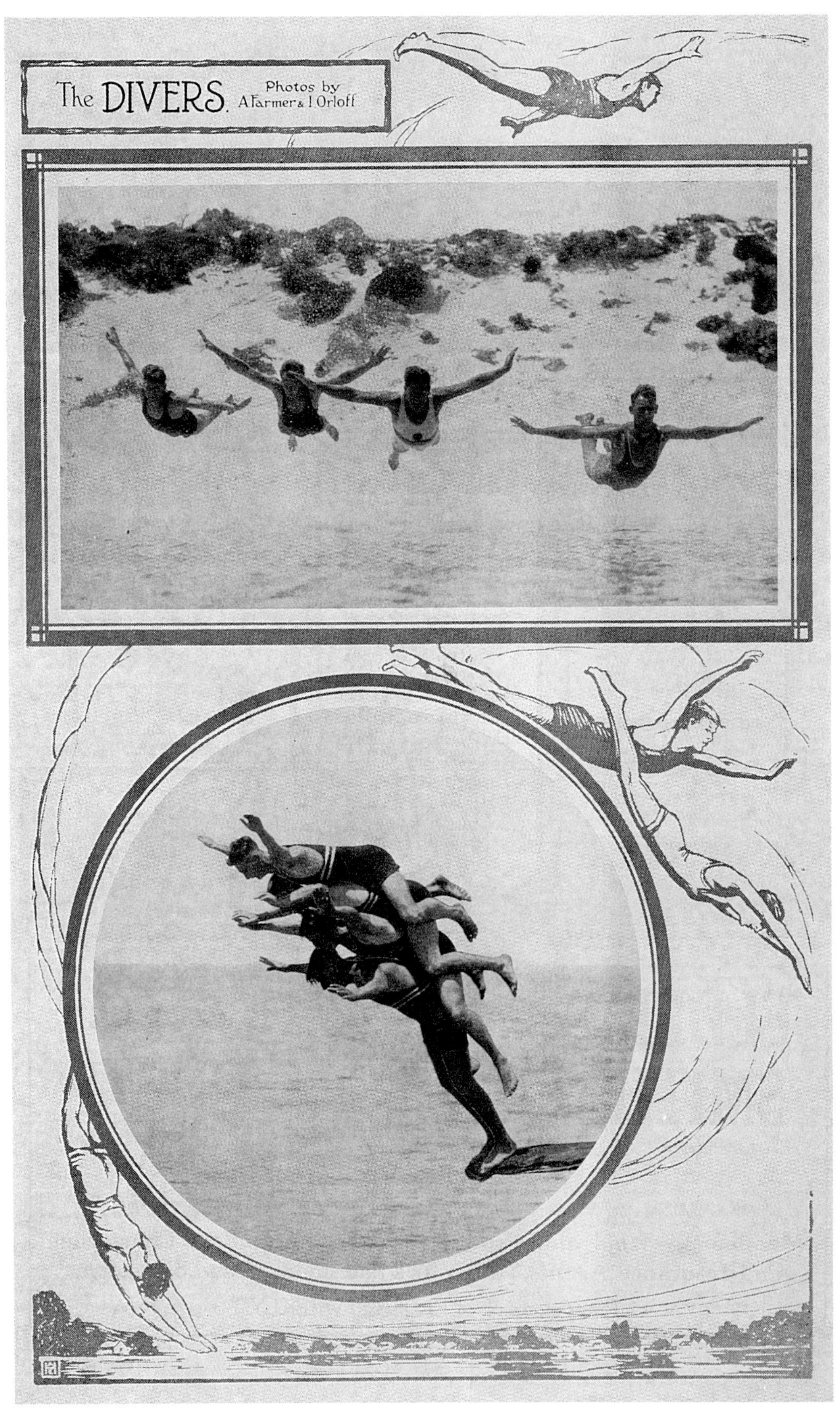

The interwar years saw the emergence of a cult of masculinity based on beach activities like life-saving. Amy completes a swirl of movement through the divers.
She, like them, enjoys the occasion.

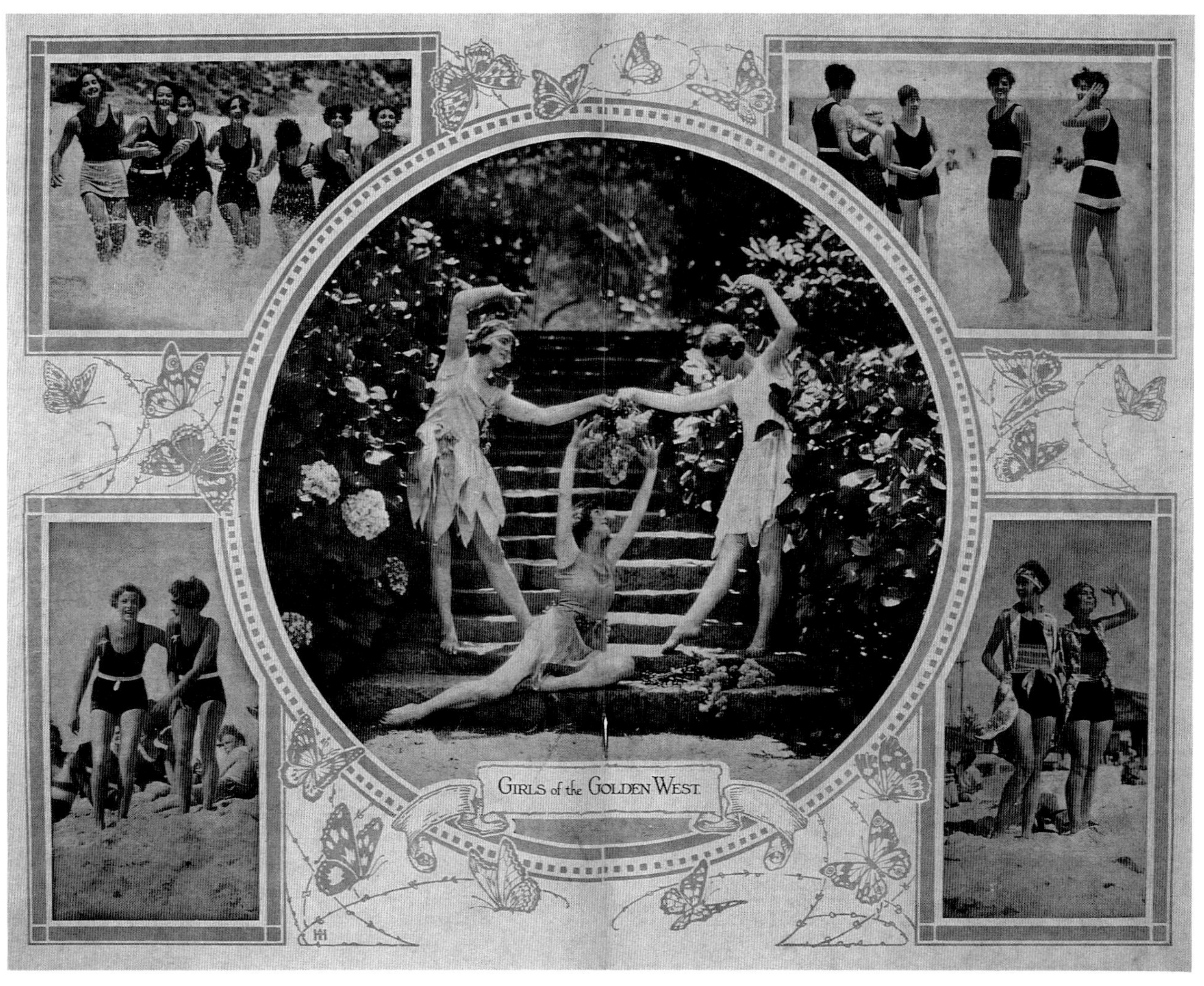

Amy's patience with both photographer and subject wears thin. Are the girls of
Western Australia merely butterflies?

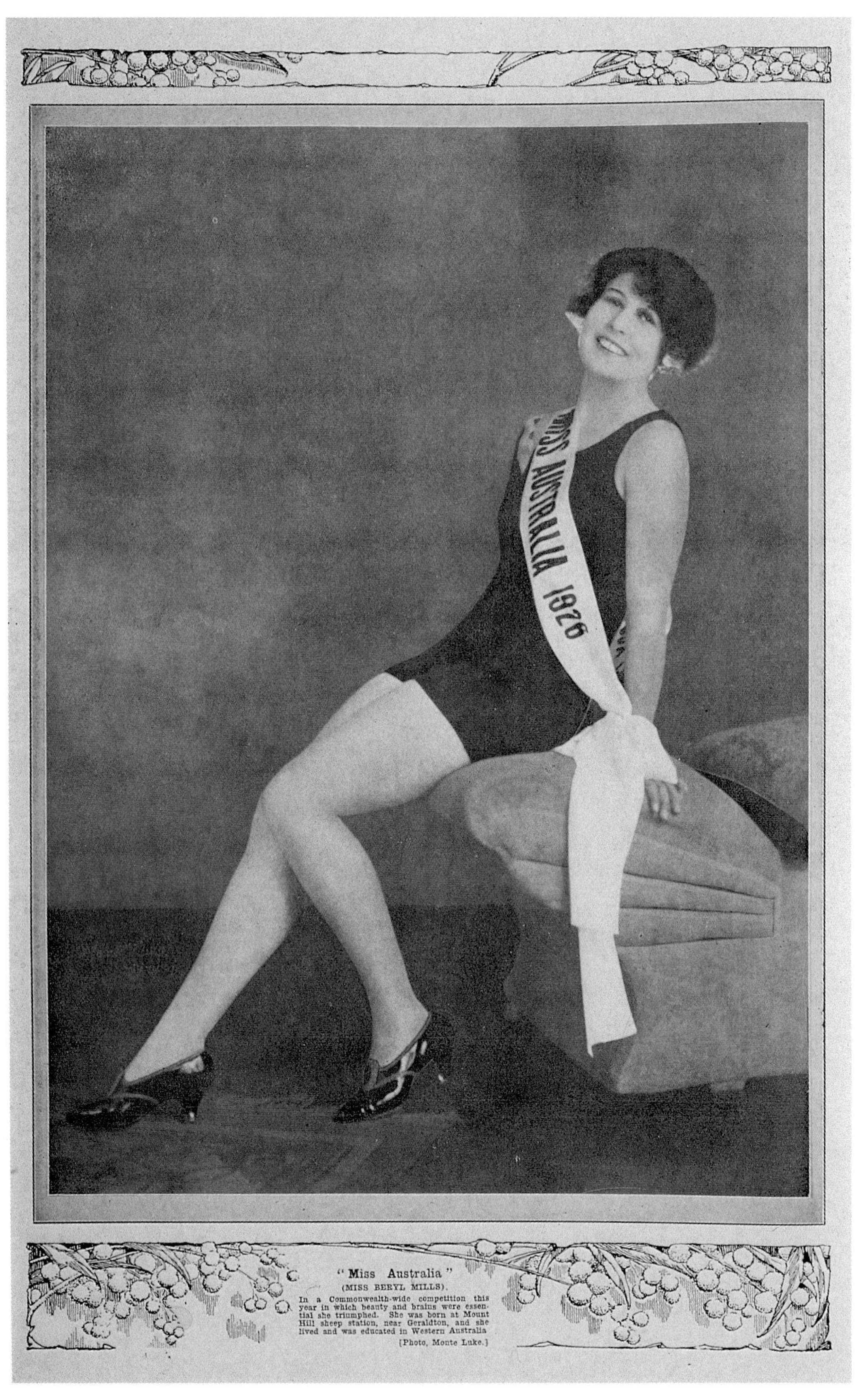

"Miss Australia"
(MISS BERYL MILLS).

In a Commonwealth-wide competition this year in which beauty and brains were essential she triumphed. She was born at Mount Hill sheep station, near Geraldton, and she lived and was educated in Western Australia

[Photo, Monte Luke.]

How can the artist embellish Beryl Mill's beauty? Amy finds the appropriate response in Australia's golden Wattle blossom, so fleeting, sweet and colourful in nature.

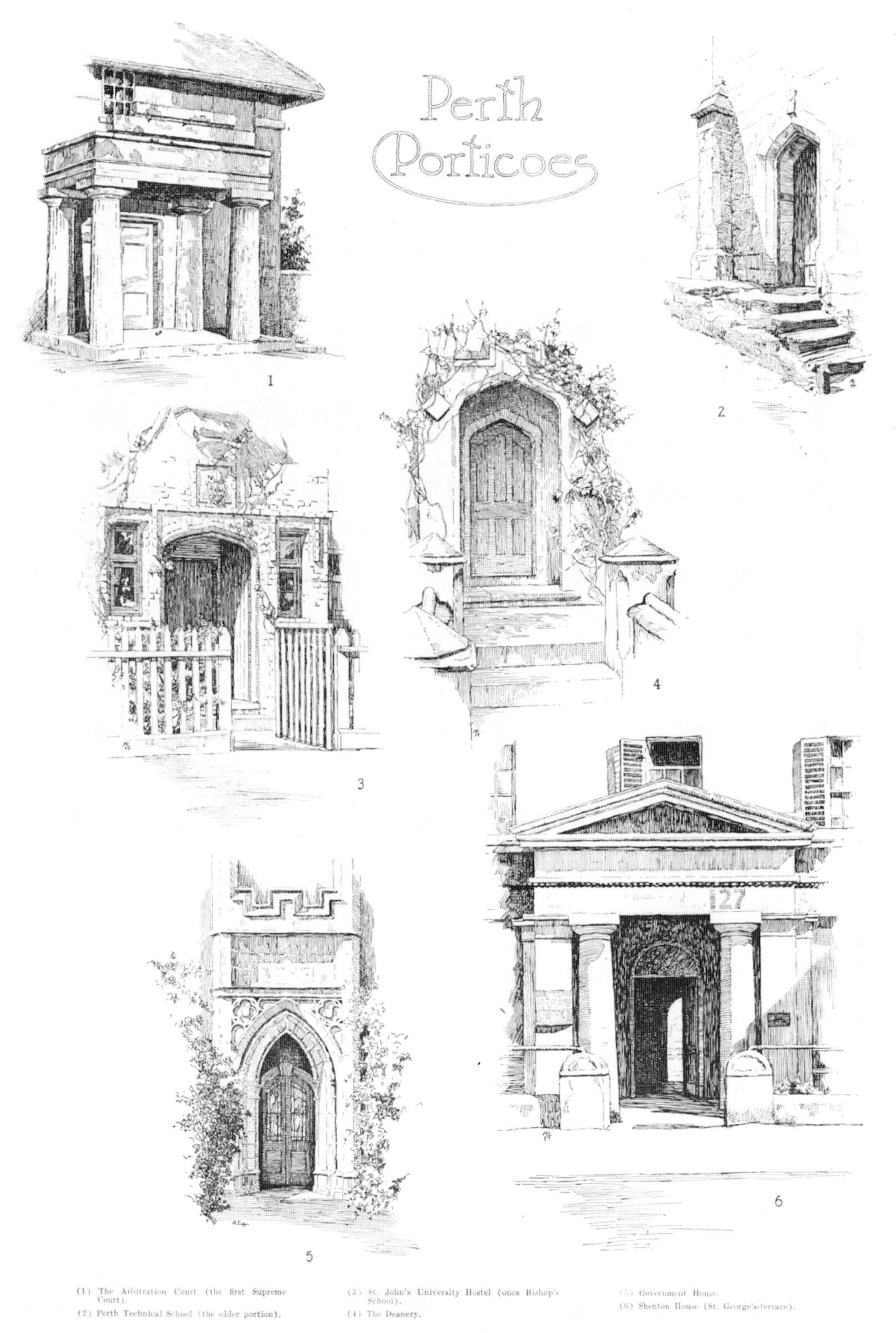

Like her journalist colleagues at the *West Australian* in St George's Terrace, Amy came to know Perth well. Here she imbues the city's porticoes with a comforting mix of classicism and romanticism.

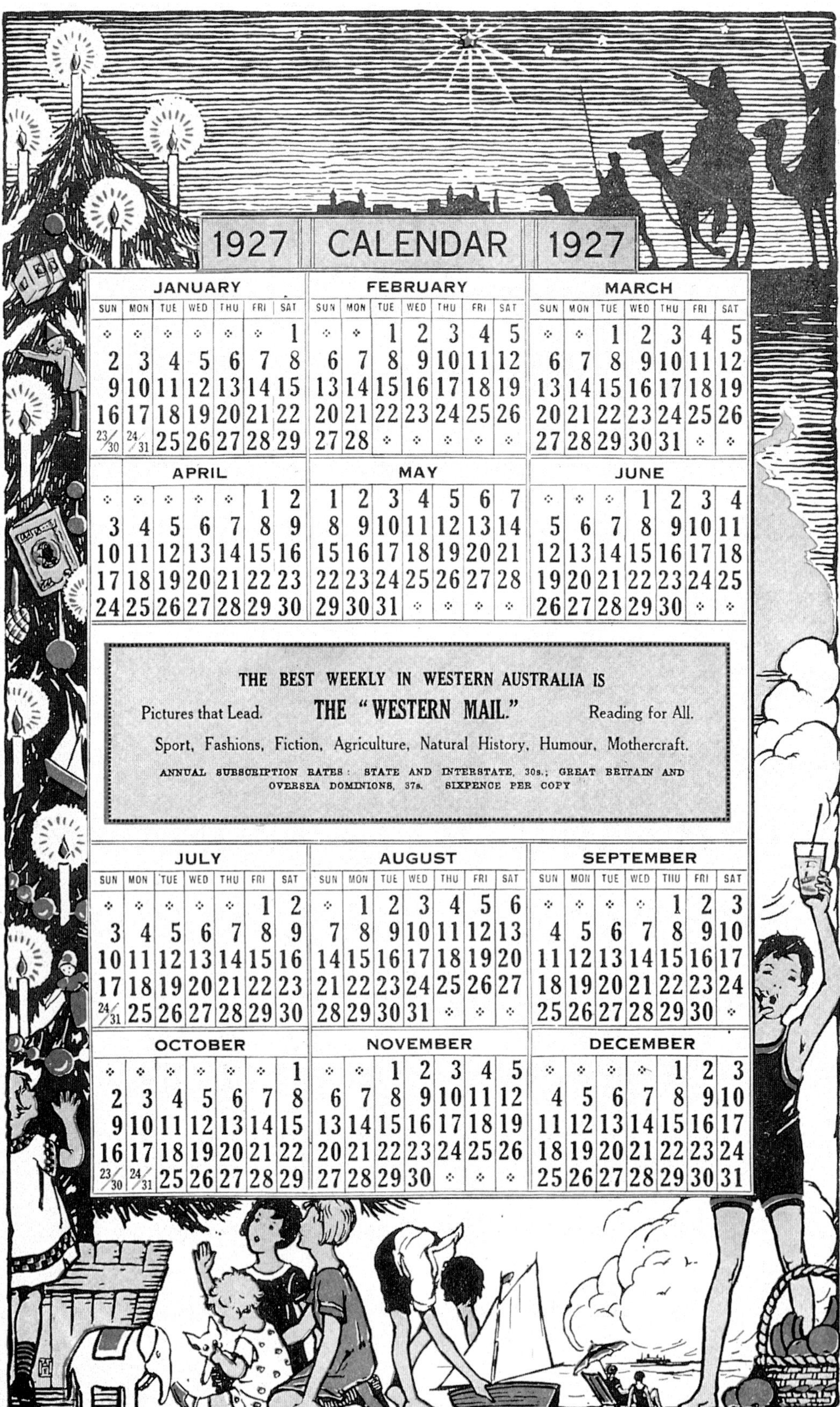

1927 CALENDAR 1927

JANUARY
FEBRUARY
MARCH
APRIL
MAY
JUNE

THE BEST WEEKLY IN WESTERN AUSTRALIA IS
Pictures that Lead.   THE "WESTERN MAIL."   Reading for All.
Sport, Fashions, Fiction, Agriculture, Natural History, Humour, Mothercraft.
ANNUAL SUBSCRIPTION RATES: STATE AND INTERSTATE, 30s.; GREAT BRITAIN AND
OVERSEA DOMINIONS, 37s.   SIXPENCE PER COPY

JULY
AUGUST
SEPTEMBER
OCTOBER
NOVEMBER
DECEMBER

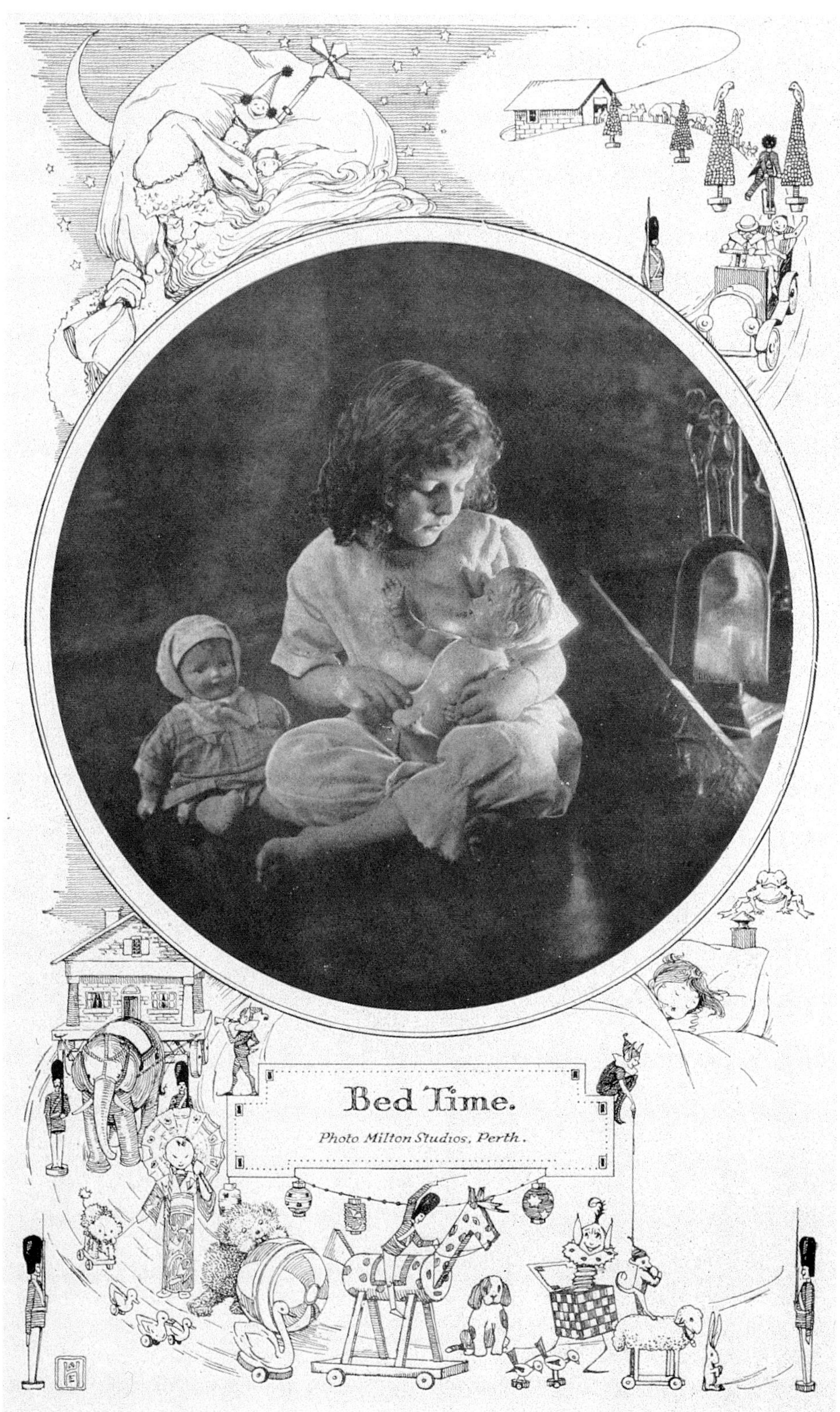

In her 1927 calendar and her Christmas bed-time drawings, Amy captures the universal child's
hopes and dreams. There are the toys of Empire in soldiers and elephants; there are elves, yachts,
Christmas trees and candles and Saint Nick himself. There is the Star in the East. What a year to
look forward to! Amy's images predate the Arthur Rackham edition of Clement Clarke Moore's
The Night Before Christmas (1931) and Joan Gale Thomas's popular
My Book About Christmas (1946).

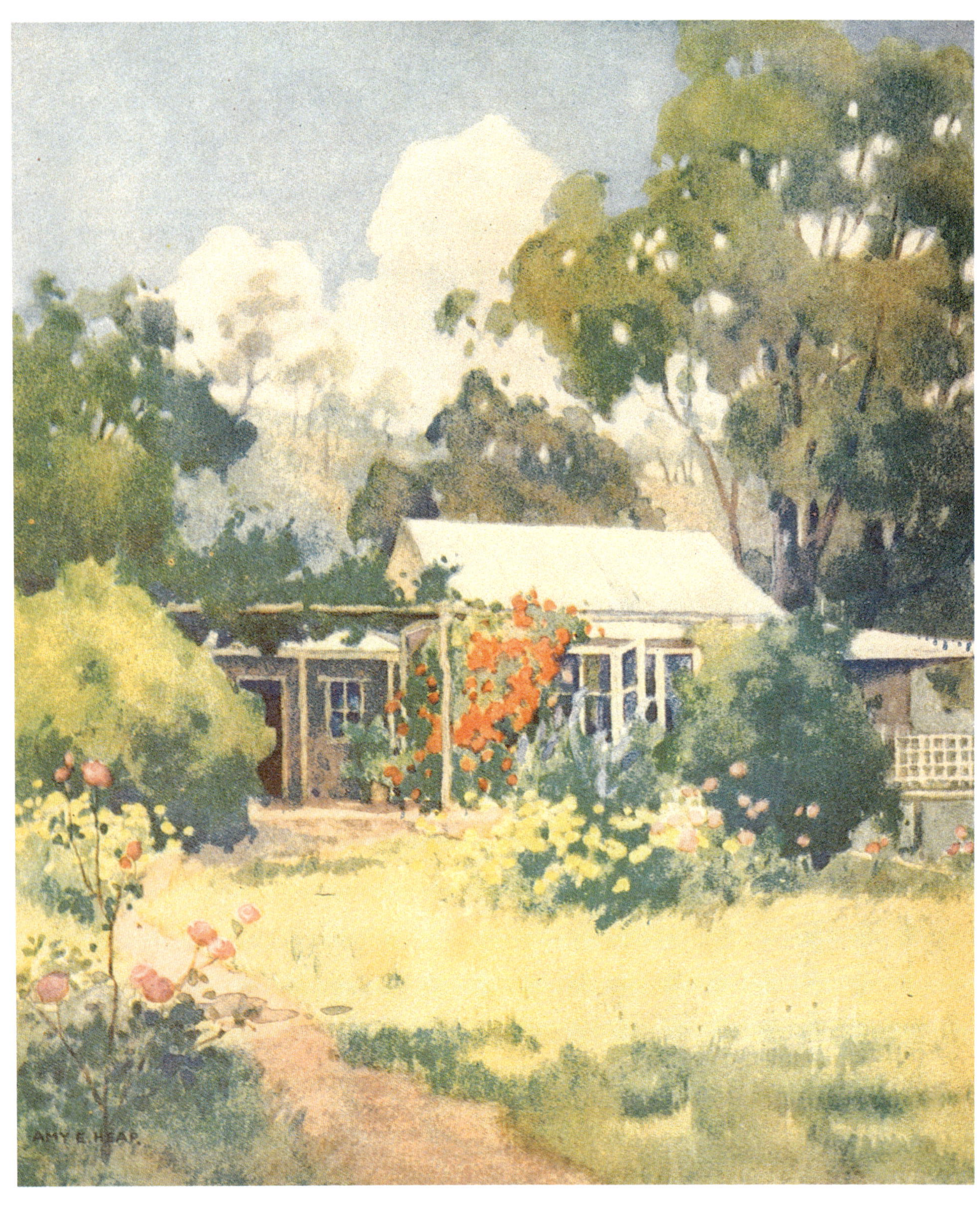

And for romanticism pure what could be lovelier than a flower-bedecked cottage in the hills of Darlington, home for Amy for many years.

THE IMAGES

FRED FLOOD

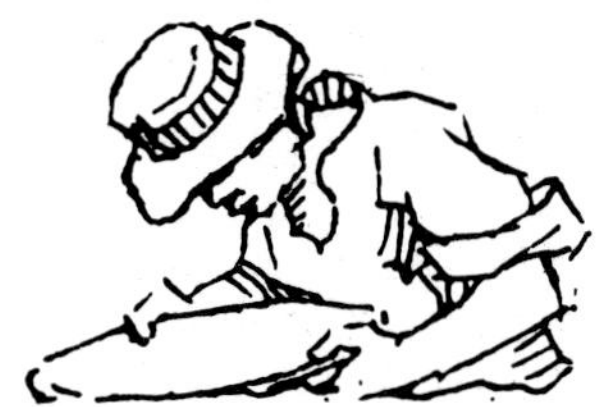

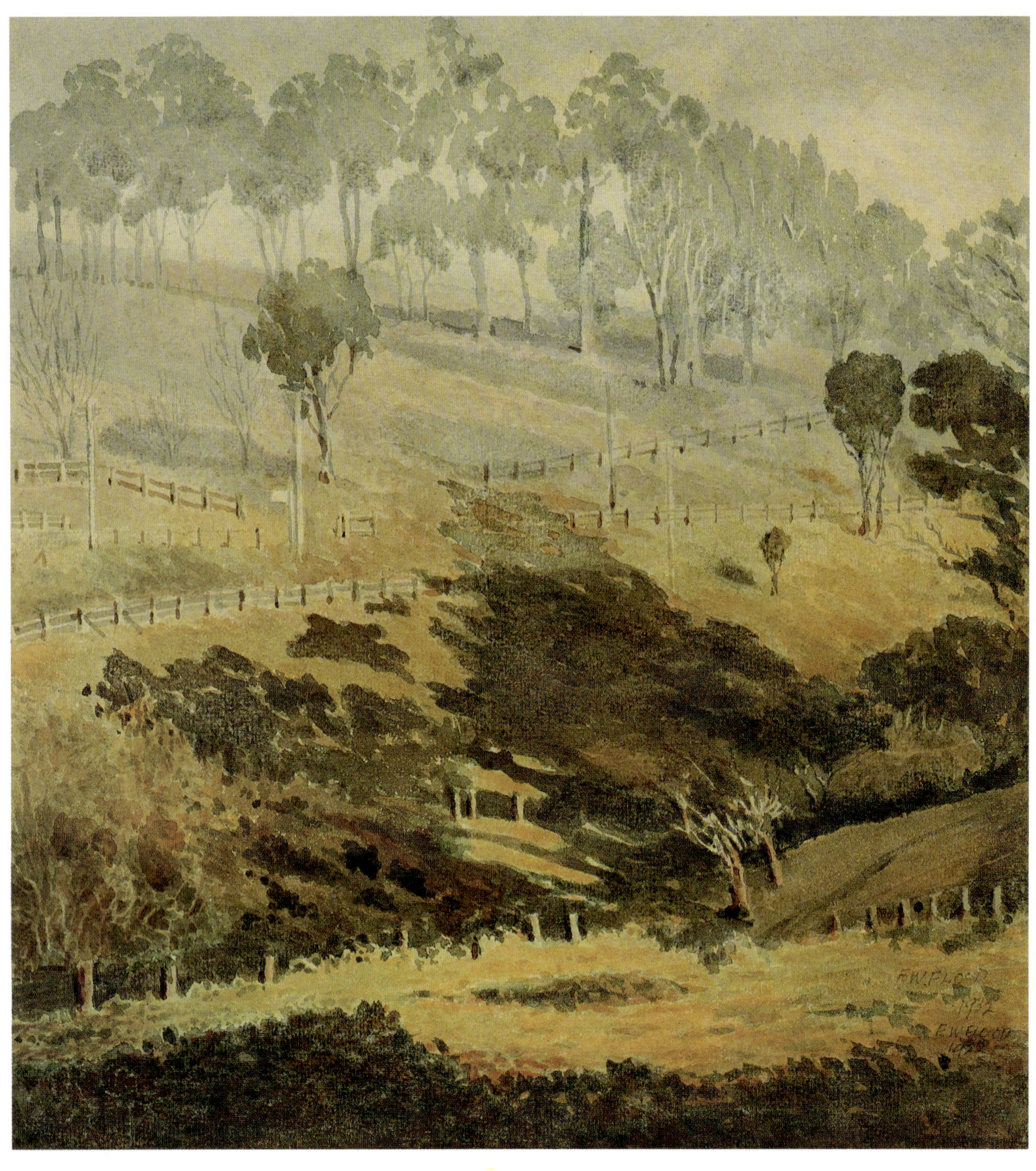

Fred's watercolours from the 1930s stress the beautiful and bountiful in nature. His roads lead through wild places and tamed places and never intrude on the landscape. They are places of solitude and reflection. Painted at the height of the Depression they are devoid of the displaced labourers who frequented them. Instead they, and the landscape observed from them, form a reverie of the golden west.

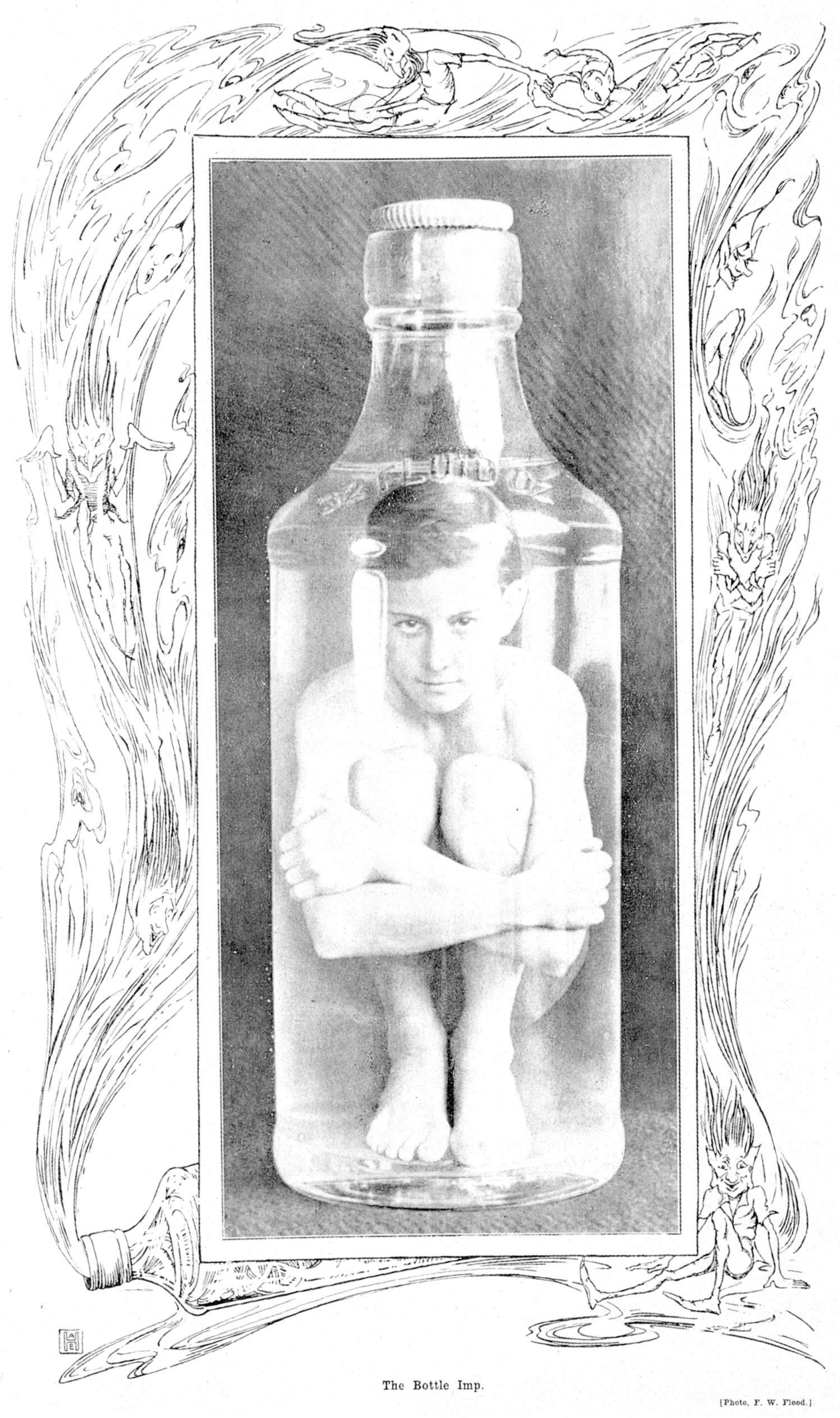

The Bottle Imp.

[Photo, F. W. Flood.]

Throughout his career Fred put the peoples and landscapes of Western Australia into a beautifully scented bottle. Crouched and looking out at us Fred's images are of elves in a fairyland. From his bottle came the genii of progress and prosperity, of love and laughter, of a world youthfully smiling at its future.

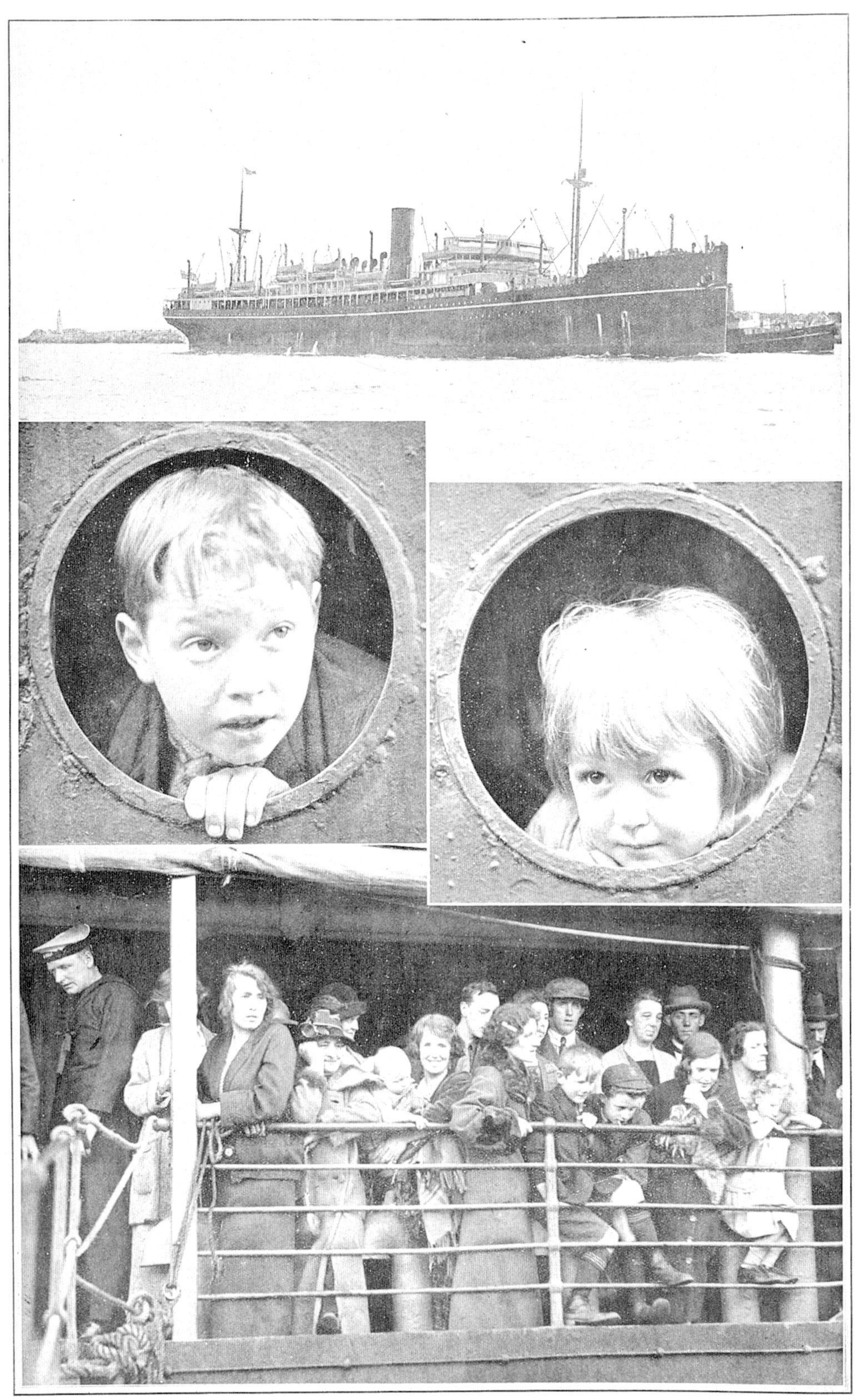

Out of England into Here.

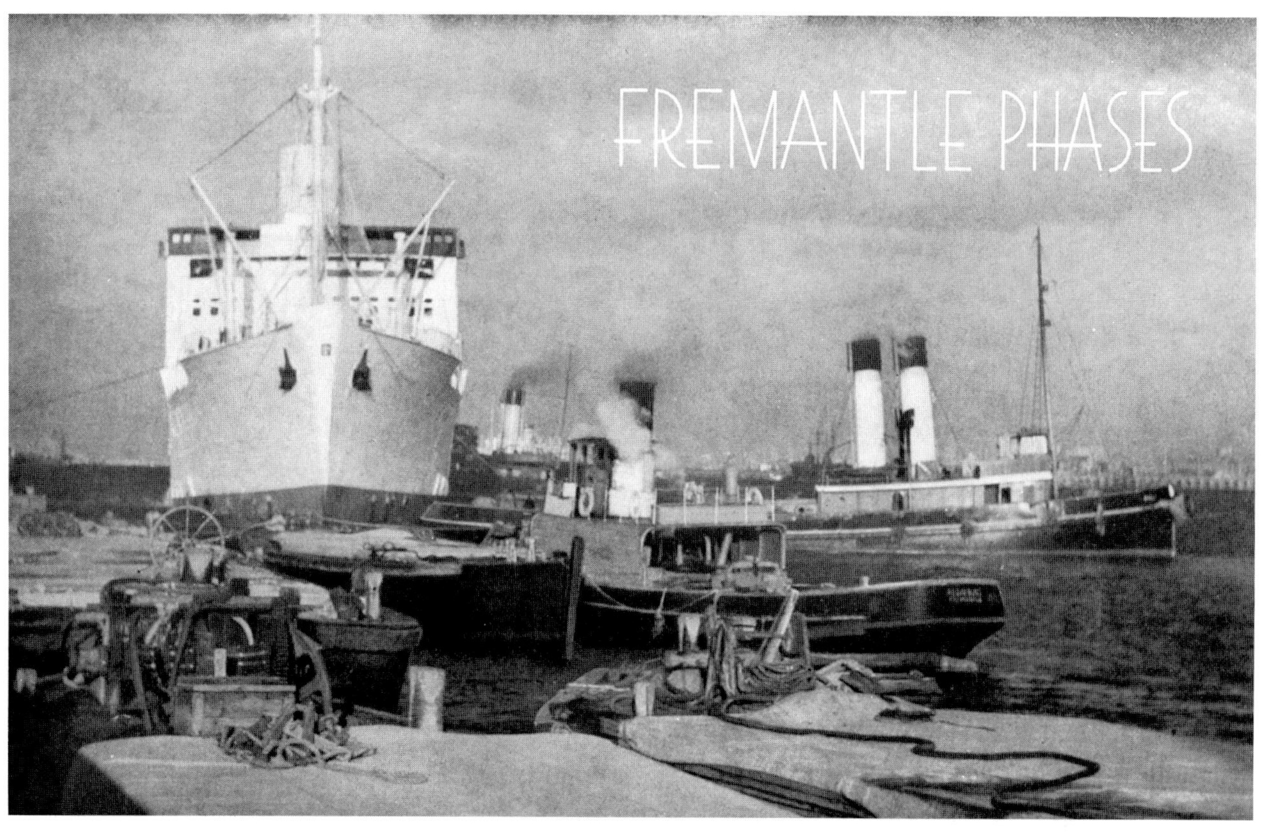

Fred was an immigrant and he loved photographing Fremantle Harbour, especially the arrival of liners carrying mail and migrants from England. Here children arrive under the Empire Immigration Scheme in the mid 1920s; here too the great liner *Strathnaver* berths in the late 1930s.

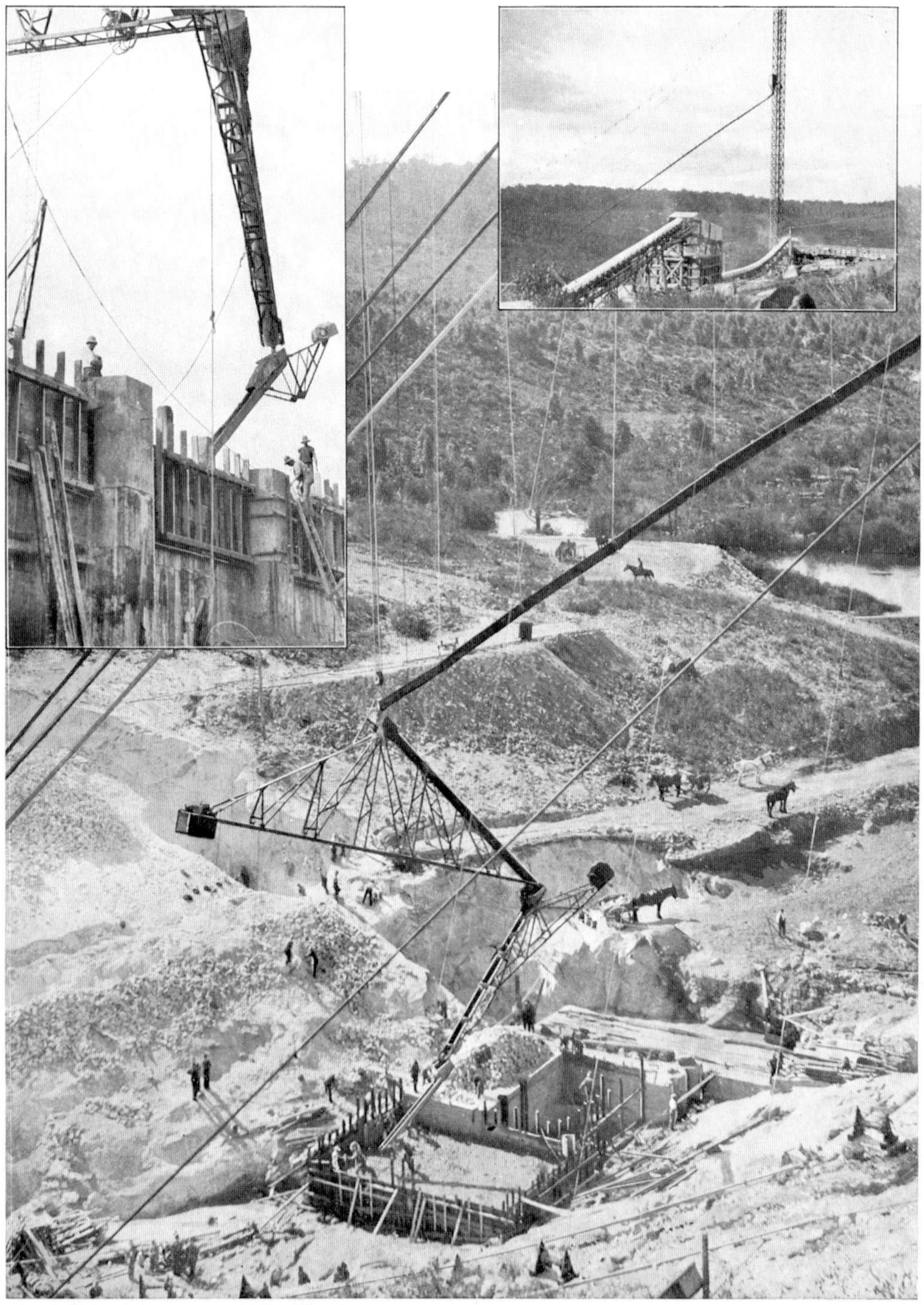

Construction of Canning Dam began in 1934. Fred photographed the work on several occasions. Rivers then were for 'harnessing', beasts to be brought under control, like horses and oxen. Here Fred catches the Dam not long after its commencement. His image is positive and welcoming, almost certainly in part because the early 1930s saw little economic advance in Western Australia. There were lives lost on the concrete chutes of the Canning, and men and women suffered low wages and the extremes of seasons in poor family cottages, and men's quarters. At the opening of Canning in September 1940 Premier J.C. Willcock proclaimed it as 'almost a 100 per cent West Australian achievement!' (Information J. Gregory.)

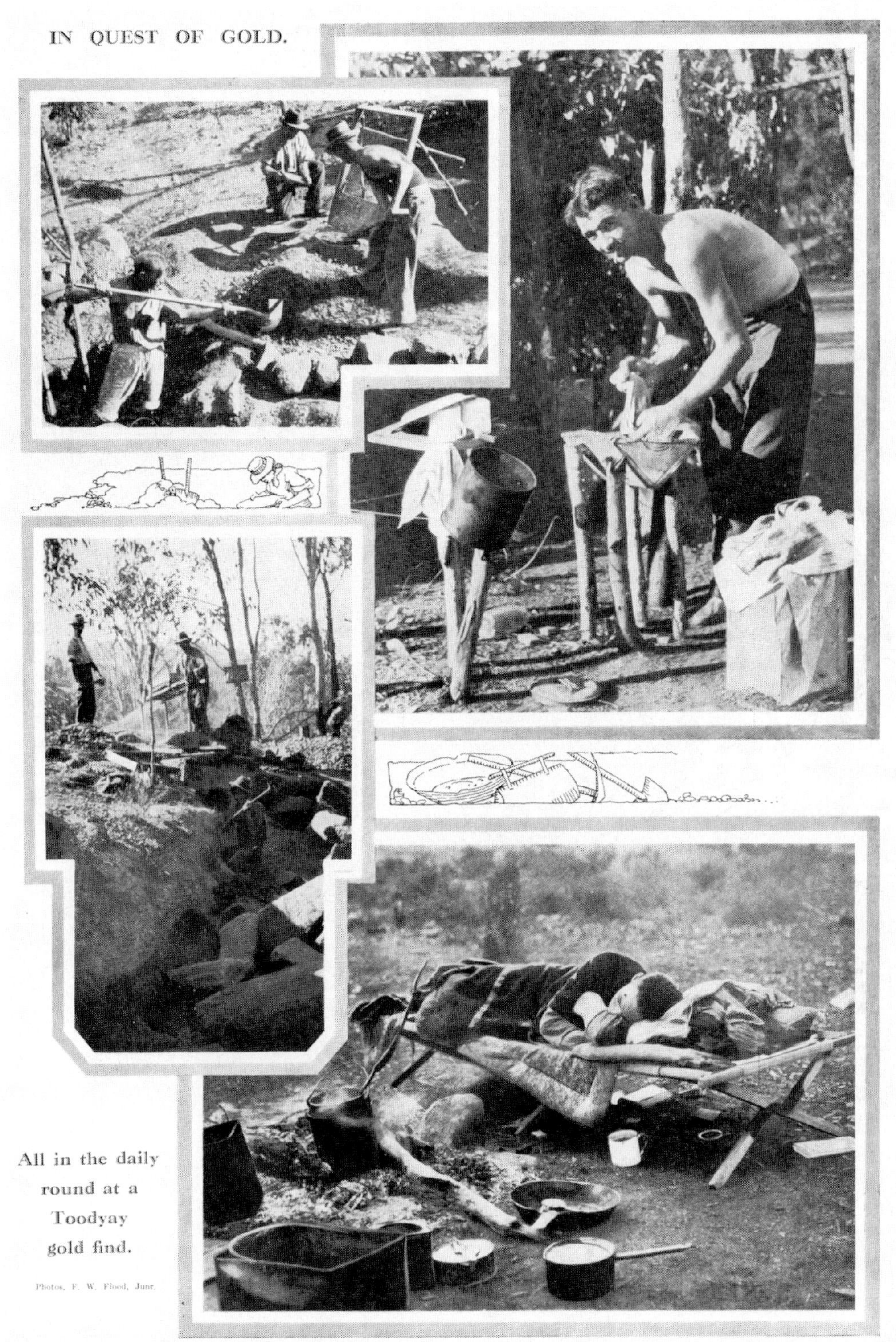

All in the daily
round at a
Toodyay
gold find.

Photos, F. W. Flood, Junr.

Gold led Western Australia out of the Depression — especially the gold of Wiluna and Kalgoorlie. But desperate men sought gold everywhere, even in the long settled and deeply conservative Avon Valley farming heartland. In their daily round the men made the best of their conditions; and Fred made light of it for them.

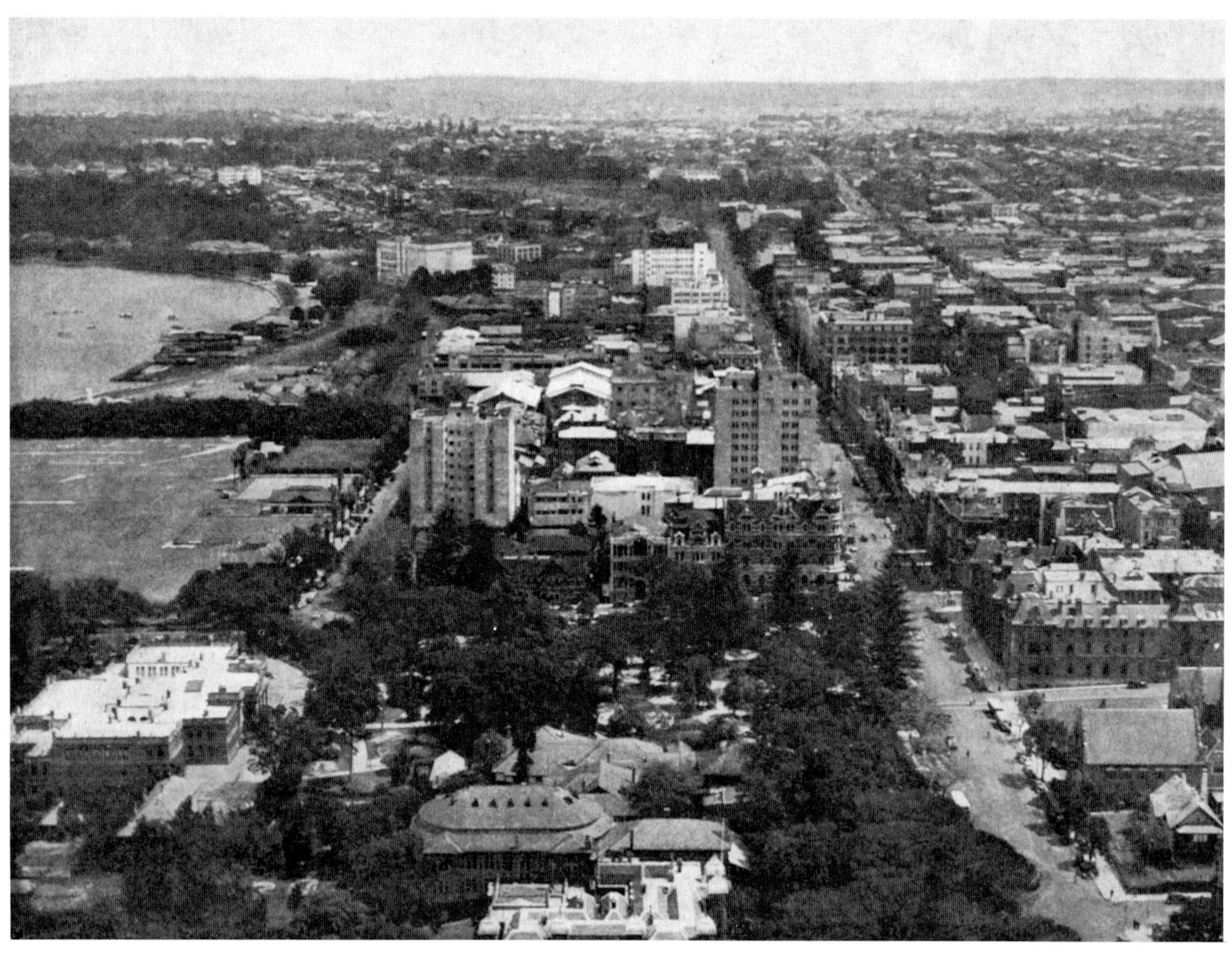

Like Amy, Fred imaged the city in which he worked. He photographed Perth in all its moods.
He took to the air with a camera strapped to the side of Norman Brearley's aeroplane. They took
off from Langley Park, buzzed the city with Fred producing this shot looking west up St George's
Terrace, before heading down the river to Fremantle.

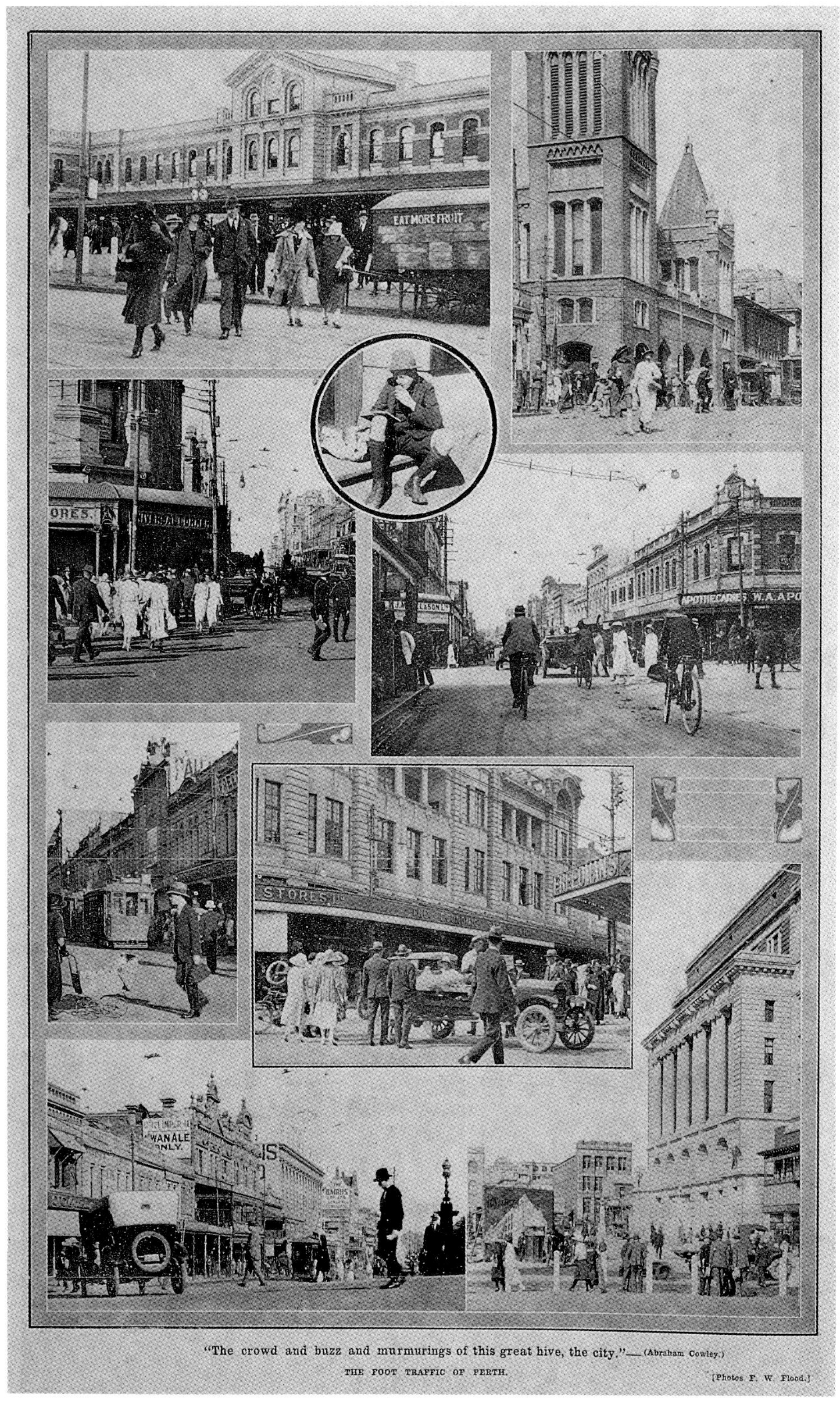

"The crowd and buzz and murmurings of this great hive, the city."— (Abraham Cowley.)

THE FOOT TRAFFIC OF PERTH.

[Photos F. W. Flood.]

Fred had a wonderful eye for the vibrancy of the 'great hive'. In this 1924 photograph of the foot traffic of Perth, Fred celebrates the arrival of people from the suburbs at Perth railway station and their dispersal through the streets: pedestrians, trams, cycles and cars jostle for space on the streets. The image represents normalcy after the trauma of the Great War and the post-war riots and strikes. This is a community which lived to eat more fruit.

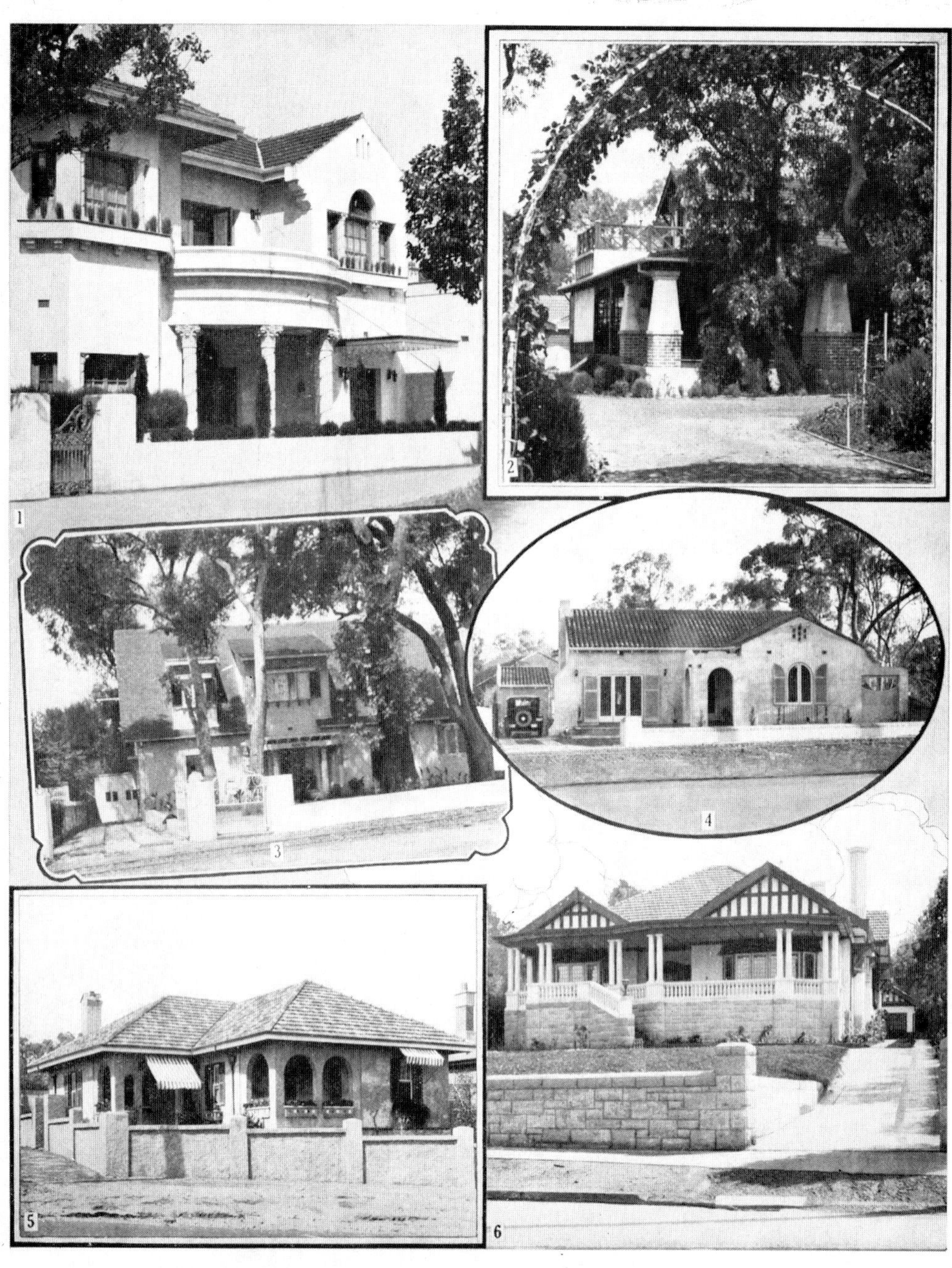

(1) Mrs. F. Piesse's flats in Bellevue-terrace, West Perth.
(2) Mr. W. Drabble's home on the Perth-Fremantle-road, Nedlands.
(3) Mrs. C. D. Everett's house on the Perth-Fremantle-road, Nedlands.
(4) Mr. Theo Taylor's house on the Perth-Fremantle-road, Nedlands.
(5) Mr. R. Summerhayes's house on the Perth-Fremantle-road, Cottesloe.
(6) Mr. T. C. Villiers's home, Mount's Bay-road, Crawley.

Photos, F. W. Flood.

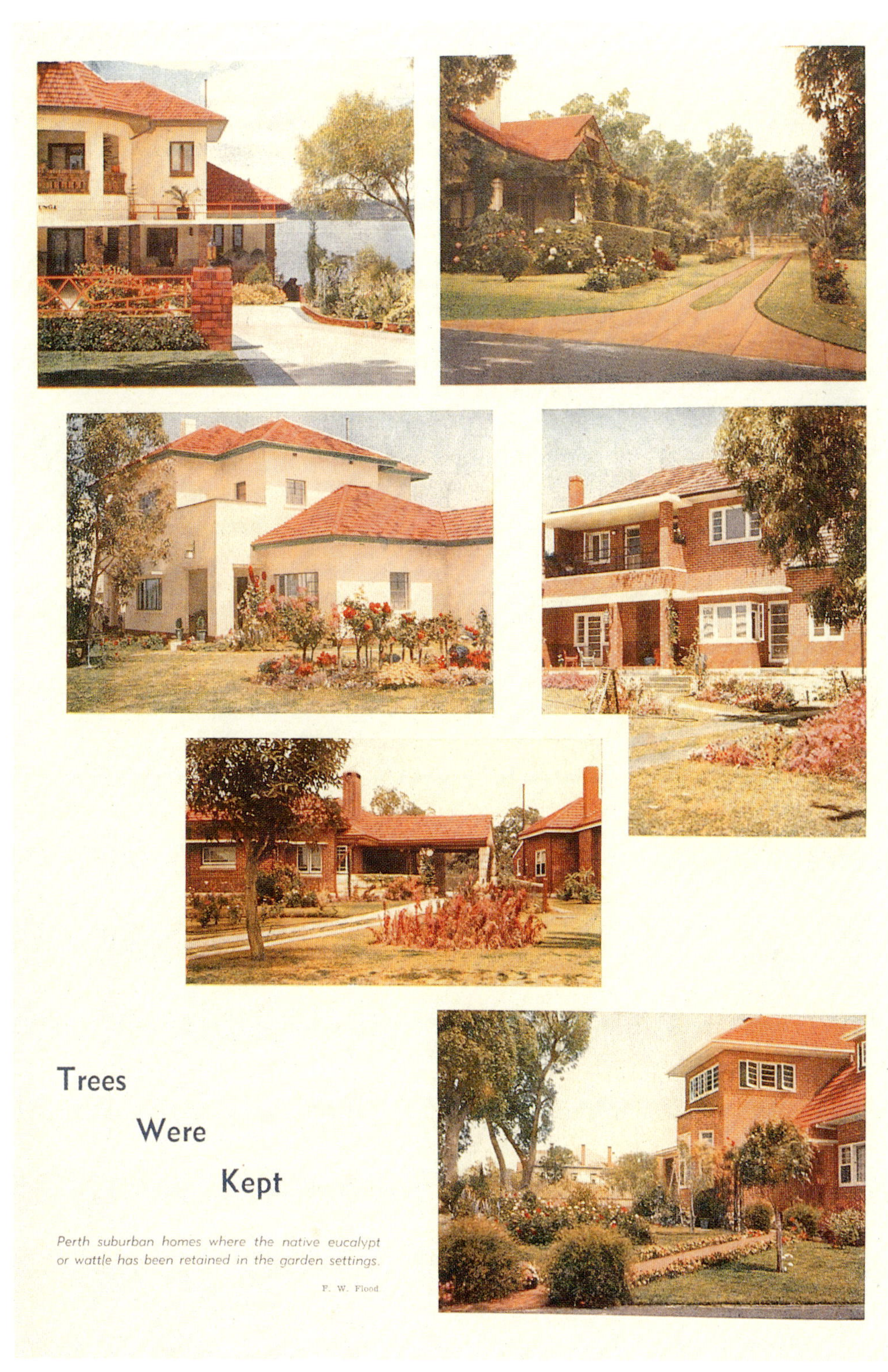

Perth suburban homes where the native eucalypt
or wattle has been retained in the garden settings.

F. W. Flood

Fred left an outstanding record of housing development in the more affluent suburbs of Perth.
The interwar years saw the rapid development of Nedlands (once the Workers' Home Scheme
had been wound up for the district), and the continued growth of Cottesloe as a commuter and
seaside resort suburb. West Perth, as ever, remained a desirable address,
in colour or black and white.

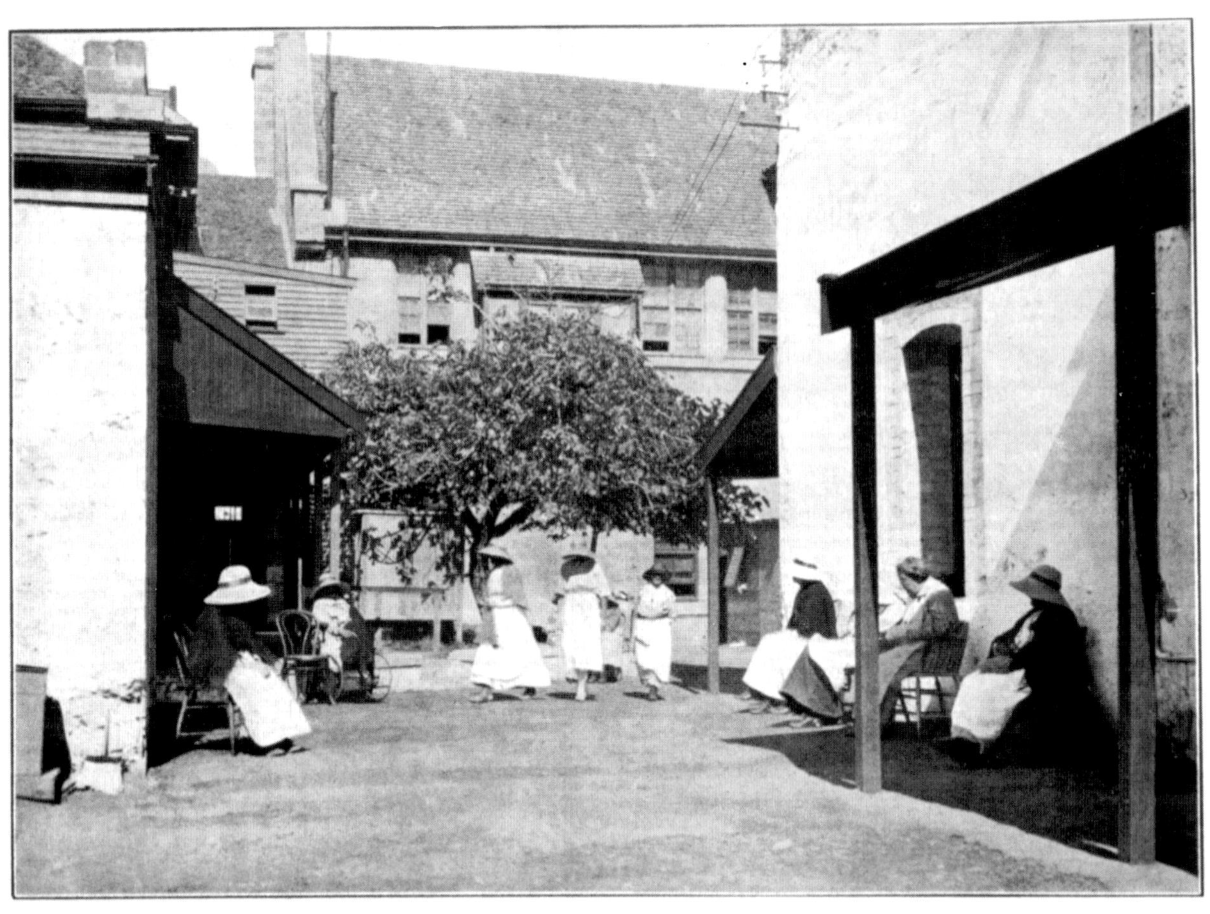

"We bring our years to an end as a tale that is told."
A GLIMPSE OF THE OLD WOMEN'S HOME, FREMANTLE.

[Photo F. W. Flood.]

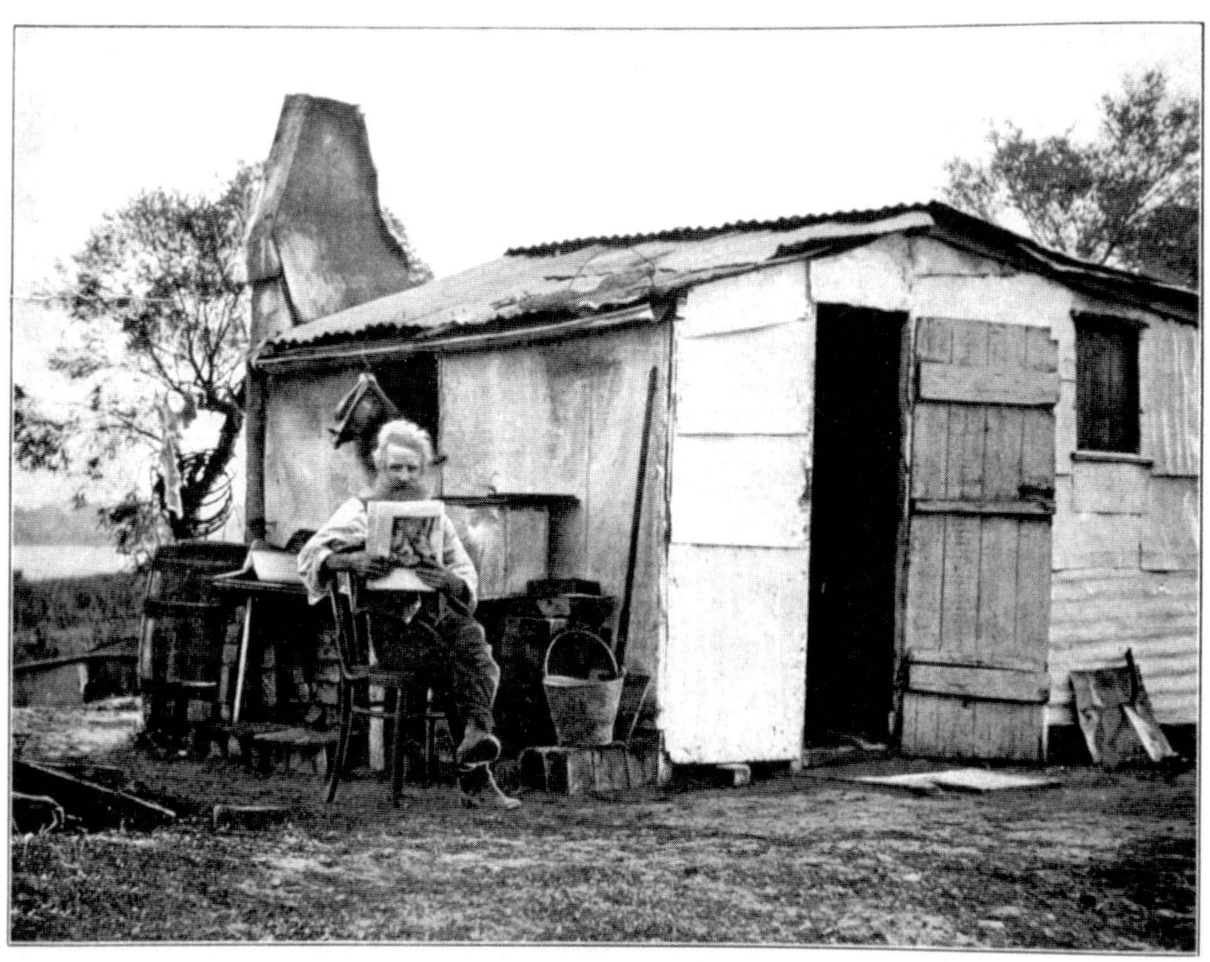

Home. Sweet Home.

Fred gave dignity to nearly everyone he photographed. He liked people and he sought out their better qualities in his images. It was a nice trait in Perth's most significant interwar photographer-interpreter. Old age could be represented cruelly; but not by Fred in these sympathetic images of the 'Old Women's Home, Fremantle' (with lines from Psalm 90), and 'Home Sweet Home' for an old man down by Perth's Causeway: 'yet is their strength then but labour and sorrow; so soon passeth it away, and we are gone'.

Sailing

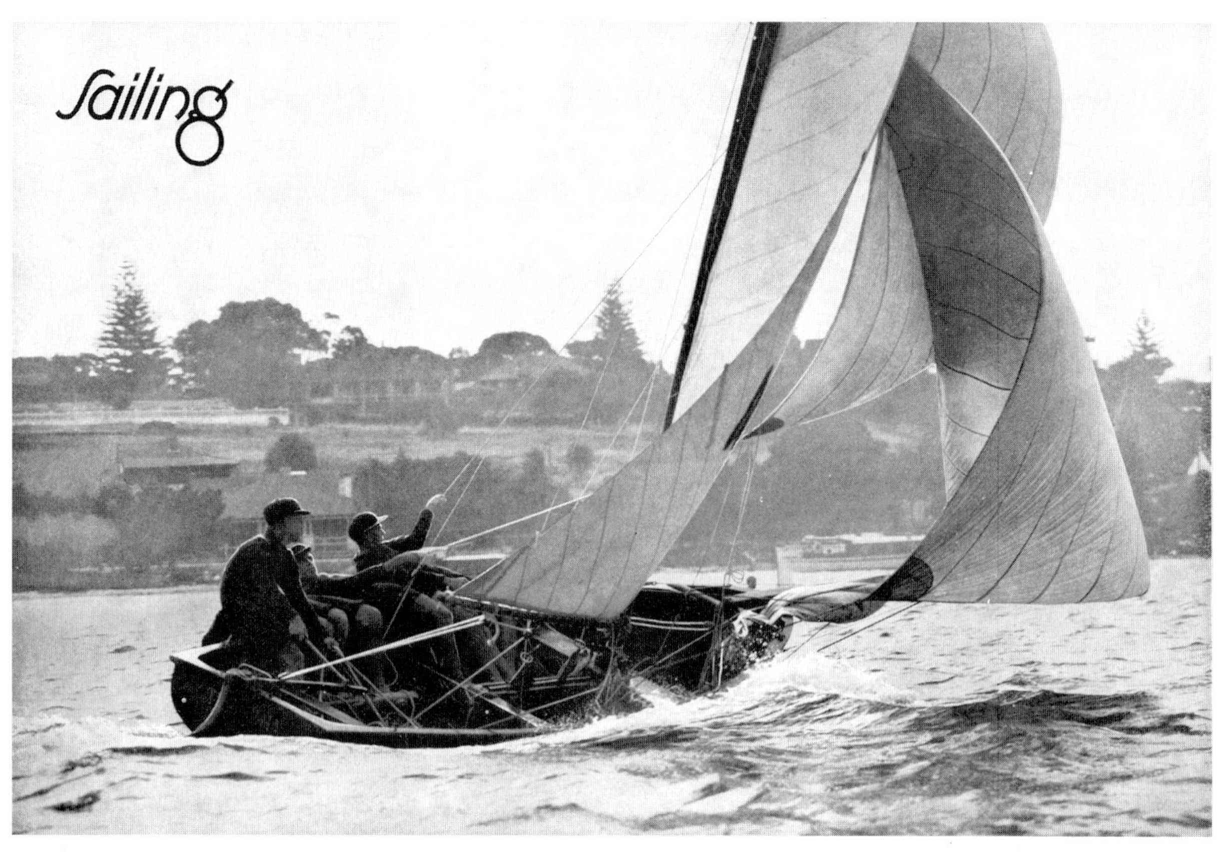

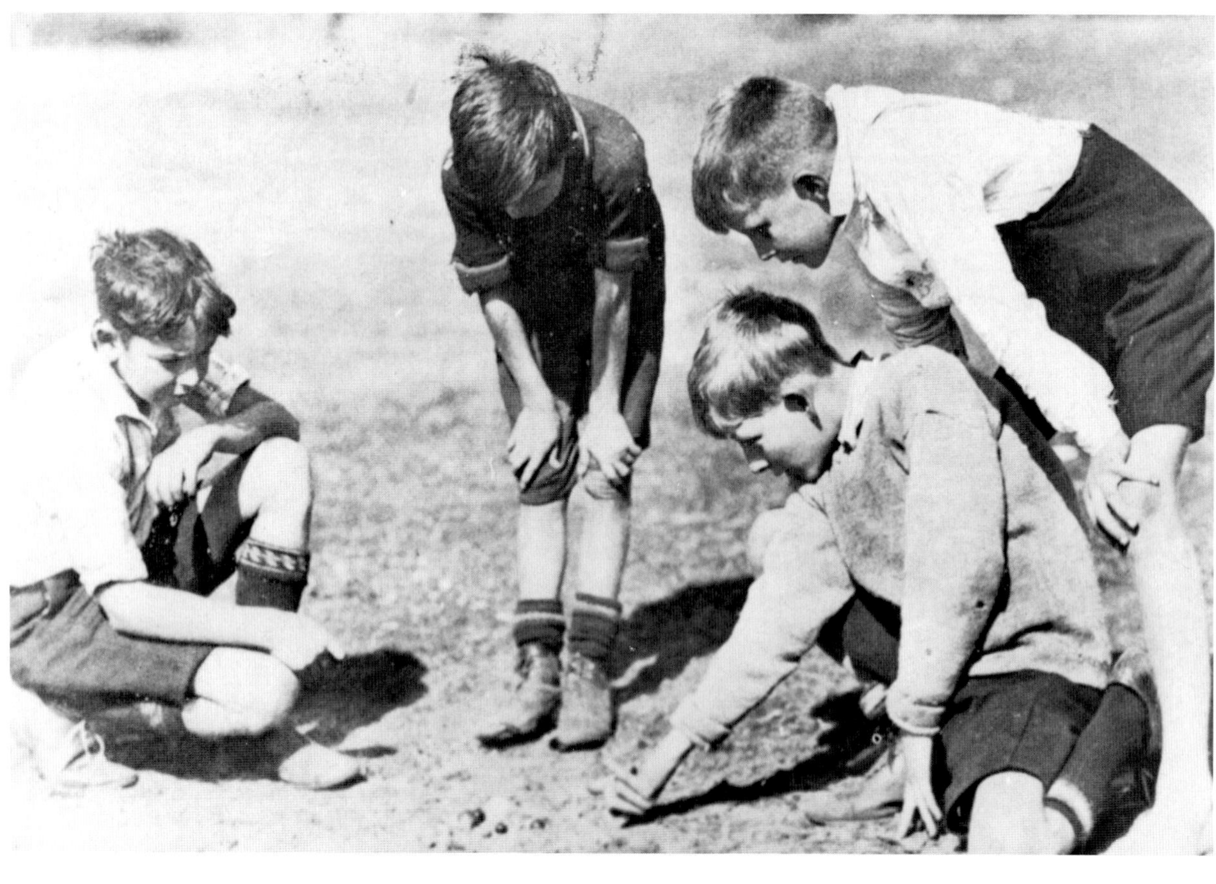

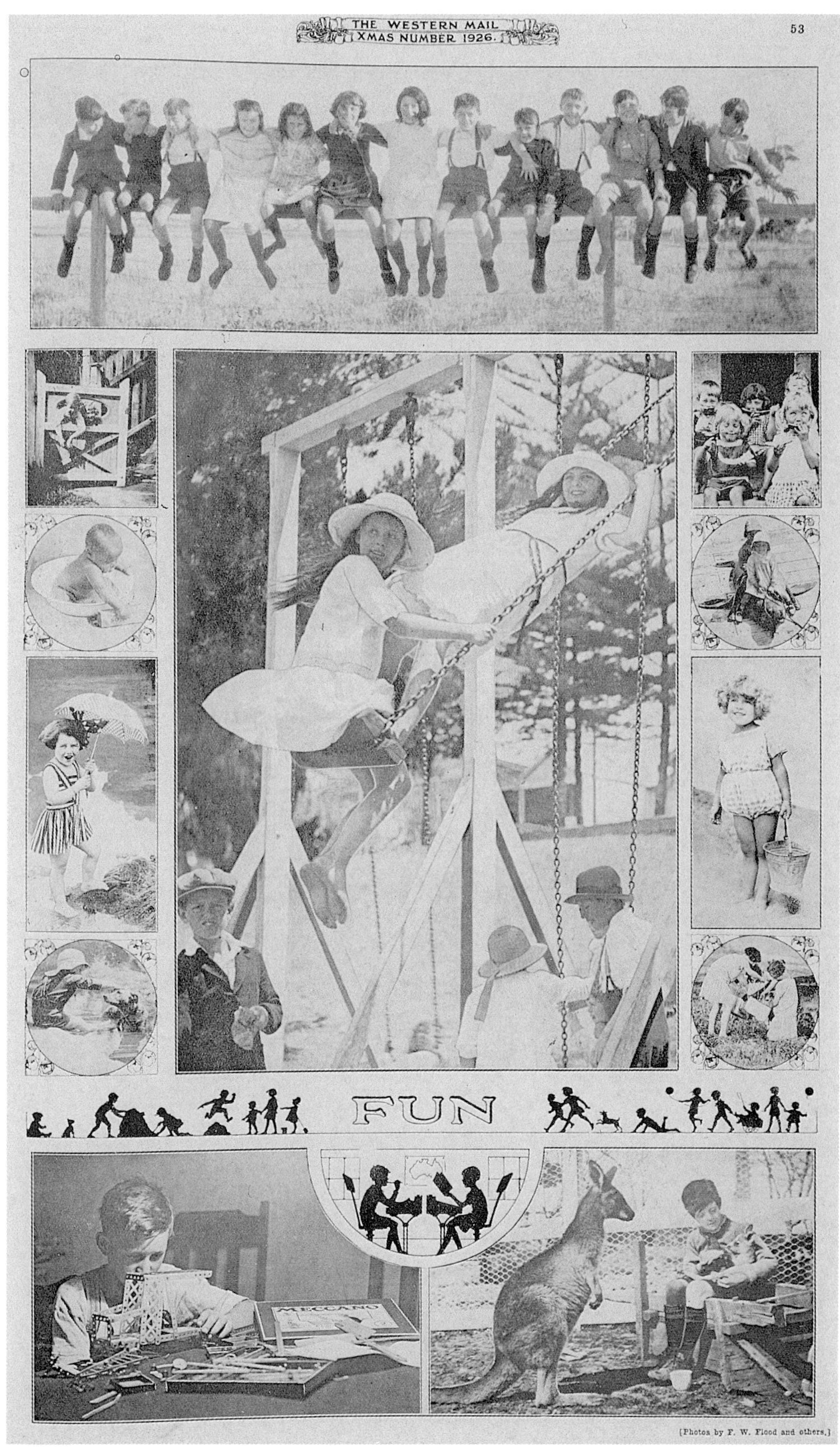

[Photos by F. W. Flood and others.]

But for the young of Perth, life would be wonderful, whether sailing on the Swan, playing marbles, or just having fun. Fred was eternally young, and his imagery ensures that forever life in Perth shall be seen as Fun.

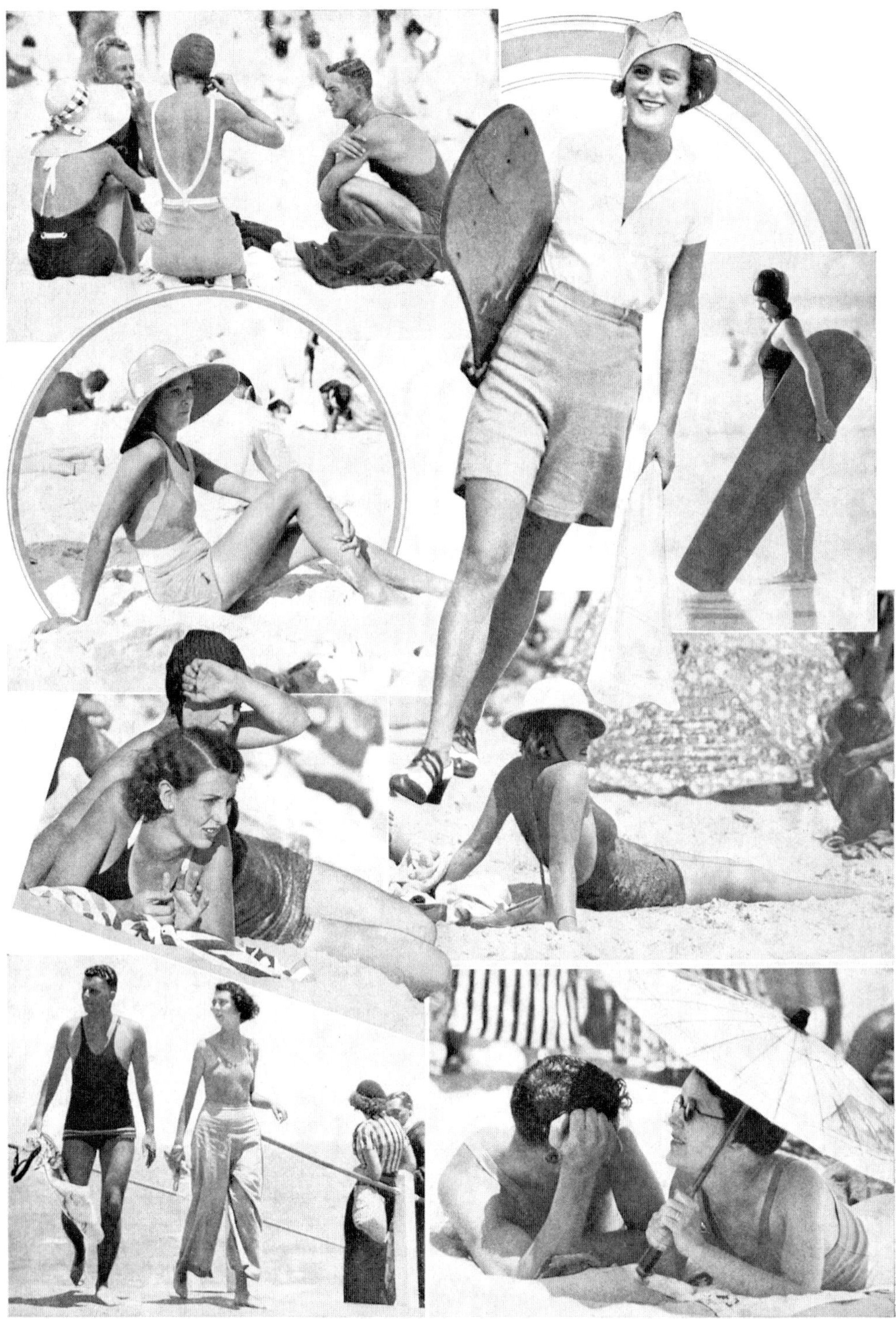

Photographs, F. W. Flood.

Some visitors to metropolitan beaches last summer.

Fred's camera was as devoted to the beach as it was to family, city and land. The beaches of interwar Perth were filled with gods and goddesses. Incredibly, the year is 1934, the secession movement and the height of the Depression are only six months behind us. The image is a reminder that for most people in Perth the Depression did not exist, or, if perceived dimly, was a time of low prices and easy pickings. The beaches were free for all;
but they were not enjoyed equally.

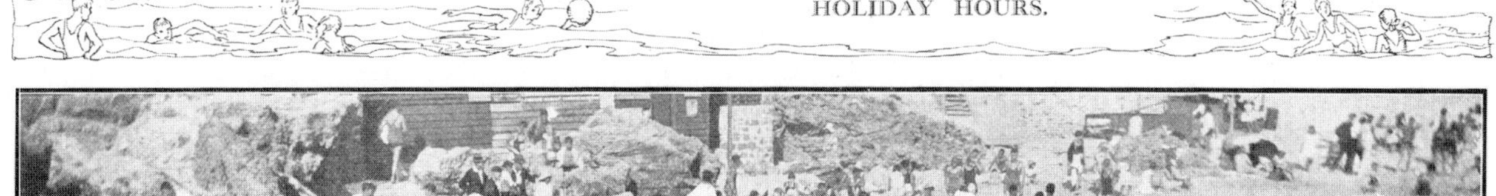

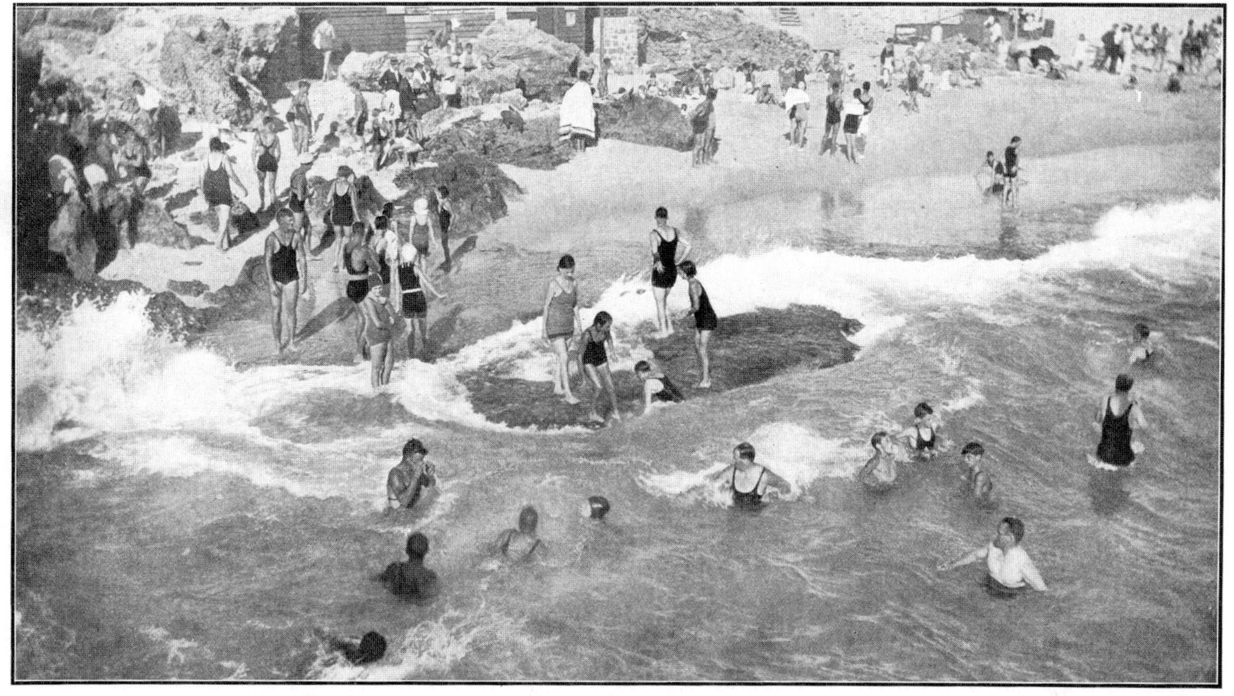

Bathers at North Beach.

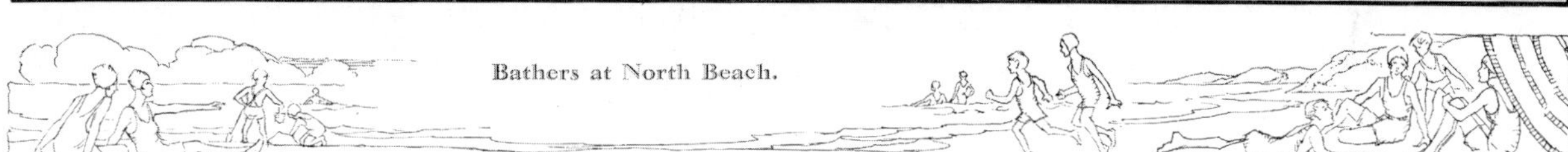

Amy embellishes an interwar holiday scene at popular North Beach.

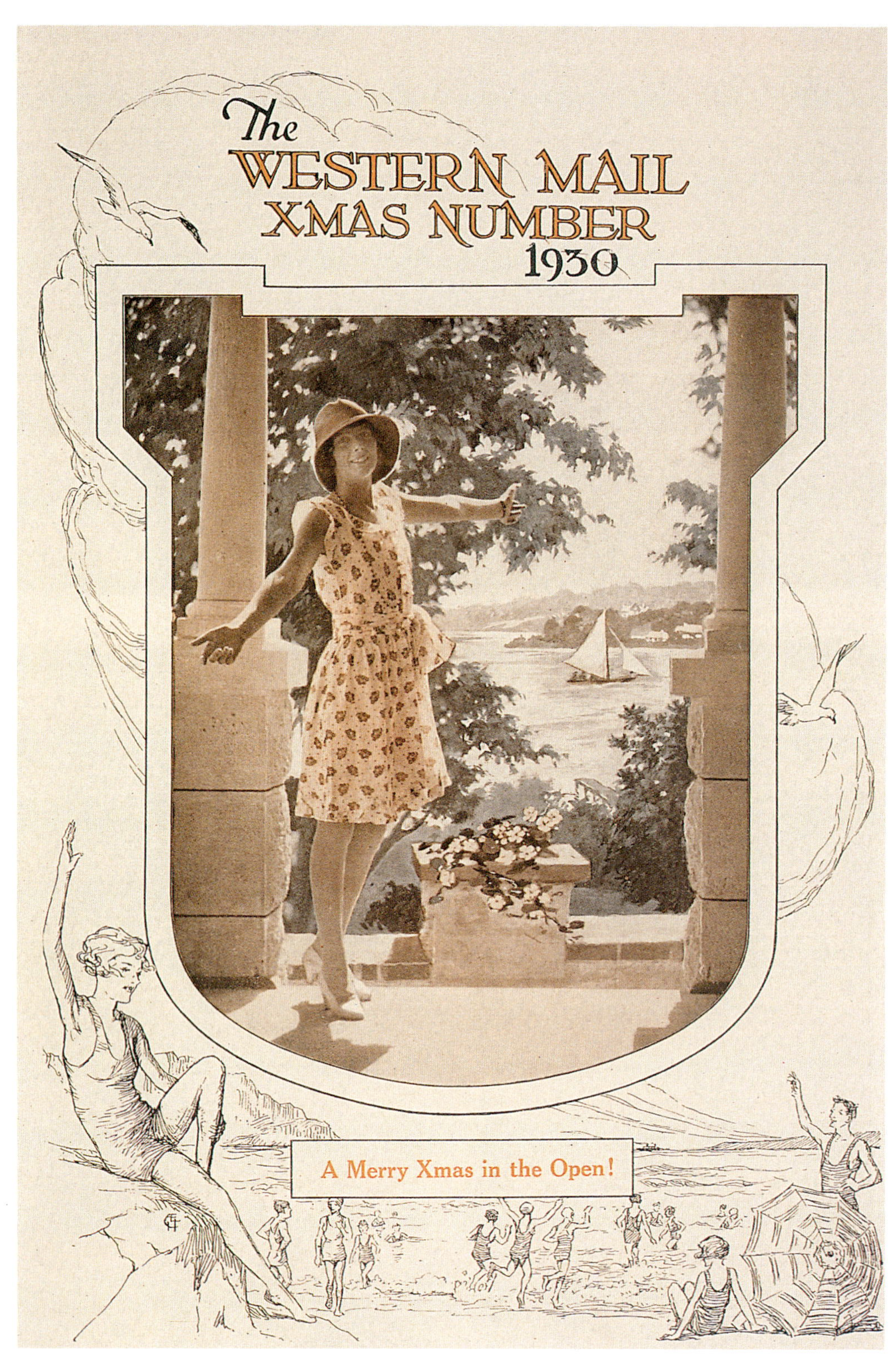

The
WESTERN MAIL
XMAS NUMBER
1930
A Merry Xmas in the Open!

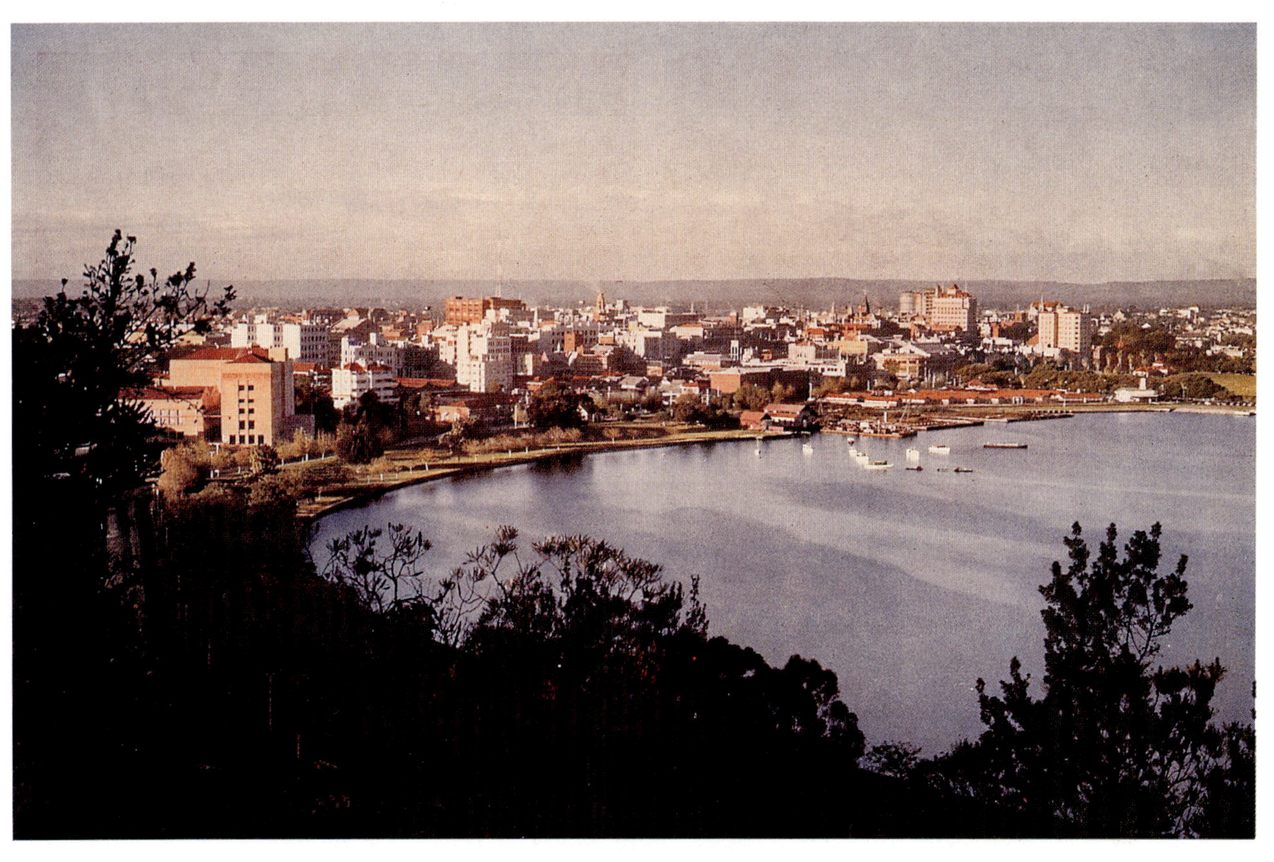

'Earth has not anything to show more fair.'

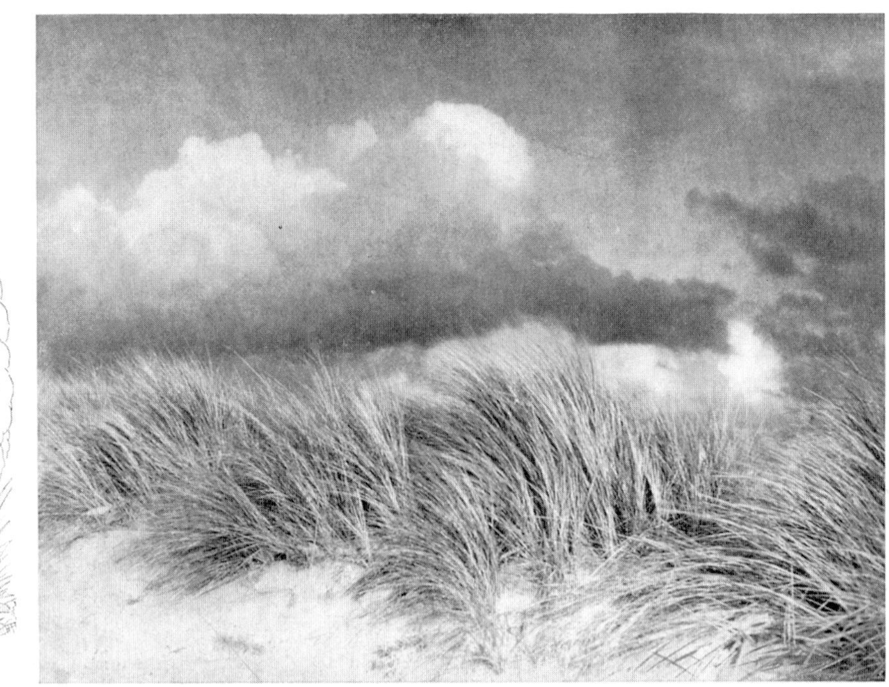

Grass upon the dunes at Swanbourne.

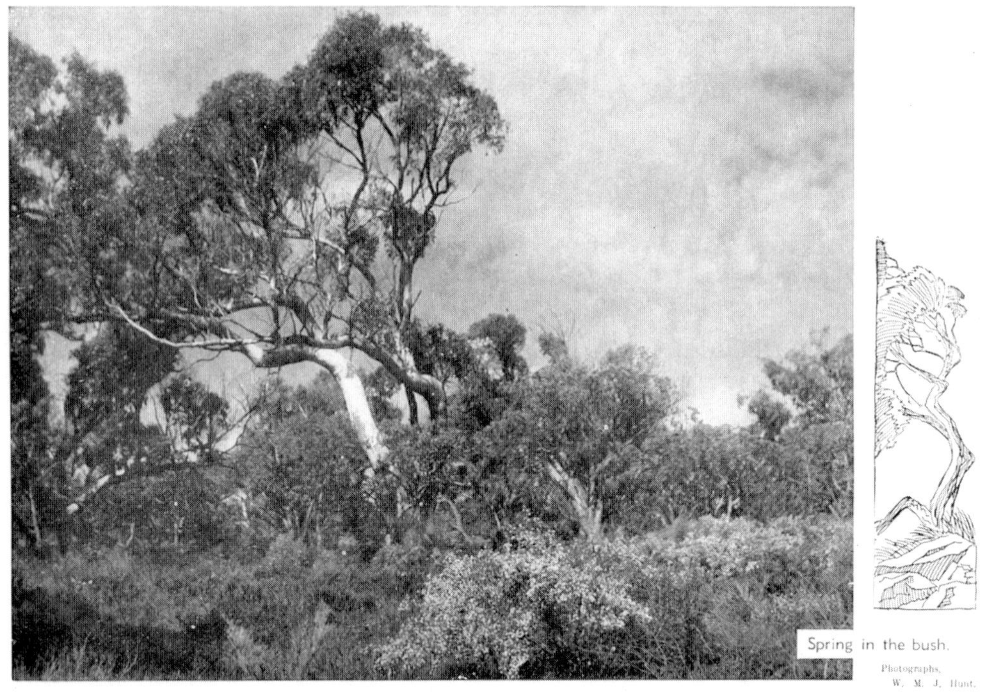

Spring in the bush.

Photographs,
W. M. J. Hunt.

The inspiration may be William Ernest Henley's lines, 'Between English earth and sky', but the scenes are antipodean and affectionate.

THE IMAGES

HEAP AND FLOOD

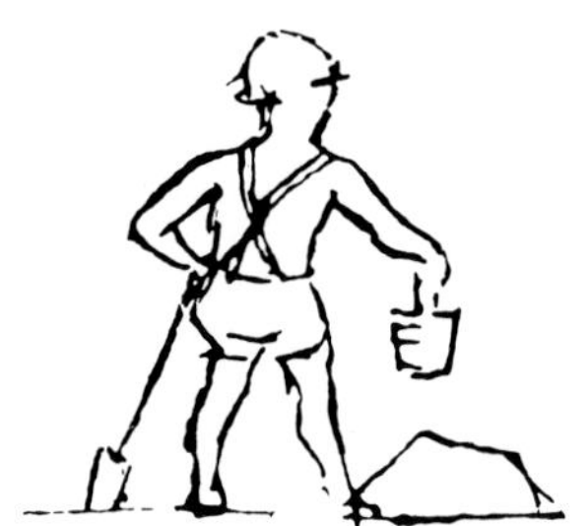

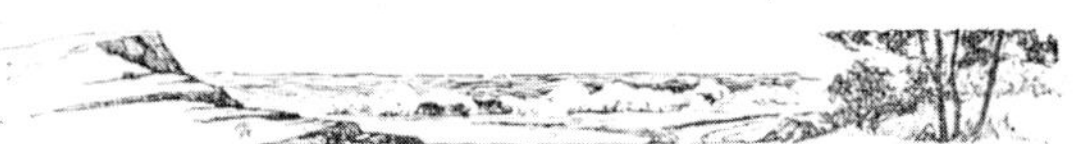

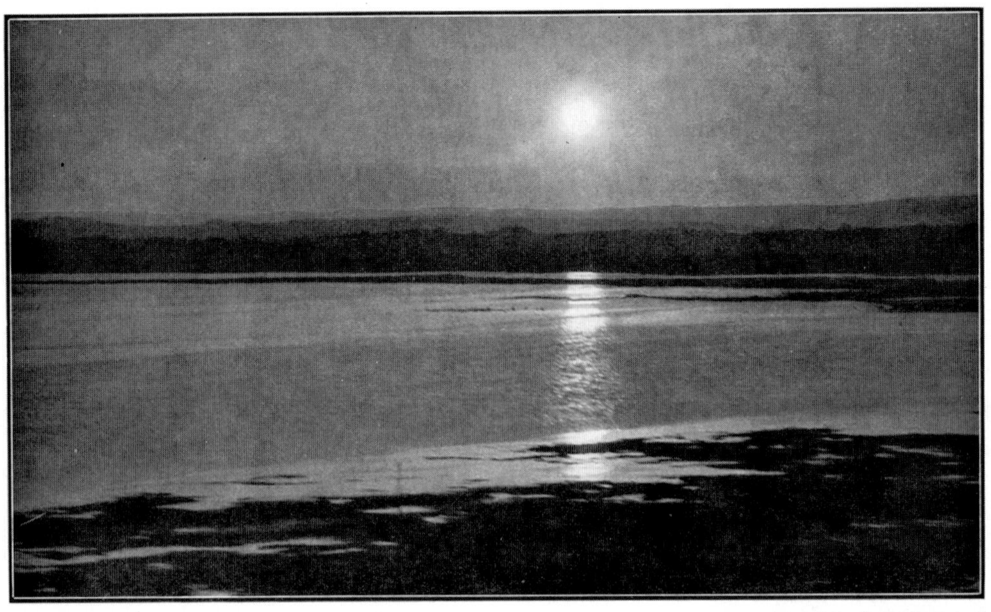

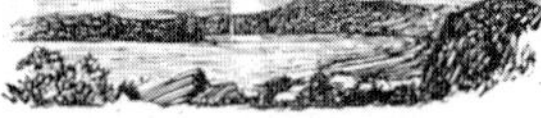

"Close by the Moon" at Albany.

Photo, F. W. Flood.

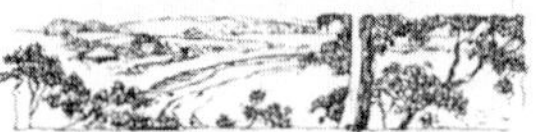

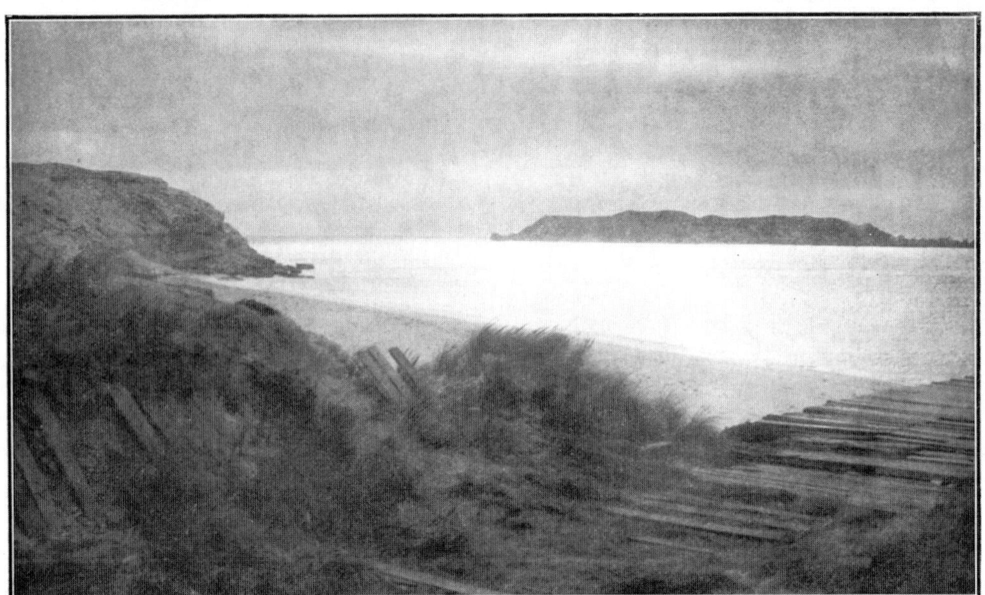

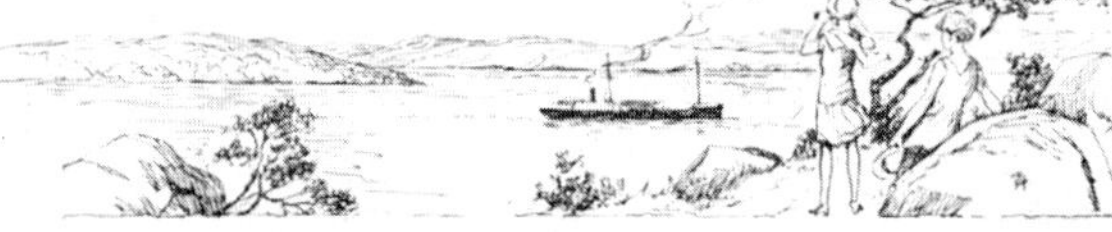

Hamelin Bay, showing Rabbit Island
and the Approach to the Old Jetty.

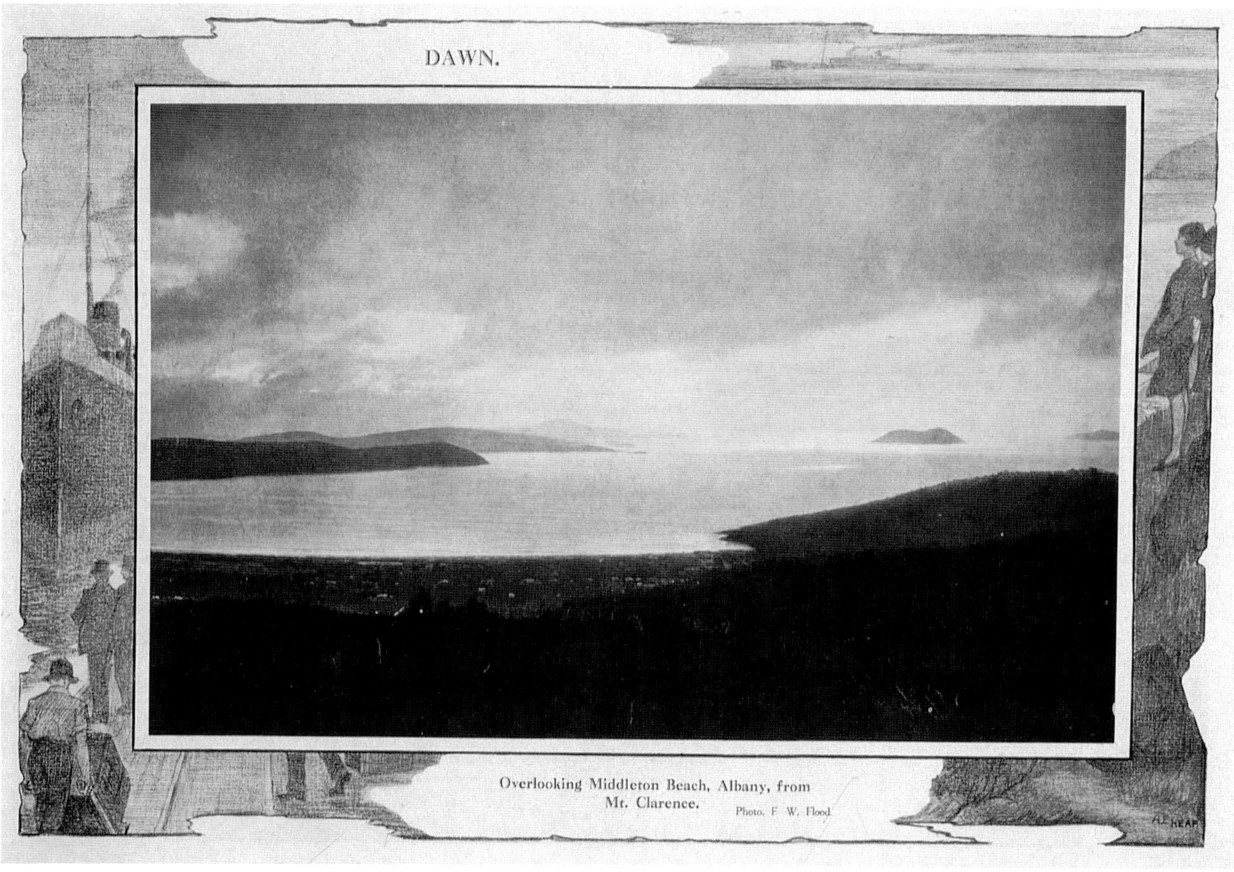

Overlooking Middleton Beach, Albany, from
Mr. Clarence.

Photo. F. W. Flood.

Sunrise and moonrise over Albany, that most English of towns, a temperate and drizzly place, complete with Sir Richard Spencer's 'Strawberry Farm' to transport the willing back into King William's time: Fred's and Amy's images from 1929-1930. Amy's women watch the men at work in the ships. Amy retired to live at Albany in the mid 1930s.

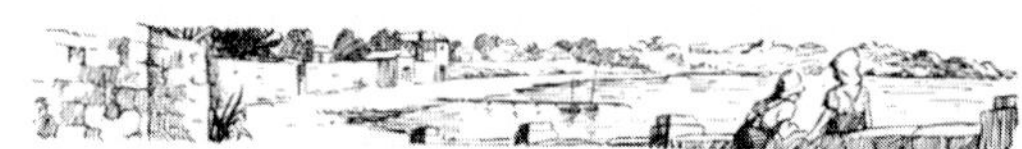

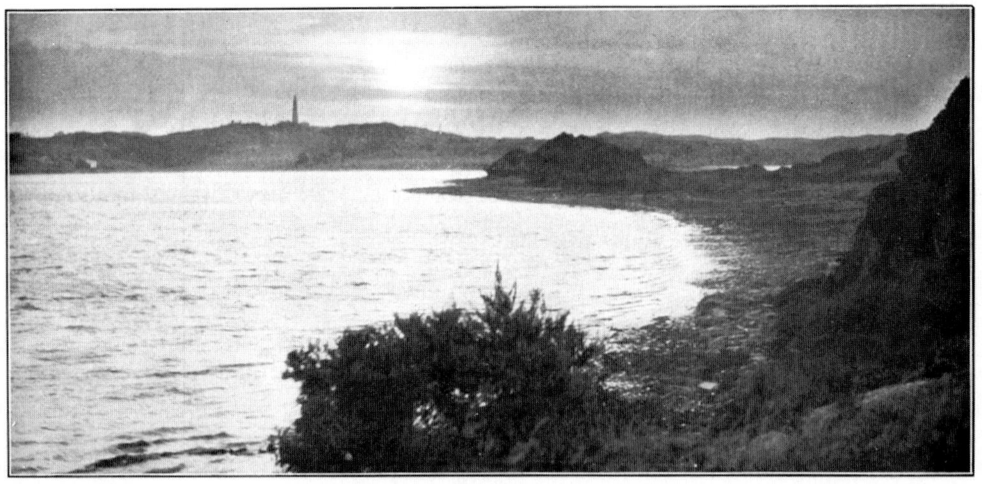

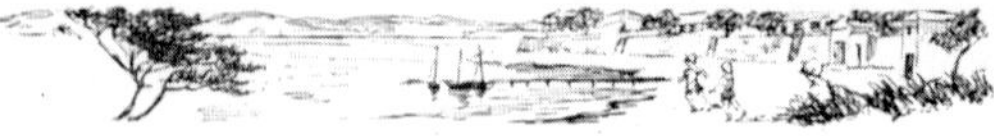

The Salt Lakes, Rottnest Island.

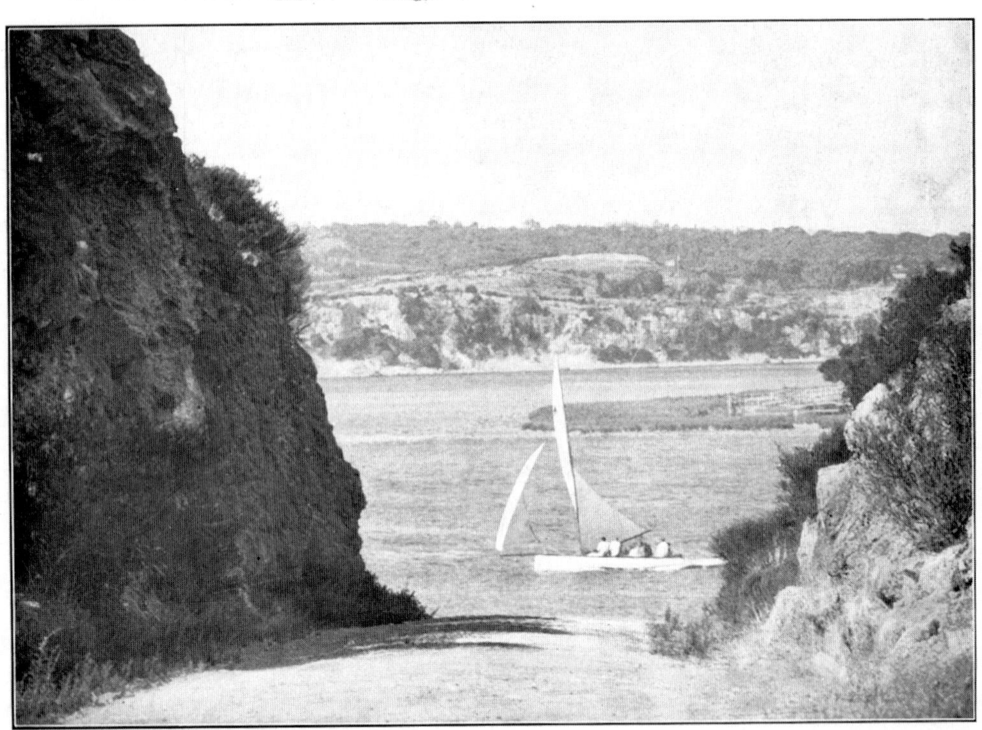

Rocky Bay, on the Swan River.

Photos, F. W. Flood.

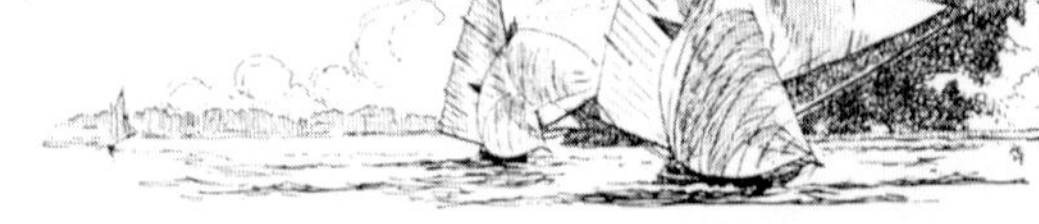

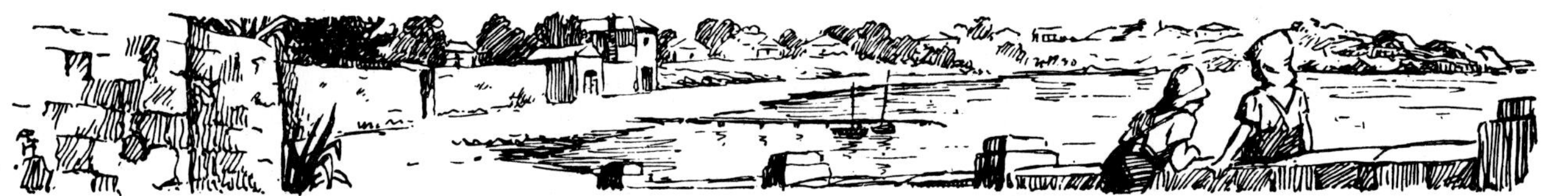

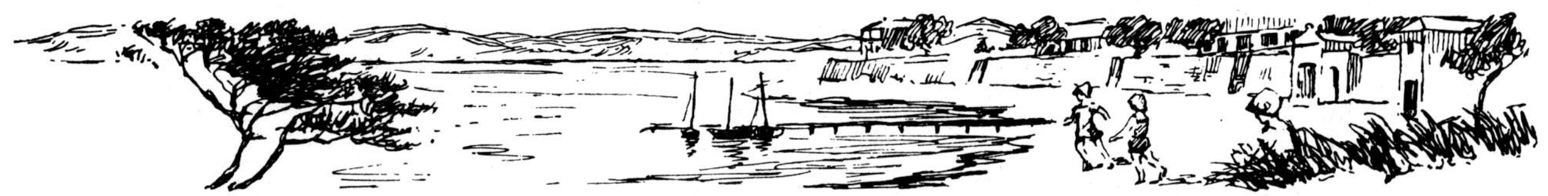

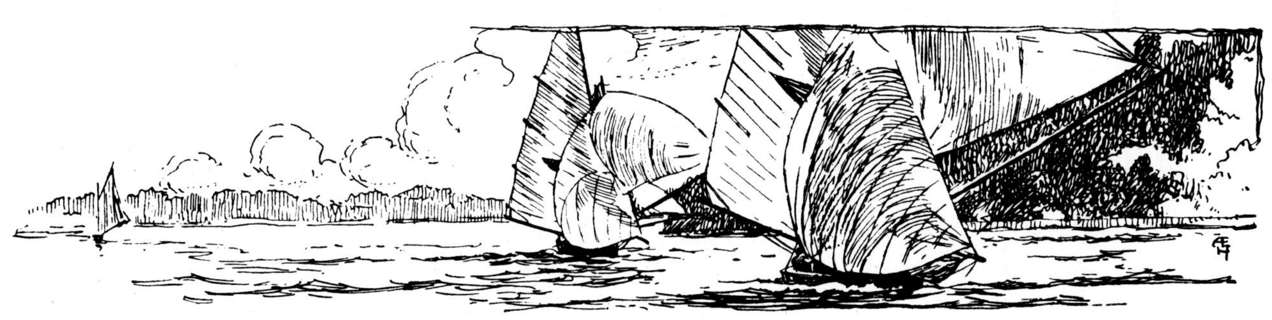

Fred and Amy understood that the Swan River and Rottnest Island were pleasuregrounds for West Australians. Amy's border drawings enliven Fred's panoramas with children playing and boats flying.

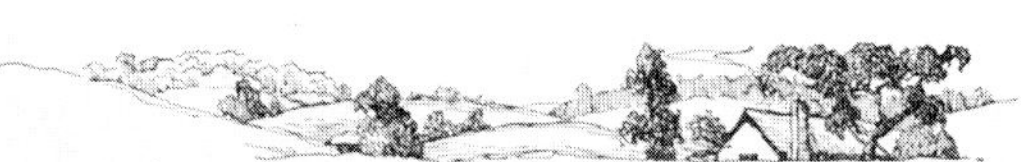

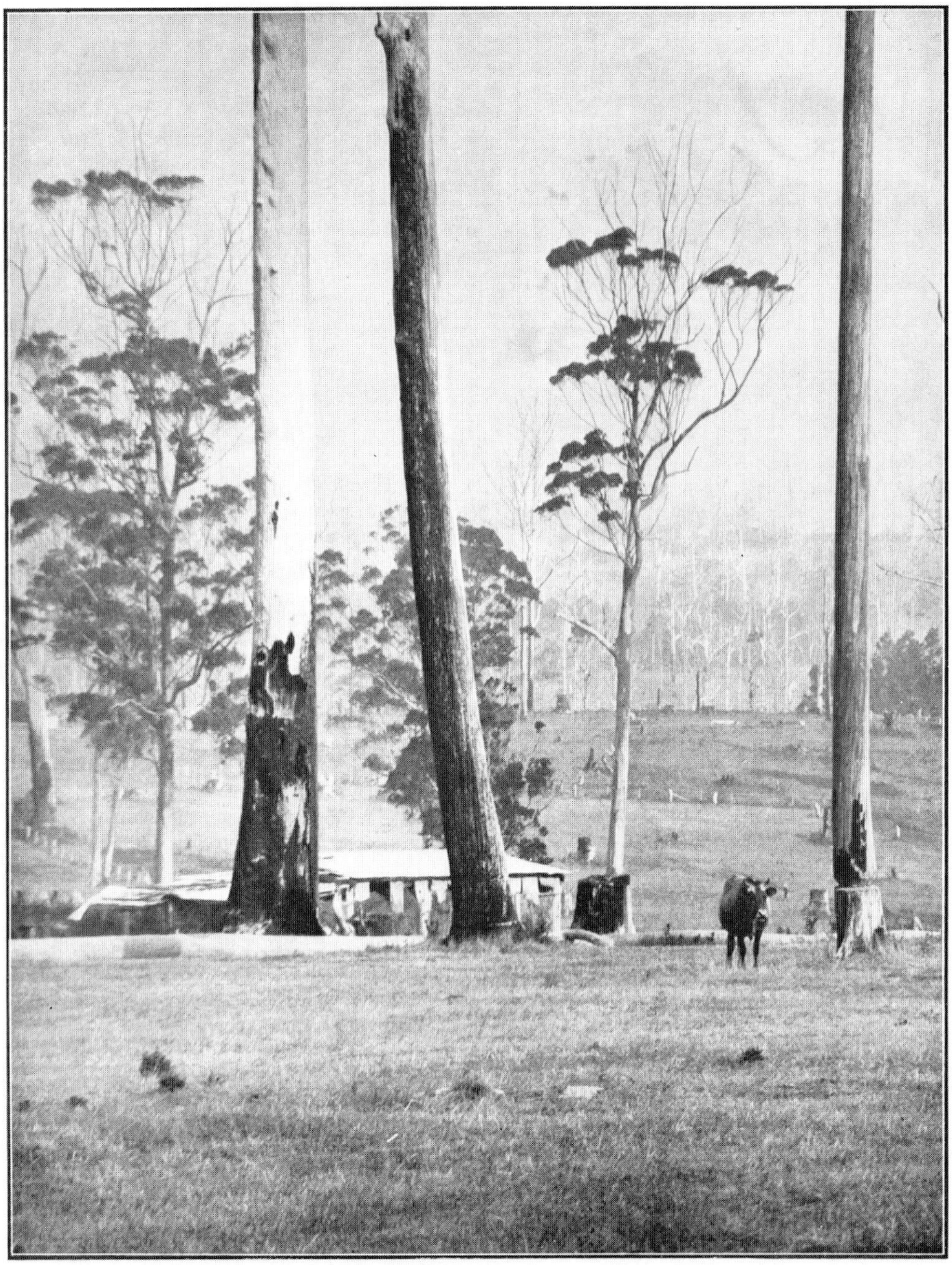

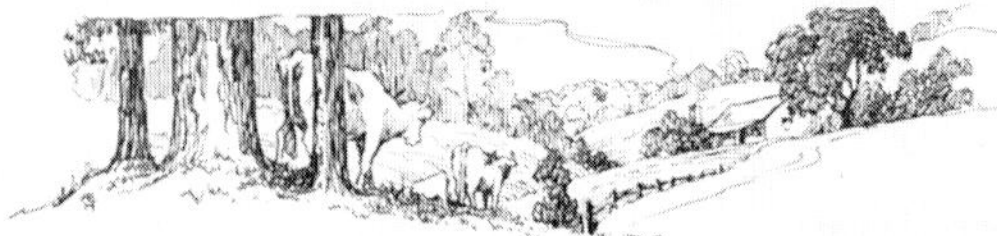

A Well Grassed Holding at Denmark.

Photo, F. W. Flood.

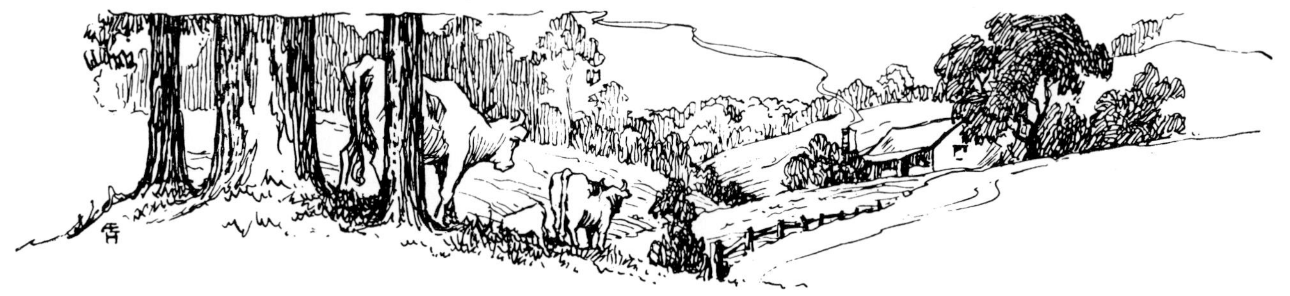

Even as wool and wheat prices plummeted internationally in 1930, Western Australia's Premier James (Moo-cow) Mitchell urged families on to rural holdings. In Fred's photograph the cow stands disconsolately among the ring-barked trees. Amy, who knew something of the tough life of group settlers near Busselton, knows also that Fred's image won't do. With brilliant control of space she softens the experience: her cows head for a homely cottage through the strong and leafy trees, guided in by an ancient fence. The caption 'Farms Out of Forests' is true to the Emigrants Guide; but in this case it is Amy who reconciles nature and history and economic development.

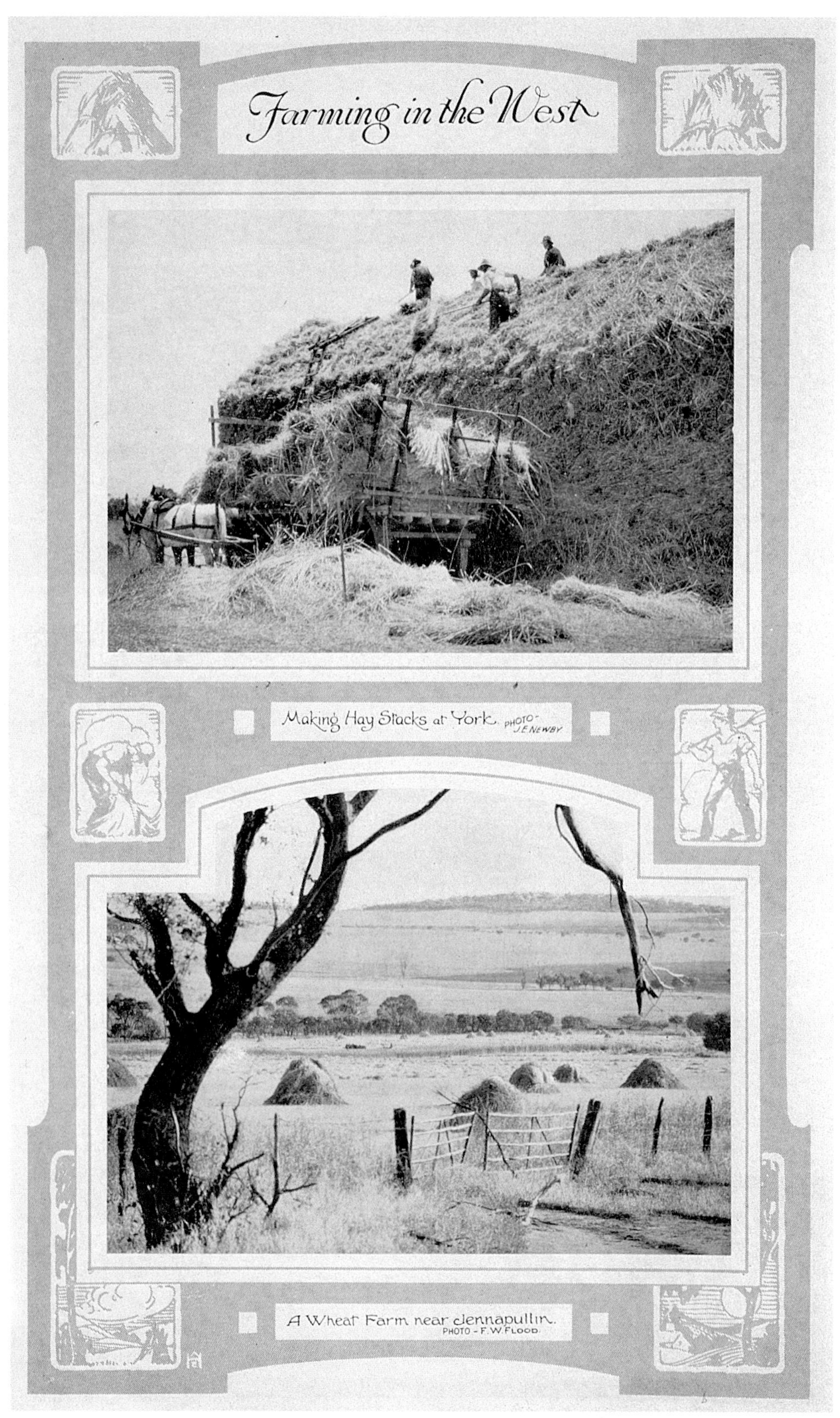

Boom conditions or depression conditions? Fred's and Amy's images were bound by the seasons, not the economic seismograph. They tended to be timeless and universal. Jennapullin is a place-name; the year is 1928; but in a golden summer Australia is a place of peace and plenty peopled here with Amy's contented workmen.

 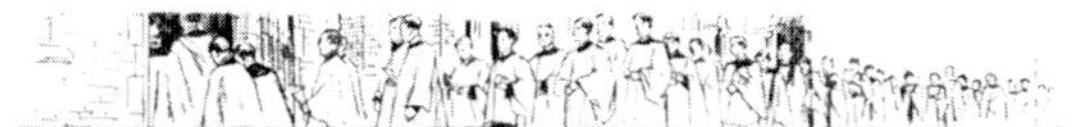

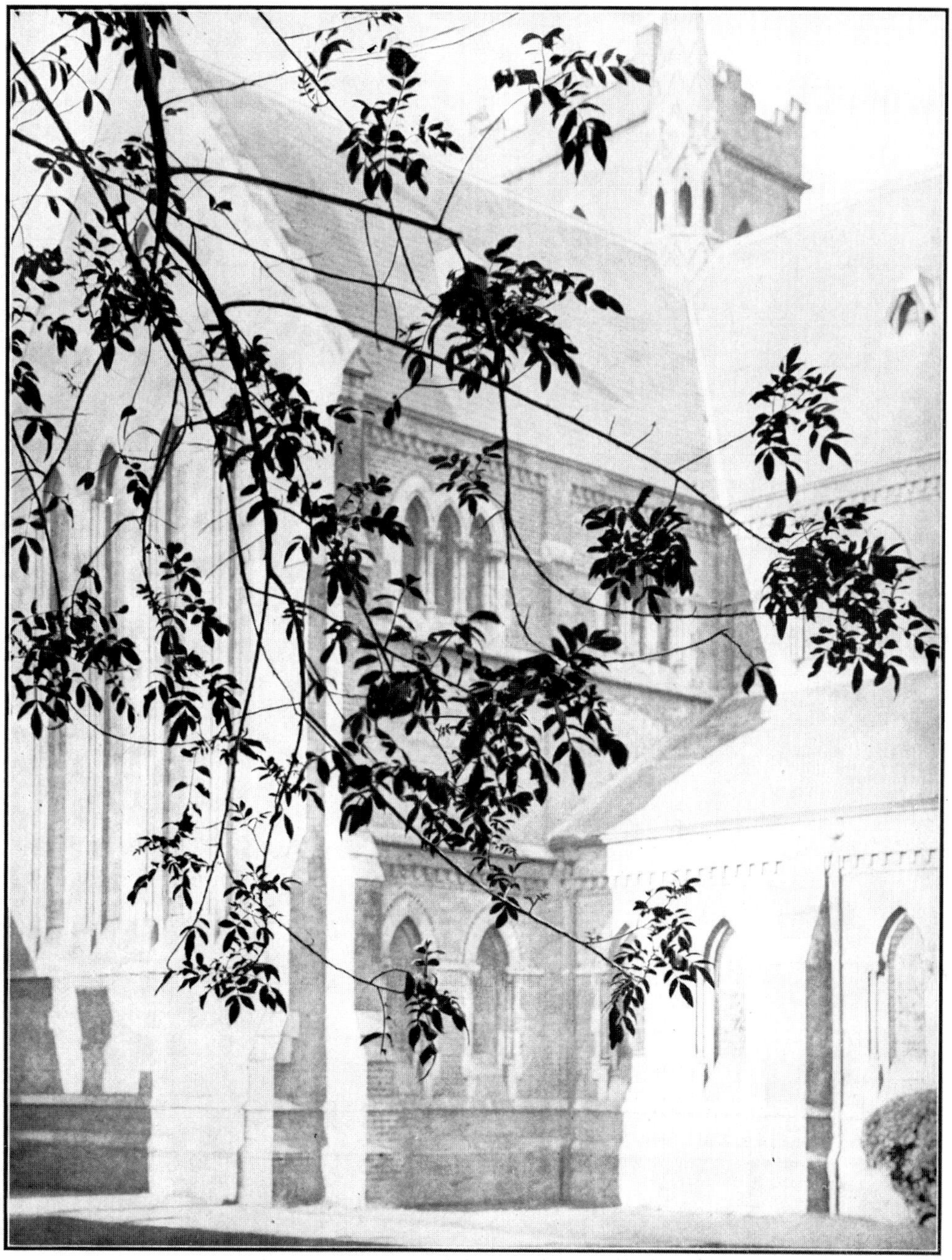

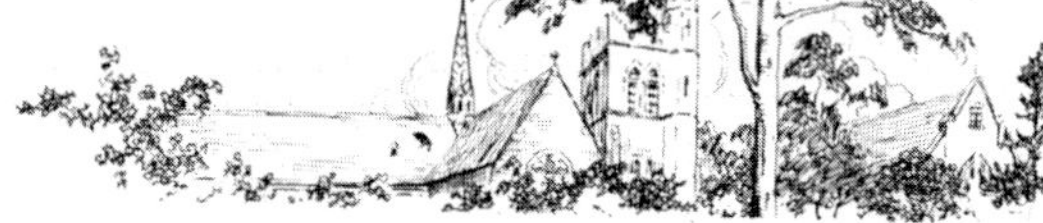

St. George's Cathedral, Perth.

Photo, F. W. Flood.

The Westralian sun shone not only on the land but brightly also on the English Church in Perth. Viewed here through the 'latticed leaves' of a tree in spring, St George's Cathedral intoned its morality to the Treasury Building opposite. In two years time the trees would screen the Church from the violence of a demonstration of the unemployed 'army'. But for now Amy's army of choristers and clergy occupy the neo-Gothic cathedral and chant the rites of old English inspiration.

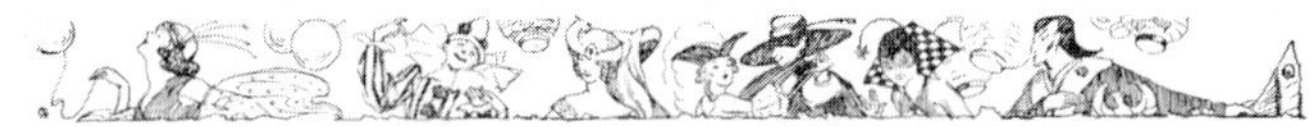

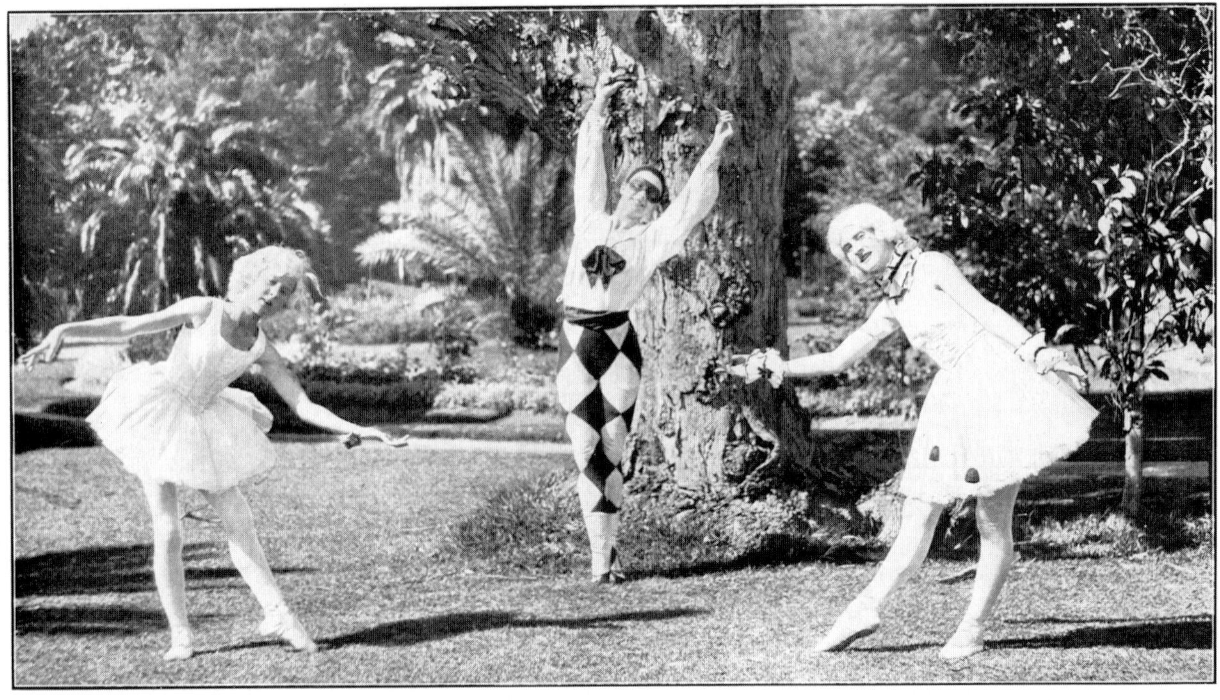

In Government House Gardens, Perth.

Photo, F. W. Flood.

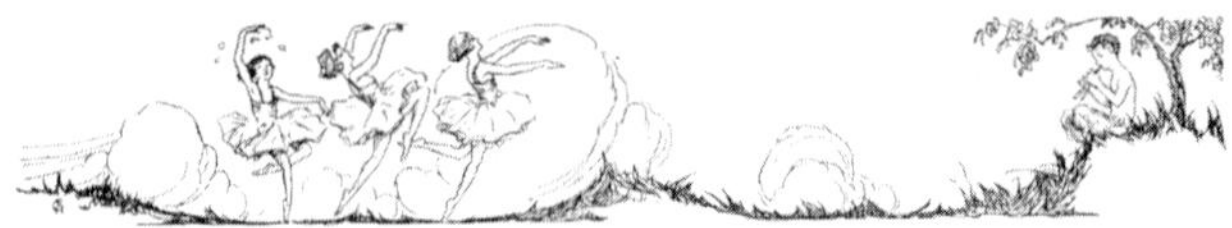

As a visual partnership Fred and Amy shared a love of fantasy and fun. While Fred's costumed youngsters perform in Government House Gardens, Perth, Amy's fairy dancers leap in Virgil's arcady to the music of Pan's flute.

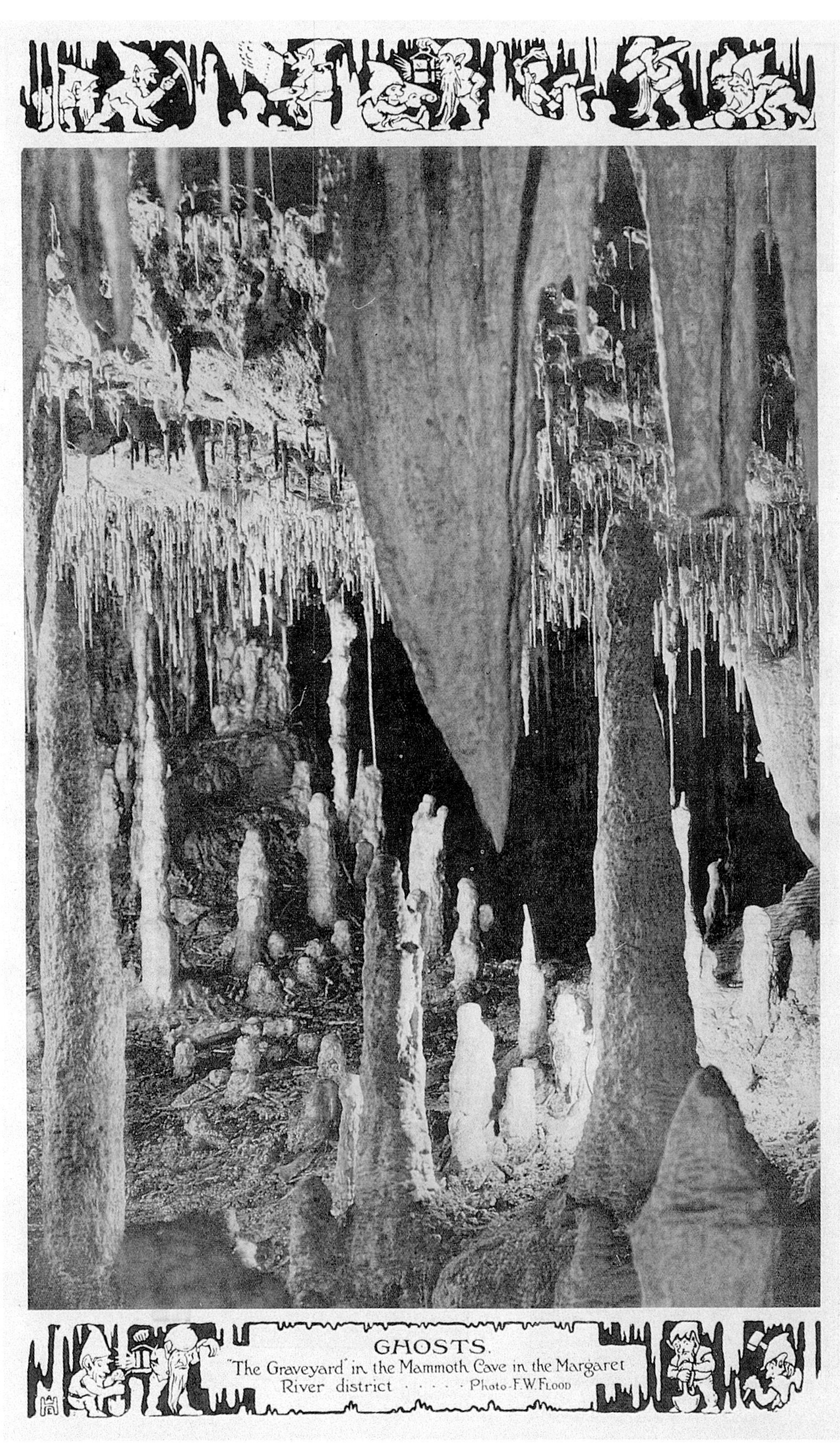

While Fred ventured down to Margaret River's Mammoth Cave to photograph 'The Graveyard', Amy's elves busy themselves among the stalactites and stalagmites.

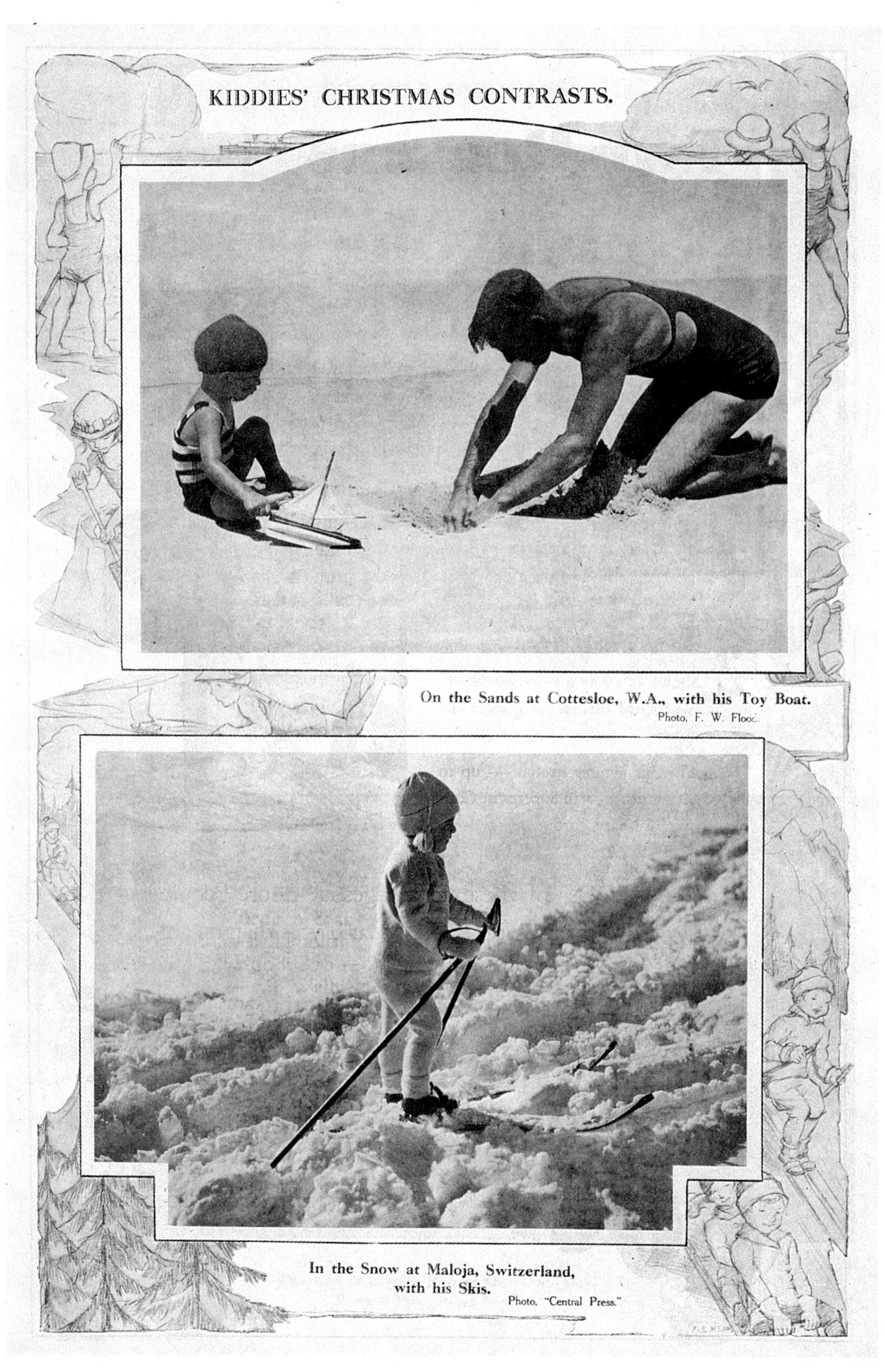

On the Sands at Cottesloe, W.A., with his Toy Boat.
Photo. F. W. Flooc.

In the Snow at Maloja, Switzerland,
with his Skis.
Photo. "Central Press."

Fred with several children, and Amy with none, shared a delight in seeing children at play; the contrast between the old and new worlds for little boys at Christmas was a constant theme.

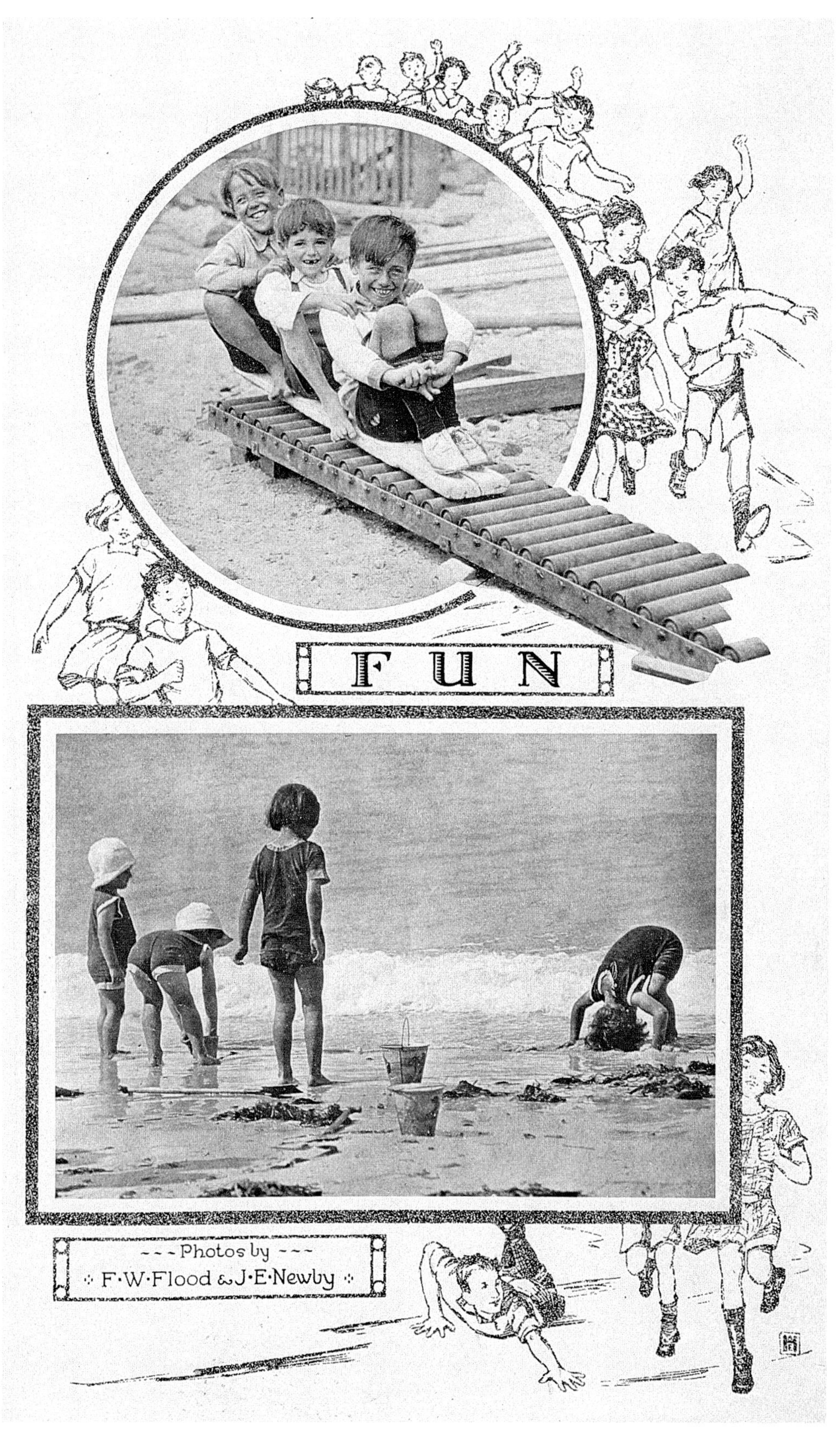

In these sunniest of images, Amy's and Fred's 'children' revel in a Westralian world their parents
fought for a decade earlier. Amy is pleased to note that little girls sometimes beat
little boys in foot-races.

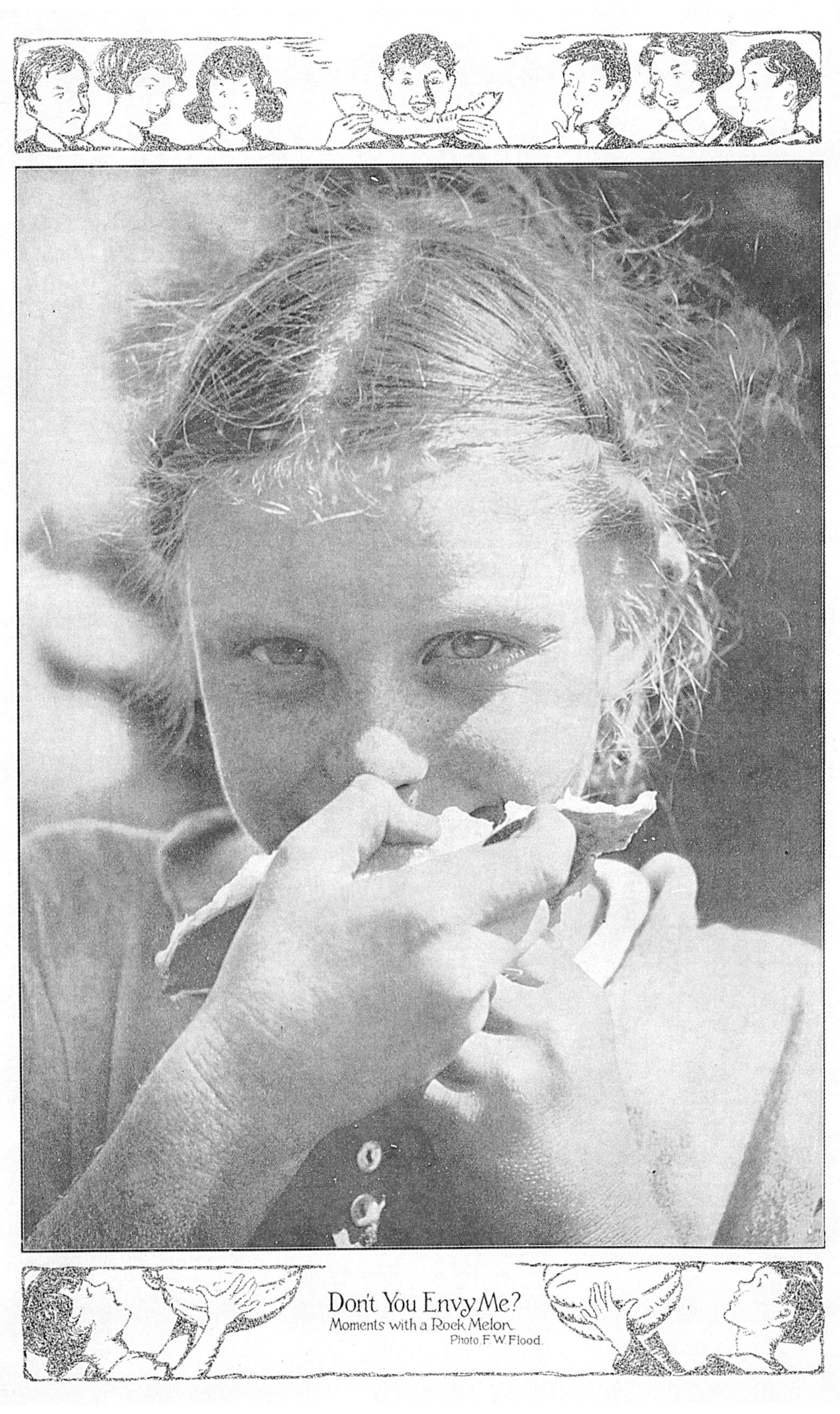

The fun continues for Amy and Fred and a little girl and all of us.

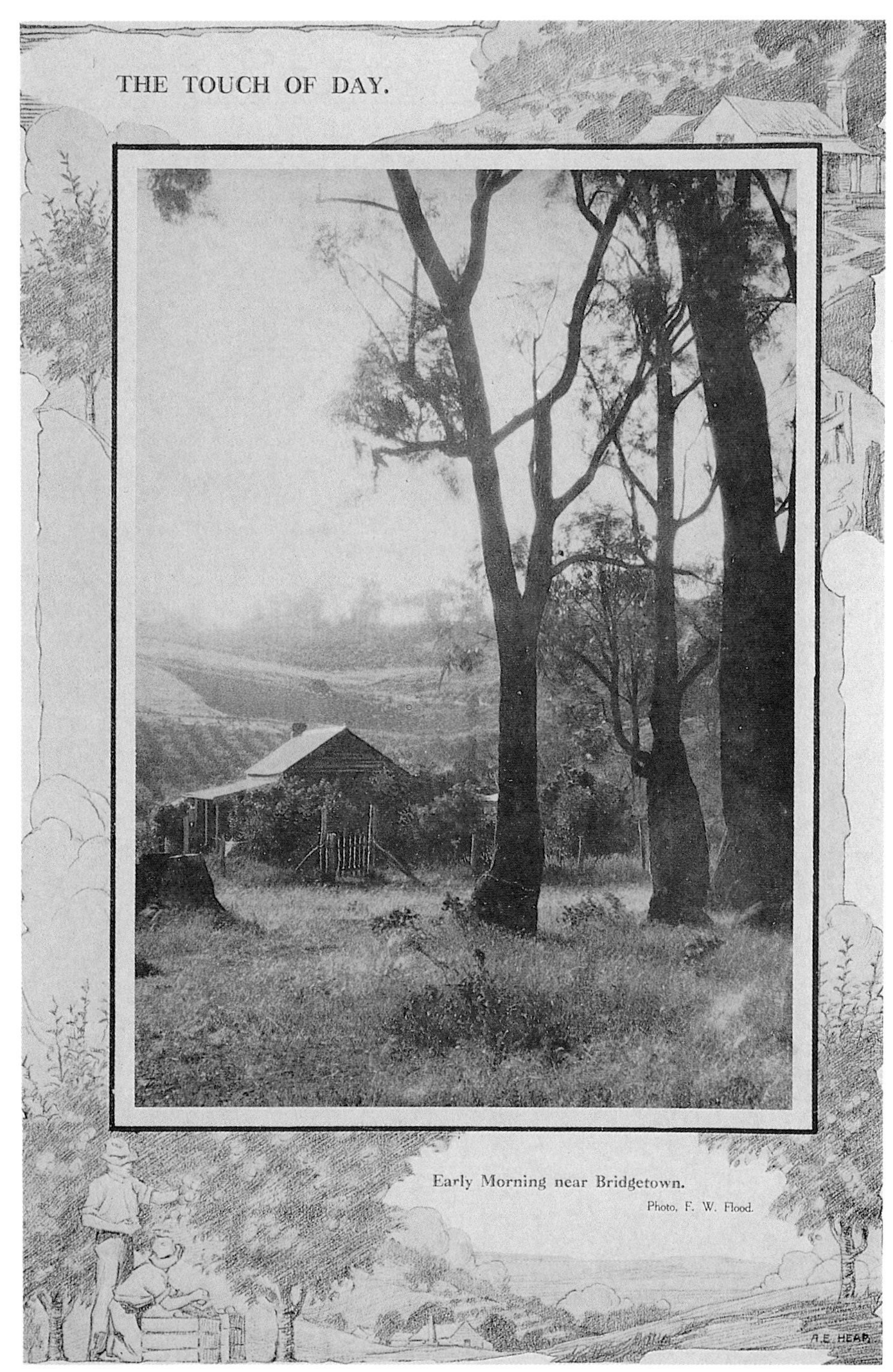

Early Morning near Bridgetown.
Photo. F. W. Flood.

In this, the greatest page of their artistic history, Fred and Amy distil the essence of the power
and beauty of a landscape embellished.

The year's at the spring,
And day's at the morn;
Morning's at seven;
The hill-side's dew-pearled;
The lark's on the wing;
The snail's on the thorn;
God's in his heaven —
All right's with the world.

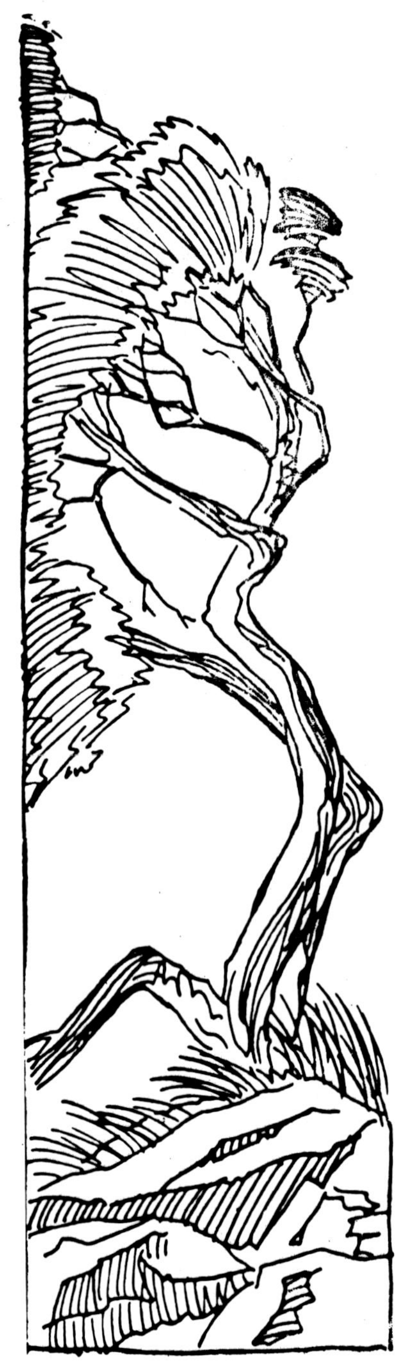

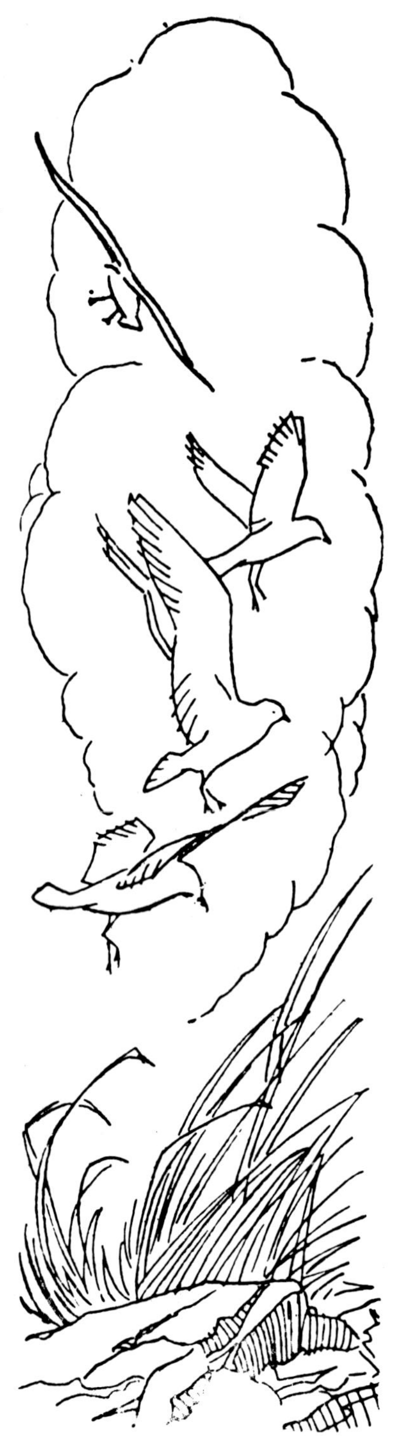

REFERENCES

1. The Interwar Years

Western Mail 1885-1955; J.S. Battye (ed.) *Cyclopedia of Western Australia*, Adelaide 1912-13, and *Western Australia: a History from its Discovery to the Inauguration of the Commonwealth*, Oxford UP 1924; F.K. Crowley *Australia's Western Third*, Macmillan 1960; G.C. Bolton *A Fine Country to Starve In*, UWAP 1972; Paul Hasluck *Mucking About: An Autobiography*, MUP 1977; J. Gregory (ed.) *The Interwar Years*, being *Studies in Western Australian History* No. 11, 1990; for Battye's role in the Art Gallery see *Acquisitions 1975-1977*, a publication of The Art Gallery of Western Australia; B. Chapman *The Colonial Eye: A topographical and artistic record of the life and landscape of Western Australia 1798-1914*, Art Gallery of Western Australia 1979; Roderick Anderson *Early Western Australian Art: From the Robert Holmes à Court Collection*, Heytesbury Holdings 1983; D. Bromfield *Paintings and Ceramics by John Barker 1867-1943*, Centre for Fine Arts, UWA, 1984; *Elise Blumann: Paintings and Drawings 1918-1984*, Centre for Fine Arts, UWA, 1984; Anne Gray *Line, Light and Shadow: James R. Linton: Painter, Craftsman, Teacher*, Fremantle Arts Centre Press 1986; D. Bromfield with J. Goddard *Aspects of Perth Modernism 1919-1942*, Centre for Fine Arts, UWA, 1986; J. Gooding *Western Australian Art and Artists 1900-1950*, Art Gallery of Western Australia 1986.

2. Beauty and Power

Official Yearbook of Western Australia, Australian Bureau of Statistics, 1985; D. Richards *An Illustrated History of Modern Europe*, Longman's 1938; W. Murdoch *Oxford Book of Australian Verse*; also J. Mackaness and G. Mackaness *The Wide Brown Land: An Anthology of Australian Verse*, Angus and Robertson rev. ed. 1946; W. Murdoch (ed.) *The Poet's Commonwealth: A Junior Anthology for Australasian Schools*, 1926; *Fifth Pacific Reader: Southern Cross Series*, 1925; R.K. and M.I.R. Polkinghorn (eds) *The Romance of Reading*, Oxford UP 1936; Mary Webb *Precious Bane* and *Gone to Earth*, Cape 1930, illustrated by Norman Hepple; Ian Jeffrey *The British Landscape 1920-1950*, Thames & Hudson 1984; *Westerly* Number 4 December 1986 'Special Issue: the 1930s'; Frances Spalding et al *Landscape in Britain 1850-1950*, Arts Council of Great Britain 1983; Susan Compton (ed.) *British Art in the 20th Century*, Royal Academy of Arts, 1987; Sadie Ward (ed.) *The Countryside Between the Wars 1918-1940: a Photographic Record*, Batsford, London 1984; *Thirties: British Art and Design before the War*, Arts Council of Great Britain, 1979.

3. Amy Heap

Birth Certificate, St Catherine's House, London; Death Certificate, Registrar General of W.A., Government Office, Perth; Teachers Certificates for Instruction, Art Gallery of Western Australia on loan from National Trust of Western Australia; 'Painters of Perth: Thirty Years in Retrospect' *West Australian*, 23 October 1937; interviews with John Brackenreg and Clem Ambler, October, November 1985; listings of painters and painting titles of exhibitions of the Western Australian Society of Artists and Perth Society of Artists 1912-1944, Art Gallery of Western Australia; paintings by Amy Heap at 'Woodbridge', for the National Trust; paintings by Amy Heap at the Albany Town Council; Walter Murdoch (ed.) *The Westralia Gift Book*, 1916; T. Glascock (ed.) *Jarrah Leaves*, 1933; Janda Gooding *Western Australian Art and Artists 1900-1950*, Art Gallery of Western Australia, 1986, especially pp. 48 and 94 on Amy Heap; *Western Mail*, 1918-1940; Amy Heap biographical notes, Art Gallery of Western Australia; also Amy Heap correspondence re gifts to Gallery, Art Gallery of Western Australia; *Western Australia: its early vicissitudes, romantic awakening, development, and progress*, issued by the authority of the Premier, Hon. J. Mitchell C.M.G., Perth 1920; *Dictionary of British Artists 1870-1970*, Society of Antiquaries, London, 1974 — Heap's 1938 Manchester Exhibition.

4. Fred Flood

Birth and Marriage Certificates, St Catherine's House, London; C. Booth *Life and Labour in London*, 1892-5; S. Nowell Smith (ed.) *Edwardian England*, Oxford 1964; P. Thompson *The Edwardians*, 1979; D. Farr *English Art 1810-1940*, Oxford 1978; interviews with Wally Flood, October 1985, February 1986, October 1989; K. Spillman *Identity Prized: A History of Subiaco*, UWAP 1985; interview with Clem Ambler, October 1985; general photographic information, Colin Murphy; *Western Mail*; 'Cameraman's unique coverage of rural life', *The Countryman*, 10 April 1986; Kathryn Reed *Pictorial Photography*, Flinders University, South Australia, 1980; Australian National Gallery *Highlights and Soft Shadows: Pictorialism in Australian Photography*, 1985; John Taylor *Pictorial Photography in Britain 1900-1920*, Arts Council of Great Britain, 1978; Sue Smith *Queensland Pictorialist Photography 1920-1950*, Queensland Art Gallery 1984; 'The Nature of Art: Van Raalte Club Paper', *West Australian* 14 July 1934; 'The Making of a Picture' by A. Knapp *West Australian* 27 July 1935; D. Bromfield 'Modernism's Back Alley — Perth's Streets as Signs of the Times', *Westerly* Vol. 31, No. 4, December 1986.